D0436835

AUDIENCE

MARKETING IN THE AGE OF SUBSCRIBERS, FANS & FOLLOWERS

JEFFREY K. ROHRS

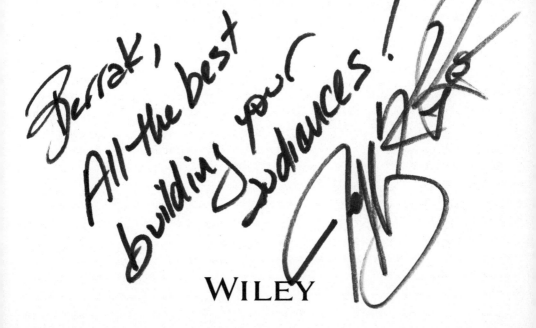

WILEY

To the weird, wonderful, and loving audience
that energizes me every single day,
Jenny, Declan, & Bailey Kate.

And to the entire ExactTarget family,
may you always be Orange.
—j.k.r.

Contents

Foreword   Scott Dorsey   ix

   Introduction: Why AUDIENCE?   1

Part I: The Audience Imperative   5

Chapter 1

   Audiences as Assets: Think Like The Boss   7

Chapter 2

   The Audience Imperative: Our Hybrid Source of
Business Energy   17

Chapter3

   Your Proprietary Audiences: Seekers, Amplifiers & Joiners   26

Chapter 4

   The VIP Joiners: Subscribers, Fans & Followers   41

Chapter 5

   Beyond Don Draper: Paid, Owned & Earned Media   56

Chapter 6

   Increase What Matters: Size, Engagement & Value 70

Chapter 7

   A Larger Font: Our Long-Term Responsibilities   91

Part II: The Audience Channels   101

Chapter 8

Website: Marketing's Magnetic Center   103

Chapter 9

Email: The Bedrock Audience   109

Chapter 10

Facebook: Making It Personal   114

Chapter 11

Twitter: Real-Time Characters   121

Chapter 12

Blogs: A Website by Another Name   127

Chapter 13

Mobile Apps: Audiences on the Go   133

Chapter 14

LinkedIn: The Professional Audience   139

Chapter 15

YouTube: Internet Built the Video Star   144

Chapter 16

Google+: The Great Unknown   149

Chapter 17

Pinterest: A Collection of Beautiful Followers   153

Chapter 18

SMS: Cutting through the Clutter   158

Chapter 19

Instagram: Moving Pictures   163

Chapter 20

Podcasts: Listen Carefully   168

Chapter 21

Other Audience Channels: More? You Want More?!?   172

Part III: The Audience Roadmap   177

Chapter 22

Map & Align: Strategy and Team   179

Chapter 23

Build & Engage: Audiences on Demand   200

Chapter 24

Serve, Honor, Deliver, Surprise & Delight: The Red Velvet Touch   228

Chapter 25

Test & Evolve: What Marketers Can Learn from 5,000 Years of Football   238

Conclusion   247
Notes   249
Acknowledgments   273
Index   275

Foreword

I first met Jeff Rohrs back in 2004 when he was president of Optiem, a digital marketing agency in Cleveland, Ohio, and one of ExactTarget's first reseller partners. His keen eye for business trends, passion for digital marketing, and sense of humor made an immediate impression on me—and it wasn't long after that I found myself asking Jeff if he'd be interested in joining our team. In 2007 he made the leap, and both of us couldn't have been happier with the results.

As producer of our award-winning *SUBSCRIBERS, FANS & FOLLOWERS Research Series* (*SFF*), Jeff was one of the first to highlight the fragmenting nature of consumer/brand relationships. Whereas many were taking a one-size-fits-all approach to their cross-channel marketing efforts, Jeff and his team were urging companies to better understand and meet the consumer expectations created by each channel. As the *SFF* research demonstrated, SUBSCRIBERS wanted different things than FANS and FOLLOWERS—and vice versa.

In early 2013, Jeff approached us with a new idea—one that seemed revolutionary at the time but has proven to be true: There's a hole in our marketing organizations. Advertising, brand, content marketing, demand generation, interactive marketing, product marketing, and sales all have leaders; but no one leader is responsible for building, engaging, and nurturing our proprietary audiences. Sure, there are great folks on the front lines of email, mobile, and social, each developing audiences specific to those channels. However, companies that don't have a singular voice to speak for the needs of proprietary audiences will be hard-pressed to deliver on the promise of today's convergent marketing technologies—true one-to-one relationships with consumers across all channels.

AUDIENCE is a wake-up call for every company today. Before you acquire a *customer* . . . before you can build a *relationship* . . . there must first be an *audience* for you to address. Your company may be content simply buying advertising to reach audiences, but Jeff and our entire team see a different future—one in which companies embrace an asset-based approach to marketing and work to constantly improve the size, engagement, and value of their own proprietary audiences. This is not an either/or proposition. Paid, owned, and earned media can and should work together to produce more revenue at lower cost wherever possible. And that's the simple, powerful message of *AUDIENCE*: It is within our ability *today* to leverage data, permission, and technology to better sell to *and serve* consumers across all channels and devices.

Frankly, I don't think there's a more important book that companies can read today. Jeff has laid the groundwork for the responsible, long-term, profitable development of proprietary audiences. The structure you choose to build upon that foundation is up to you. However, if you build wisely, you'll find yourself with a competitive advantage that will last for years to come.

—Scott Dorsey (@ScottDorsey)
CEO and Cofounder
ExactTarget, a salesforce.com company

Introduction: Why AUDIENCE?

It requires a very unusual mind to undertake the analysis of the obvious.[1]

—Alfred North Whitehead

Welcome to the audience of *AUDIENCE*, the book! The moment you began flipping through these pages, you became a READER. I'm hoping you'll soon purchase a copy and graduate to my CUSTOMER audience.* And if the subject matter really strikes a chord with you, perhaps you'll become a website VISITOR (www.AudiencePro.com), email SUBSCRIBER, or a FAN of the book on Facebook. Who knows, you may even become one of my FOLLOWERS on Twitter, LinkedIn, or Google+, where I ponder how to build and engage audiences while masking a lifetime of pain caused by rooting for the Cleveland Browns (@Browns).

Ultimately, the choice is yours because you—the consumer—determine whether or not to become a part of any audience. *You are not owned.* Your attention, action, and loyalty have to be *earned* by all those who want it.

That's how it works today. We *like, follow,* and *subscribe to* our favorite brands, companies, and people any time we want. We usually do so when

---

*I use ALL CAPS throughout to refer to specific, proprietary audiences that are detailed in Chapters 3 and 4. My hope is that it will avoid confusion and help you refer back to key audiences of interest.

1

it brings us joy, saves us money, or provides us with timely information. As consumers, we are in control. We decide which audiences to join, leave, or ignore altogether.

Unfortunately, not all businesses appreciate this dynamic. They operate under the false assumption that paid media still rules the roost and provides all of the audiences needed to fuel their business. That may have been the case at one point in time, but no longer. Consider that as you read this, there are the following phenomena:

- A cookie (the edible kind) with over 34 million FANS on Facebook
- A landscape designer with over 3.5 million Pinterest FOLLOWERS
- An actor with 13 times the Twitter FOLLOWERS of his TV show
- An oral care startup with 100 times more YouTube SUBSCRIBERS than competitors with over 100 times the revenue
- A local restaurant with over 20,000 email SUBSCRIBERS—over 500 of whom have restaurant-inspired tattoos

Each of these entities has a distinct advantage over their competitors who rely on driving business through paid media alone. With a push of the button, they can message their audiences directly in cost-effective ways that drive measurable sales, response, and engagement. In these pages, I'll share their stories and those of other brands that illustrate the simple fact that:

Proprietary Audience Development is now a core marketing responsibility.

If you embrace this responsibility, you'll be a part of the team that turns audiences into long-term, profitable assets for your company. However, if you neglect it, you will fall behind competitors with less dependency on paid media thanks to their development of audiences that they—and they alone— can access on demand.

The choice is obvious, but many companies will fail to embrace the tenets of this book because it requires a consistent, long-term effort. Marketing staff turnover, campaign-based mentalities, and siloed objectives all work to undermine your audience development efforts—and this will never change. It will always be far easier to call your media buyer, rattle off some target demographics, and rent audience attention than it will be to command your own.

But we know the truth. Always doing what's easy is a path to poverty, not prosperity. Just as consumer behaviors are changing thanks to mobile and social technologies, so too must our marketing organizations evolve to reflect our new realities. The time has come to stop treating proprietary audiences as afterthoughts and instead embrace them for what they are—a source of critical business energy in need of investment, leadership, and support.

AUDIENCE is as much a book for CEOs as it is for marketing professionals. Its lessons and advice are as relevant to small businesses as they are to Fortune 500 companies. You should feel free to read it from end to end or jump straight to the parts that interest you most. After all, you're the audience; you're in control.

In Part I, we'll explore *The Audience Imperative*. Through its mandate, I explain what proprietary audiences are, what they have to offer our companies, and why it is more important now than ever before for your company to build them.

In Part II, I provide a deep dive into the top *Audience Channels* for Proprietary Audience Development. My goal here is to help you understand how these channels might fit your strategic needs, and how to pursue additional resources to aid in your use of them.

In Part III, I present an *Audience Roadmap* that you can use to build, engage, and value your proprietary audiences in ways that will deliver measurable results. I conclude with thoughts on what marketers committed to *Proprietary Audience Development* can learn from 5,000 years of football (yes, football—trust me, you'll enjoy it).

One quick note—in the spirit of helping all of those whose stories, support, and encouragement have helped me make this book a reality, you will find that any mention of a specific individual or brand is accompanied by their Twitter handle (if they have one). I would encourage you to follow the folks that interest or inspire you. I know they'll appreciate you joining their audiences as much as I appreciate that you've joined one of mine.

So welcome! Grab a seat, settle in, and let's learn how to build your proprietary audiences for the long haul.

Part

The Audience Imperative

Audiences are all around you. They are direct, responsive, and extremely cost-effective. They're also new, constantly evolving, and quick to anger if you cross them.

Your company needs audiences to survive. If you aren't building, engaging, and activating proprietary audiences of your own, you're falling behind.

It's high time you discovered why.

Audiences as Assets: Think Like The Boss

[T]he audience is not brought to you or given to you; it's something that you fight for. You can forget that, especially if you've had some success. Getting an audience is HARD. Sustaining an audience is HARD. It demands a consistency of thought, of purpose, and of action over a long period of time.[1]

—Bruce Springsteen

Quick! What are the most important assets of your business today? Your brand? Intellectual property? Physical facilities? Inventory? Employees?

All of these are likely answers; however, there's one asset that is constantly missing when I ask companies this very question. Audiences.

Yes, audiences.

This answer tops your list if you're in the media, sports, or entertainment industries, because you're in the actual business of putting people in seats. You build audiences for a living and know the competitive advantage to be gained if your audience is bigger, better, and more energetic than the competition's. Media companies build READERS (print), LISTENERS (radio), and VIEWERS (television). Football teams feed off of FANS. And Lady Gaga . . . well, she loves her "Little Monsters."

Even lay consumers who aren't in media or entertainment inherently understand that each of these audiences has monetary value. Loyal FANS pay cash for tickets to a live event, and a percentage of that money goes to the performers. The equation is simple: *bigger audiences = more revenue.*

You may think that this equation doesn't apply to you if you work outside of an audience-centric industry, but it does. Do you pay for advertising? Then audience matters. Do you have a website? Then audience matters. Do you want to grow your business? *Then audience matters.*

Audience is the bedrock upon which every business is built. After all, what were your customers *before* they were customers? They were members of some audience that was exposed to your products and services.

Not that long ago, companies were totally dependent on print, radio, and television gatekeepers to reach audiences. Today, however, every company can build its own global audiences via websites, mobile apps, email, Facebook, Twitter, YouTube, Instagram, and Pinterest (just to name a few). The rapid adoption of mobile devices and social media also gives those same audiences the ability to communicate right back to companies—often, in *very* public fashion.

Ahh . . . that sounds familiar. You've got "a young gal" who works on social media, "a guy" who is in charge of email—and you have some videos on YouTube. Your website "kind of" works on smartphones and you've got a LinkedIn profile for your company, so you must be building audiences correctly. Right?

Wrong. These are siloed tactics that produce siloed audiences. Moreover, they're often managed by people with conflicting objectives and few organizational incentives to collaborate. What I'm advocating—what this book is about—is the creation of an entirely new marketing discipline focused solely on *Proprietary Audience Development.* To fully appreciate the importance of this cause, we had better check in with *The Boss.*

The Boss Is Worried

Bruce Springsteen (@Springsteen) is no stranger to proprietary audiences. With over 120 million albums sold worldwide and thousands of live concerts under his belt, he lives for them. And while you might think a veteran performer would be the last person to worry about finding an audience—you'd be wrong. After four decades as a performer, Bruce remains concerned about his ability to build and sustain an audience for his product (i.e., his music) in the Internet age. His quote at the beginning of this chapter sums the challenge up perfectly:

> Getting an audience is HARD. Sustaining an audience is HARD.
> It demands a consistency of thought, of purpose, and of action
> over a long period of time.

If The Boss is worried about getting an audience, shouldn't you be worried? Shouldn't *your boss* be?

The question of where the next sale will come from has always dogged businesses. Indeed, the entire field of capital-M Marketing rose up to address such fears head on. Over the years, marketers have used a combination of creativity, messaging, and well-placed advertising to help their companies generate the vast majority of their sales—so much, in fact, that we completely lost any fear about on-demand audiences disappearing. After all, there were always print publications, radio stations, and television networks out there, all willing to put your product in front of an audience at a moment's notice in exchange for cold, hard advertising dollars.

And then, the Internet happened.

New, interactive channels fragmented consumer attention, toppled traditional information gatekeepers, and decimated the business models of traditional media. Consider that:

- From 2008 to 2012, daily newspaper circulation dropped 26.6 percent in the United Kingdom and 14.9 percent in the United States.[2]
- Twenty-nine percent of TV viewing is time-shifted thanks to DVRs, VOD, and Web-streaming platforms (and 41 percent of recorded shows go unwatched).[3]
- By 2020, the average consumer will own 50 Internet-enabled devices.[4]

In Bruce's industry, once all-powerful, taste-making radio stations now stand as homogeneous shells of corporate efficiency where fewer owners play fewer artists to fewer listeners. Record stores are on life support, sustained by a few die-hard music enthusiasts, vinyl addicts, and the resale market for CDs. As for the music-buying experience, it has shifted from tactile and personal to virtual and impulsive. Practically overnight, the biggest artists went from selling entire albums to pushing MP3 singles for 99 cents a pop.

This is why The Boss is worried. The Internet, mobility, and social media have drastically altered a formerly stable and profitable means of manufacture, distribution, and promotion. Traditional influencers who propelled his albums to platinum-level sales have lost power. And if Bruce can't find new, cost-effective ways to reach audiences, his records won't sell, his concerts won't sell out, and his cash register won't ring.

But we know this hasn't happened. The Boss is doing just fine. His 2012 album, *Wrecking Ball*, topped the charts—his tenth album to do so.

He has amassed an incredibly loyal audience over the course of his 40 years in the music industry, and as times have changed, so have the ways they follow him. Instead of learning about his new album from a radio DJ, they hear about it directly from his website, email, or Twitter account. Or they hear about it from a new tastemaker—a blogger or fellow FAN on Facebook. Whatever the case, The Boss has retained his following because his management understands the absolute necessity of *Proprietary Audience Development* over the long term.

The Audience Imperative

Proprietary Audience Development is a comprehensive, collaborative, and cross-channel effort to build audiences *that your company alone can access*. This new marketing practice is built upon a mandate that I call *The Audience Imperative*:

Use your Paid, Owned, and Earned Media not only to sell in the short term but also to increase the size, engagement, and value of your Proprietary Audiences over the long term.

When you build bigger and better proprietary audiences than your competition, you gain a tremendous advantage in the marketplace. You're able to drive consumers to your doorstep with the push of a button—while your competitors are left fighting for better ad placements and bidding up keywords. Proprietary audiences allow you to:

1. Reach CUSTOMERS and PROSPECTS at a lower cost.
2. Drive sales in a more on-demand fashion.
3. Treat consumers as individuals instead of faceless masses.
4. Optimize your budget across Paid, Owned, and Earned Media.*

Proprietary Audience Development *is a comprehensive, collaborative, and cross-channel effort to build audiences that your company alone can access.*

---

*I've elected to capitalize the terms Paid, Owned, and Earned Media from here on out to better highlight how they support *Proprietary Audience Development*.

While few could discount these tremendously beneficial outcomes, *Proprietary Audience Development* is a discipline without a champion in most companies today. In Chapters 3 and 4, we'll explore the different audiences in greater detail, but for now, take a look at all of the potential proprietary audiences at your disposal:

SEEKERS	AMPLIFIERS	JOINERS
BROWSERS	ADVOCATES	CUSTOMERS
LISTENERS	ANALYSTS	DINERS
PROSPECTS	COMMENTERS	DONORS
READERS	CREATORS	EMPLOYEES
SEARCHERS	INFLUENCERS	FANS
SHOPPERS	REPORTERS	FOLLOWERS
VIEWERS	REVIEWERS	PARTNERS
VISITORS	SHARERS	SUBSCRIBERS

Now ask yourself this: Who manages the acquisition, development, and performance of these audiences in your company? Is it one person? Two? Five? Fifteen?

If your company is like most, your proprietary audiences lie strewn across a variety of different channels, databases, and teams—there's no primary leader as with advertising, branding, and even content marketing. As a result, your efforts to drive audience engagement through your Paid, Owned, and Earned Media are neither as seamless nor as profitable as they might be. Your messaging is also probably far from optimized since your website, email, mobile, and social databases aren't fully integrated with one another.

As if this weren't bad enough, your company runs another huge risk absent a commitment to *Proprietary Audience Development.* Your audiences—critical business assets that they are—become subject to abuse at the hands of the loudest, most desperate executives, inexperienced newbies, and all manner of well-intentioned colleagues who seek to achieve their personal objectives regardless of the *unsubscribes, dislikes,* and *unfollows* they cause. This leads your company (often unknowingly) to sacrifice long-term audience profitability in service to short-term, ill-gotten gains.

This is not the fearmongering of a deranged marketer; it's a story I've seen play out time and time again.

- The email marketing team directed by management to "blast" all of their SUBSCRIBERS (and sometimes even those who unsubscribed) regardless of the impact on opt-out rates and long-term email ROI

- The social media manager told to "sell, sell, sell" even though self-centered posts suppress FAN and FOLLOWER engagement
- The mobile app developer who fails to ask SUBSCRIBERS to opt-in to push messaging or email, thereby leaving their company without any means to trigger mobile app reengagement

Sound familiar? Want to help stop the madness and embrace *The Audience Imperative*? Then it's time to help your company understand proprietary audiences as the incredibly valuable business assets they are.

The Audience as Asset

Say it with me. Audiences are assets—*valuable business assets*. They may not be tangible assets, but with the right message to the right person at the right time, proprietary audiences can quickly turn into paying customers.

Of course, a company's physical assets are more readily appreciated precisely because everyone in the organization can see them. We know the value of a piece of land because of what we paid for it or what the market will bear. We have the common sense to hire security to guard our physical facilities because the alternative is to let thieves or vandals disrupt our business. And we know to invest money in the maintenance of our physical facilities, because otherwise that small leak will become a far more costly problem overnight.

Audiences are assets—valuable business assets.

Unfortunately, we lack the same organizational common sense when it comes to audience assets. Few executives fully appreciate the lifetime value of proprietary audiences and yet, as we'll see, many of them could be worth *millions of dollars in future revenue*. Does your company just let anyone walk around with access to accounts containing millions of dollars? Heck, no! We entrust such assets to people who are well trained, well screened, and well compensated. If your proprietary audiences possess such inherent value, shouldn't the people who are a push button away from your audiences be some of your brightest, most trusted, and most valued people?

This strikes me as common sense, but overall businesses fail to hold audience assets in the same regard as physical assets for a few reasons:

1. *The whole concept of proprietary audiences is very new.* Prior to the Internet, a proprietary audience was a direct mail database hidden in some huge, distant server. Today, proprietary audiences exist inside and outside of our databases as well as across a vast array of public and private channels.

2. *We're focused on channel management instead of audience development.* Many companies have Facebook, Twitter, and YouTube strategies, but few have comprehensive *Proprietary Audience Development* strategies. This leaves marketing pigeon-holed into tactical discussions instead of debates about strategic priorities.

3. *Channels are still evolving.* The channels that support proprietary audiences haven't evolved to the point where they provide market-ers with simple, consistent ROI measurements. This makes it difficult sometimes to provide leadership with more than anecdotal stories of positive audience engagement.

Today, your proprietary audiences aren't reviewed as part of your company's financial statements, but you need to begin preparing for the day when they will be. Indeed, I envision a future in which the people who manage a company's proprietary audiences command the same respect and scrutiny as the VP of Sales. They do, after all, manage assets (audiences) that account for a huge portion of your company's future sales if managed appropriately.

Netflix: When Audiences Are Your Most Important Assets

For a glimpse at a future where corporate fortunes rise and fall on the size and quality of their proprietary audiences, look no further than Netflix (@Netflix). The company's ill-fated 2011 plan to split SUBSCRIBER accounts (one for streaming and one for DVD delivery) caused the loss of 800,000 SUBSCRIBERS in a single quarter. As a result, Netflix stock dropped from a high near $300 per share to the $60 range in a matter of months.[5]

Granted, Netflix is in the audience business. However, its plight—and subsequent recovery in terms of SUBSCRIBER count and stock price—underscores that when audiences are viewed as assets, their rise and fall can dramatically impact the fortunes of any company.

Proprietary vs. Owned

You may have already noticed that I've been going out of my way to say "proprietary" instead of "owned" audiences. Audiences are *proprietary to* your company and not *owned by* your company because no audience is owned; members can leave any time they want. Whether at a concert, using a mobile app, or subscribing to an email list, the audience member always has the option to leave the venue, delete your app, or unsubscribe from your email. The same rule holds painfully true for traditional media. If it didn't, we'd all still be reading printed copies of *Newsweek* (@Newsweek) while waiting to watch *Must See TV* Thursday nights on NBC (@NBC).

While not owned, audiences can be *proprietary* in that the right to communicate with them belongs to a single entity. To better understand this distinction, let's take a look at someone who's not quite as famous as Bruce Springsteen but commands a loyal FAN base today, Joel McHale (@JoelMcHale).

For those unfamiliar with Joel, he's a talented actor, comedian, and "Proud Mom" according to his Twitter profile. In reality, he's one of the hardest-working men in show business, with a starring role on NBC's *Community*, a long-standing role as host of *The Soup* on E! Entertainment Television, and a lucrative stand-up career built in part on making fun of Ryan Seacrest (@RyanSeacrest). Joel and each of his shows have an active presence on Twitter, and as I write this, their FOLLOWER counts stand at:

- 3,272,374 @JoelMcHale
- 241,996 @TheSoup
- 234,997 @NBCCommunity

No audience is owned; members can leave at any time they want.

You read that right. Joel McHale has over 13 times more Twitter FOLLOWERS than each of his shows. In fact, as I write this, he also has over 11 times the Twitter audience of the NBC Network itself (@NBC—364,945 FOLLOWERS)! "Must See TV" has definitely seen better days.

But here's the twist: Not one of those FOLLOWERS is *owned* by Joel. He must work to retain their attention with each new tweet. Still, Joel's Twitter FOLLOWERS are his *proprietary audience* in that he is the only person that can message them in the aggregate. E! and NBC can't. They can message their own FOLLOWERS; but to reach Joel's, they must ask (or pay) him to message them.

As it turns out, Joel does encourage his Twitter FOLLOWERS to watch both of his shows. This is of tremendous benefit to NBC and E! as it extends their promotional efforts for zero cost. Similarly, Joel has to love it when NBC and E!'s main accounts (@NBC and @Eonline, respectively) include his Twitter handle (@JoelMcHale) in their promotions. This helps him build his Twitter following—an asset that he will take with him long after he departs from *Community* and *The Soup*.

Audience Exercise #1: Check Yourself

If you want to understand audiences as assets, look no further than your own behavior.

Write down the brands you currently *like* on Facebook or *follow* on Twitter, LinkedIn, Pinterest, or elsewhere. Now check your personal inbox. What brands did you give permission to send email to you? Which ones do you still look forward to? If you have a smartphone, pick it up and browse your open apps. How many are provided by companies you do business with?

Now ask yourself this: Is your company doing all it can to build its proprietary audience across these channels?

Twitter definitely provides Joel with his largest proprietary audience, but it's not the only one that he commands. He also has a website audience (www.joelmchale.tv), a Facebook FAN audience (www.facebook.com /joelmchale), and a live audience of CUSTOMERS when he headlines as a stand-up comedian.

Does this sound familiar? It should, because aside from being an actor/ comedian, Joel is really a business—a business seeking to increase the professional opportunities and income for one Joel McHale. He does this when he can create *energy* in the form of buzz, interest, and ultimately sales around his projects. The same thing holds true for Bruce, and the same thing holds true for your company.

In fact, if you're in marketing in any capacity today, it's time to embrace the fact that you, my friend, are in the energy business.

The Relationship between Audience and Customer

As I've hammered out the concepts in AUDIENCE, I found myself referring back to three books that helped to shape many of my beliefs as a marketer:

1. *The One-to-One Future* by Don Peppers (@DonPeppers) and Martha Rogers (@Martha_Rogers)
2. *Permission Marketing* by Seth Godin (@ThisIsSethsBlog)
3. *Flip the Funnel* by Joseph Jaffe (@JaffeJuice)

Each of these works envisions a future where marketers could increasingly leverage technology to build deeper, more meaningful, and more human relationships with consumers. Each also values consumer permission as the key to unlock both the channels (email, SMS, Facebook, etc.) and the data to power more personal, relevant, and timely communications.

AUDIENCE stands on the shoulders of these giants, seeking to remind marketers that before you can gain a CUSTOMER or build a relationship with a PROSPECT, you must have an audience—preferably one that's bigger, better, and more responsive than the competition's. That's the heart of *Proprietary Audience Development*—and hopefully, a worthy heir to the fine work of Don, Martha, Seth, and Joseph.

Chapter

The Audience Imperative: Our Hybrid Source of Business Energy

[T]he difference between a theatre with and without an audience is enormous. There is a palpable, critical energy created by the presence of the audience.[1]
—Andy Goldsworthy

As Britain's foremost environmental artist, Andy Goldsworthy doesn't usually perform with an audience. He works alone or with his team, assembling often fragile sculptures out of natural materials including sticks, stones, leaves, and even snow. However, Goldsworthy changed his approach in 1996 when he partnered with ballet choreographer Régine Chopinot to produce *Végétal*, a piece of performance art that married dance and with environmental sculpture.[2] Goldsworthy reflects on the experience in his book *Midsummer Snowballs*, which perfectly captures what an audience provides to the artist:

Critical energy.

Picture an empty arena. Quiet. Still. Serene. Now picture it full of people overflowing with excitement for the sporting event they're about to see. Even in the abstract, the difference is palpable—because we've all been there. Each and every one of us has been a part of an audience that's chanting, singing, and stomping our feet for more.

There's a reason comedians, stage actors, musicians, and athletes say they "feed off the crowd." It's because audience energy can literally make or break their performance.

Think about when you're more energized in your own business. Are you sitting alone in your office or interacting with prospects and customers? And which room is more "electric": an empty store or one filled with people? The answers may be self-evident, but I raise them to point out a fundamental truth:

Consumers are the fundamental source of business energy.

When consumers channel their energy into your business, the cash register rings. When they don't, it's lights out. What separates the winners from the losers is the ability to keep consumer interest (i.e., energy) flowing when and where your business needs it to propel sales, donations, or whatever pays the bills. Of course, the corollary to this proposition intrigues me even more:

Each and every company is in the energy business.

You may not consider yourself to be akin to an *explorer* when you put on your marketing hat—but you are. You spend your professional life on a constant quest to locate, tap, and transform consumer energy into sales for your company. And frankly, the effort to convince, cajole, and coax consumers off of their couches—and smartphones—to pay attention to your products or services is no less difficult at times than drilling for oil beneath the deepest ocean.

Attention is the precious natural resource all companies are struggling to acquire and retain. The fragmentation of consumer attention across channels, devices, and locations has created a genuine energy crisis for marketers. As a result, companies are scrambling to find additional sources of energy to fuel their businesses.

Attention is the precious natural resource that all companies are struggling to acquire and retain.

Marketing's Fossil Fuel

I remember standing dumbfounded at the sight of a Sinclair Oil (@SinclairMemory) station sign as a child. It was a largely green, white, and red affair that would have been unremarkable save for one element—the green dinosaur below the red Sinclair name. You must understand one thing: Dinosaurs are irresistible to eight-year-old boys. They are big, scaly, and terrifying—in short, THEY ARE THE COOLEST THINGS EVER!!!

Now I'm not sure why Sinclair wanted to appeal to my particular demographic of dino-loving tweens, but their logo did lead me to ask my father why a brontosaurus (or another 'saurus of unknown etymology) was shilling for a gas station. A learned man, my father turned to me and said (without missing a beat), "Because oil comes from dinosaurs."

Jaw dropped. Mind blown. I probably called in sick to school the next day so my eight-year-old self could sit contemplating how many triceratops it took to fill up our Ford Econoline van.

Of course, my dad was pulling my leg. He knew full well that oil, coal, and natural gas didn't come from dinosaurs but rather from organic plant materials subject to millions of years of pressure under the Earth's surface.[3] Granted, it's far less cool than the dinosaur theory, but it's still pretty amazing to think that the majority of our energy comes from ancient resources that companies extract from the ground, refine, and sell to us.

Sort of like advertising.

Yes—you heard me right. Advertising is the *fossil fuel* of marketing. I say that without any intent to cast aspersions. In fact, there's a strong argument to be made that advertising has never been more alive than it is today.

Advertising is the fossil fuel of marketing.

Companies today run ads via traditional print, radio, and television outlets as well as all manner of Web, video, mobile, and social-powered networks. With the help of tracking cookies, advertisers can use consumer demographic, Web surfing, and purchase data to better target and retarget those ads to increase their performance in ways that look like something straight out of the science fiction film *Minority Report*.

Yet no matter how geo-targeted, data-driven, or socially infused today's ads are, they still rely on a basic economic exchange:

An advertiser pays a fee to receive a limited amount of time in front of an audience whose attention is obtained by a third party.

With fossil fuels, big energy companies drill and mine the earth in order to lay claim to vast repositories of oil, coal, and natural gas. With advertising, media companies mine consumers for their attention that they then sell back to advertisers in pages, impressions, clicks, and 30-second increments. In both situations, a middleman controls access to the natural resource, adding cost and building an addiction of convenience.

The Rising Cost of Super Audiences

There is perhaps no more public barometer of the value of audiences than the Super Bowl. As the game has become a cultural event, audiences have grown and so has the cost to reach them; however, rates are going up due to greater demand rather than bigger audiences.[4]

	AUDIENCE (U.S., millions)	30-SECOND AD COST (USD)
2004:	89.8	$2,200,000
2005:	86.1	$2,400,000
2006:	90.7	$2,500,000
2007:	93.2	$2,600,000
2008:	97.5	$2,700,000
2009:	98.7	$2,700,000
2010:	106.5	$2,500,000
2011:	111	$3,000,000
2012:	111.3	$3,500,000
2013:	108.4	$3,800,000

That's right. In just one decade, Super Bowl ad costs jumped 72 percent while the television audience grew only 21 percent. Clearly, it pays to have proprietary audiences that lots of brands want to reach.

This is why the fossil fuel analogy works. The Paid Media audience is an energy source collected by others and drawn from a finite natural resource—consumer attention. And just like fossil fuel, Paid Media also has some downsides:

1. *It puts companies at the mercy of third parties.* You are always "renting" audience attention from someone else. While some quality assurances about audience composition are provided, companies that advertise are always left feeling as if half their budget was wasted; they just don't know which half.[5]

2. *It leaves marketers subject to the whims of the marketplace.* Just as drivers cringe when prices at the pump rise, so too do marketers when the cost to reach an audience increases 50 percent year after year. CPM (cost per thousand impressions), CPC (cost per click), 30-second spot, and other advertising-unit price spikes strain budgets and force marketers to make up for sales or lead shortfalls elsewhere or miss their numbers. And nobody wants that.

3. *It "pollutes" the consumer environment.* Estimates suggest that the average American consumer is exposed to thousands of advertising messages per day.[6] That's all noise pollution that your message must break through in order to connect with consumers.

If you're not a high-volume, multichannel advertiser, it's safe to say that relying solely on the fossil fuel of advertising is a path to certain extinction. Increased competition for fewer and fewer resources has never been a great survival plan. Just ask the dinosaurs.

Renewable Marketing Energy

Renewable energy is a very romantic notion. You install a solar panel, put a wind turbine on the prairie, or tap the geothermal energy under your home, and you're no longer at the mercy of the energy barons. You can suddenly access all of the clean, abundant energy you need—without ever having to pay a third party ever again.

Only it doesn't quite work that way. At least not yet.

Solar is viable only in certain sun-soaked areas of the world. Wind turbines are great if it's windy, but they tend to kill birds and require a backup power supply when the wind stops. And while geothermal is a great system for newer homes, it's expensive to retrofit. Despite these issues, renewable energy advocates see our future not in fossil fuels but in abundant, natural resources—the sun, wind, tides, and Earth itself. With the help of technology, they hope we can harness these forces to reduce our dependency on fossil fuels.

The Internet is marketing's renewable energy source. After all:

- What is a website if not a type of marketing solar panel set out to collect attention?
- What is a viral video if not a wind turbine propelled by the collective excitement of people who want to share your content?
- What is a Facebook FAN page if not a sort of geothermal system that taps into your most loyal brand FANS' energy?

Proprietary Audience Development is built upon these renewable sources of audience energy. Instead of "paying at the pump," you build your own audiences to propel your growth. Individuals may *opt-out, dislike,* or *stop following* your brand over time. But engaging in ongoing *Proprietary Audience Development* efforts allows you to constantly add new consumers who are eager to hear from your company. To better understand this concept, let's examine the market for baby products.

Babies—or more specifically, their parents—are a renewable source of marketing energy. That first baby may stop using formula, but there's a good chance another will be on the way. And if not, then another new set of parents will be in the market for formula again soon. If you're a brand like Enfamil baby formula (@Enfamil), you understand this. You therefore concentrate on capturing the attention of those fresh, new parents through a website, great search engine optimization (SEO), email, Facebook, Twitter, and other direct online channels. And when their baby no longer needs your products, you cycle those parents out of your direct marketing efforts.*

Consumer energy (i.e., interest in your product) can shift quickly; it's driven by forces such as age, career, convenience, health, income, interests, life stage, and location. Our companies cannot control these changes; therefore, we must be constantly seeking to replenish our renewable, proprietary audiences with new members. And therein lies the rub: We cannot depend solely on fossil fuel advertising or renewable Internet marketing to fuel our companies. We must embrace a *hybrid marketing approach*.

---

*Years after my last child's birth, Enfamil sent me a free can of formula. I believe this was a mistake unless, of course, my wife is now raising a secret child with her secret second family. I'd better go check Facebook . . .

Audience Exercise #2: Desert Island Tactics

One of my favorite questions to ask marketers is this: If you could use only five tactics to grow your business, what would they be?

Inspired by the long-running BBC Radio show (@BBCRadio4), Desert Island Discs, the question gets you focused on the tactics that generate business—not just headlines. So—what are your five "Desert Island Tactics" and why? Which ones require you to pay for audiences versus building your own? Now go ask your marketing colleagues the same question, and let the debate begin!

The Hybrid Marketing Era

When *Motor Trend* (@MotorTrend) named its 2013 Car of the Year, car enthusiasts found themselves face to face with the first winner in the award's 64-year history not powered by an internal combustion engine—the all-electric Tesla Model S (@Tesla). *Motor Trend* itself called the car a "shocking winner" and "proof positive that America can still make great things."[7] That great thing, as it turns out, is a luxury sedan that seats seven and can go 265 miles on a single charge.

The Tesla Model S may be a glimpse at the future—one in which we are far less dependent on fossil fuels and increasingly powered by sustainable energy sources. That future sounds great, but I'm not blind to the truth; the all-electric Model S must be plugged in to charge, and that electricity comes straight from the coal-fired, fossil-fuel-burning electric grid. While the Model S may not technically be a hybrid car, its energy sources most certainly are—electricity from fossil fuels and renewable energy generated while driving.

And that's okay. The Model S doesn't have to solve *all* of the world's energy problems. It's enough that it is a step toward a more energy-efficient future.

We could say the same about *Proprietary Audience Development*. There's no way we're going to solve all of our marketing needs overnight. We simply face too many unknowns as to how consumer technologies, channels, and behaviors will evolve as they mature. But we do know a fundamental truth about marketing that will never change:

Proprietary audiences are a renewable source of energy that any business can develop.

So . . . what if instead of worrying whether we should pour more money into offline or online media, we concentrated on making them *work better together*? One way we can accomplish this is to ask our advertising to do more than just sell. We need to ask it to also help build our email SUBSCRIBERS, our engaged Facebook FANS, our influential Twitter FOLLOWERS—all of our proprietary audiences wherever they congregate now or in the not-too-distant future. This is the higher calling of *hybrid marketing* embodied in *The Audience Imperative*. Let's take a look at its directives once again:

> ***Use your Paid, Owned, and Earned Media not only to sell in the short term but also to increase the size, engagement, and value of your Proprietary Audiences over the long term.***

The Audience Imperative contains four key concepts you must embrace fully before you can begin your *Proprietary Audience Development* efforts:

1. Proprietary Audiences
2. Paid, Owned, and Earned Media
3. Size, Engagement, and Value
4. The Long Term

Let us begin by better understanding the different types of proprietary audiences that we can build today.

Elon Musk: The CEO Armed with Audience

Elon Musk (@ElonMusk) is not a normal CEO. Whereas most executives are content running a single business, Elon runs three—Tesla, SpaceX (@SpaceX), and SolarCity (@SolarCity)—all of which are on the cutting edge of the highly regulated transportation and energy industries.

As an early tech entrepreneur (he also co-founded PayPal and Zip2), Elon was quick to embrace Twitter and has 393,472 FOLLOWERS as of this writing. He is also one of the most active CEOs on Twitter, and regularly uses his Twitter FOLLOWERS to:

- Successfully pressure *The New York Times* (@nytimes) to correct portions of an article in which their journalist made false claims about his test drive of the Tesla Models.

- Amplify major company events such as the early repayment of governmental loans.
- Discredit Tesla skeptics with facts and data.

Elon's Twitter FOLLOWERS allow him to circumvent traditional media gatekeepers, advocate on behalf of his company, and share his thoughts on the future of energy, transportation, and the environment. So the next time your CEO asks you why he or she should tweet, just point to Elon—the CEO who managed to build his Twitter audience while leading three companies simultaneously. Oh, and did I mention he also has five children—a set of twins and triplets? They're the reason the Model S seats seven comfortably.

Your Proprietary Audiences: Seekers, Amplifiers & Joiners

With the crowds on your side, it's easier to play up to your potential.[1]

—Julius "Dr. J" Erving

Leave it to Basketball Hall of Famer Dr. J to provide businesses with the prescription for what ails them. Crowds. Audiences. Attention. As a player, Dr. J experienced firsthand how the singular focus of an audience of thousands can lift one's performance to previously unimaginable heights.

Although your company may not play in sold-out arenas, there are three principal types of proprietary audiences you can draw regularly with the right effort:

1. SEEKERS
2. AMPLIFIERS
3. JOINERS

Understanding the difference among these groups is critical to your long-term ability to build audiences as assets. Accordingly, let's take a moment to examine each in greater detail.

SEEKERS

If you're a *Harry Potter* fan, mere mention of the word *seeker* probably brings to mind Quidditch, the fictional game in which wizards fly on broomsticks in hot pursuit of the "Golden Snitch." While that's clearly not the type of SEEKER we mean to discuss here, it is an apt analogy.

What SEEKERS Want

SEEKERS are consumers in hot pursuit of information or entertainment via the Internet. Such folks may know exactly what they're seeking, or they may not have a clue. What they all *do* know is that there's something out there to serve their needs, and the Internet—accessed via a PC, smartphone, tablet, or other device—is bound to have the answer. SEEKER audiences include:

- BROWSERS
- LISTENERS
- PROSPECTS
- READERS
- SEARCHERS
- SHOPPERS
- VIEWERS
- VISITORS

The key attributes that make each of these audiences SEEKERS are:

1. They are looking for *something of personal interest*—information, a product, a service, a store location or even just entertainment.
2. You gain and retain their attention *by providing relevant content* that serves their interests.
3. They don't become a part of your SEEKER audience *until their attention is focused* on your Paid, Owned, or Earned Media.
4. *They initiate contact* with you, browse, and leave as they like. You're not able to initiate communications.

How SEEKERS Are Acquired

That last attribute is crucial to spotting a SEEKER: *You have no means to initiate communications with them directly.* This is not to say that you are powerless to attract them. Indeed, the entire fields of Content Marketing and SEO are focused on creating and optimizing content that will attract SEEKERS before the competition. However, search engines are just one tool SEEKERS use to find information. Their entire toolbox includes:

- Directories
- Location-based services
- Maps
- Mobile apps (third-party)*
- Online communities (like Quora)
- Reviews
- Search engines
- Social networks

The SEEKER audience is a slippery one; they move tangentially from search results to maps to apps and back again as their interests direct. Technically, a consumer does not become a true member of your SEEKER audience until they arrive at your:

- Blog
- Event
- Landing page
- Photos
- Podcast
- Store (office, restaurant, venue, etc.)
- Social media profile or news feed
- Video
- Website
- Whitepaper

---

*Users of your company's app are JOINERS rather than SEEKERS because they have "joined" your app—they have downloaded it, thereby enabling direct communications from you via app, push messaging, and/or email.

Audience Exercise #3: Find Yourself

Search is no longer an activity solely for those seated in front of a computer. Smartphones and tablets have transformed search such that it can take place anytime, anywhere; there's Web search, location search, social search, and video search. And if your company doesn't appear in all of these search locations, you're either invisible to consumers or a brand defined by others.

Find out how you appear to SEEKERS:

- Search for your company on Google desktop search, Google mobile search, and Google Maps. Repeat the searches after you've logged into a Google product. Document how personalized search changes your results.

- Search for your company on Facebook on the desktop. Compare that to the same search on Facebook's smartphone and tablet apps. Do the same thing using LinkedIn.

- If you have a physical location, visit one and use the AroundMe, Foursquare, and Yelp apps to see whether and how your location is portrayed. Document the accuracy of this information.

- Search for your company or products on Google Images, Flickr, Instagram, Pinterest, and Vine. Document how you appear in these visual channels.

What did you find? Did you like the results? If not, it's time to curate your online appearance as it may be the first (and only) impression you get with SEEKERS.

The Value of SEEKERS

SEEKERS are looking for immediate gratification when they arrive at one of your destinations. As a result, their membership in your SEEKER audience only lasts as long as you satisfy their needs. Your challenge as a marketer, therefore, is to convert SEEKERS into:

- A CUSTOMER (financial value)
- An AMPLIFIER (marketing value via extension of brand reach)
- A JOINER (marketing value via cost-effective, direct communications)

Clearly, our primary goal is to convert all SEEKERS into paying CUSTOMERS (the ultimate JOINER audience). Short of that, getting them to contribute positively to the growth of your AMPLIFIERS or JOINERS (SUBSCRIBERS, FANS, and FOLLOWERS) is a great outcome. Without some conversion, SEEKERS will disappear from your marketing radar without adding any value—perhaps never to return.[*]

The Great Mobile Migration

In the early days of the Internet, SEEKERS were stationary creatures, tethered to the Internet by a keyboard, mouse, and wire. Today, however, they are mobile masters of their domain—using the Internet whenever and wherever they want on smartphones, tablets, and other connected devices (Google Glass, anyone?).

The impact of Internet ubiquity cannot be understated. By 2020, more than 30 billion devices will connect wirelessly to the Internet, and the majority of users will have never known a laptop computer.[2] Today, smartphones comprise over 61 percent of the cell phones in the United States.[3] This means your SEEKERS aren't just *looking* for information; they're armed with it on your doorstep, in your store, and at checkout. They know if there's a better price across town or better food at the restaurant next door.

As a result, smart businesses are reinvesting in convenience, personal attention, and customer service as a means to convert SEEKERS immediately. BestBuy (@BestBuy) offers a best price guarantee and their helpful "Blue Shirts." Walgreens (@Walgreens) offers a mobile app that lets you refill prescriptions and print Instagram pictures. And family-owned Hi-Time Wine Cellars (@MrHiTime) offers SHOPPERS a mobile app that uses videos, special promotions, and wine recommendations to enhance their shopping experience.[4]

What does it mean when everyone inside and outside your store has a supercomputer in their pocket? It means you had better help SEEKERS find you, inspire AMPLIFIERS with superior customer service, and acquire JOINERS so you can communicate directly with them in the future.

---

[*]This isn't totally true if you're using tracking cookies. They may allow you to personalize advertising as the SEEKER moves on to other websites, thereby increasing the opportunity for conversion into a CUSTOMER, AMPLIFIER, SUBSCRIBER, FAN, or FOLLOWER away from your website.

AMPLIFIERS

Whereas SEEKERS want information, AMPLIFIERS are looking for the warm, fuzzy feeling—and social recognition—that comes from *sharing*.

What AMPLIFIERS Want

Just like a wall of Marshall amplifiers (@MarshallAmpsUK) behind a lead guitarist, the AMPLIFIER audience has the potential to spread your messaging to people you could never reach otherwise. AMPLIFIERS aren't just seeking information; they also hope to help or inform their own proprietary audiences (i.e., personal network). AMPLIFIERS raise the volume on your message and propel your content well beyond your marketing budget's reach. Sometimes, they even help branded content "go viral"—the pinnacle of AMPLIFIER audience achievement (aside from gaining some public recognition for themselves).

To put it another way, AMPLIFIERS are audience members with audiences of their own, and they want to be heard. Your AMPLIFIER audiences include:

- ADVOCATES
- ANALYSTS
- COMMENTERS
- CREATORS*
- INFLUENCERS
- REPORTERS
- REVIEWERS
- SHARERS

Amplifiers are audiences with audiences, and they want to be heard.

Basically, if you've got a mouth or hands that can type, you can be an AMPLIFIER—all of whom share a few key attributes:

1. They share—that is, amplify—content or experiences that *interest them* personally or professionally.

---

*I use the term CREATORS as a catch-all for bloggers, Instagrammers, Pinners, and all manner of consumers creating user-generated content (UGC).

2. They share content *when, where, and how they want* through both public and private channels.

3. They share content *as a service to inform or entertain* their own proprietary audiences (family, friends, followers, etc.).

4. They are AMPLIFIERS *only lasts as long as it takes them to share information* about your brand, products, services, content, or activities.

Keep in mind that your most vocal AMPLIFIERS are probably not strangers. Happy CUSTOMERS can serve double duty as AMPLIFIERS as can EMPLOYEES and PARTNERS. This is one reason why the best place to start with social media is often at home (more on that in Chapter 4).

AMPLIFIERS: The People Formerly Known as The Audience

Back in June 2006, NYU Professor of Journalism Jay Rosen (@JayRosen_NYU) penned a pointed commentary titled "The People Formerly Known as the Audience."[5] Written from the perspective of Internet-empowered consumers, the piece served as a wake-up call to media members who still believed they *owned* their audiences.

Jay not only put this notion to rest, he also enumerated how consumers had become content CREATORS capable of stealing attention away from mass media itself. As he stated:

> You don't own the eyeballs. You don't own the press [. . .] You don't control production on the new platform, which isn't one-way. There's a new balance of power between you and us.

AMPLIFIERS are the new, digitally savvy audience Jay contemplated. They are consumers with audiences all their own, and they're under no obligation to help your brand whatsoever. Indeed, it is your obligation to create experiences, products, and services that get the people formerly known as the audience working in your favor.

How to Acquire AMPLIFIERS

Two key actions create AMPLIFIERS:

1. The consumption or creation of content about a company
2. The act of sharing that content with third parties

Amplification of any kind begins with *content*. It may be something an AMPLIFIER creates, something your company creates, or something from a third party, but there must be something to share, such as:

- Blog posts
- Experiences with your brand, products, or services
- Images
- Location information
- Product information
- Reviews
- Written content (books, e-books, infographics, white papers, etc.)
- Videos

With content in hand, consumers become part of your AMPLIFIER audience only when *they choose to share* that content with their own proprietary audiences (colleagues, family, friends, etc.). Notice that as with SEEKERS, AMPLIFIERS initiate the action that makes them a part of your audience. There's no magic button you can push to force consumers to share positive messages about your company. Your best strategy is therefore the same as it is with SEEKERS: to create content and experiences that AMPLIFIERS want to share.

Why AMPLIFIERS Share

Encouraging consumers to share brand stories is nothing new to marketing. Back in the 1970s and 80s, Fabergé Organics Shampoo had a series of commercials in which women—including actress Heather Locklear—beamed that they "told two friends who told two friends and so on and so on."[6] More recently, the "Ask Me" television and online campaign from Tempur-Pedic (@TempurPedic) encouraged customers to share their unfiltered feedback with family and friends on Facebook.[7]

Each of these brands sought to tap the power of their AMPLIFIER audience to generate far more buzz and product awareness than a single television commercial could generate on its own. This is called *word-of-mouth market-ing*, and it has been the subject of study as far back as 1966 when Ernest Dichter published "How Word-of-Mouth Marketing Works" in *Harvard Business Review*.[8] In his survey of 255 U.S. consumers, Dichter identified what he called "active word of mouth recommendations." Of these, Dichter determined that:

- *Product Involvement* drove 33 percent of recommendations (i.e., a great product experience)
- *Self-Involvement* drove 24 percent of recommendations (i.e., the desire for attention or inside information)
- *Message Involvement* drove 23 percent of recommendations (i.e., for humor or information*)
- *Other Involvement* drove the final 20 percent of recommendations (i.e., to reach out and help or show friendship)

More recently in 2012, Brian Brett (@brianbrett1), managing director of customer research for *The New York Times*, spearheaded research into the topic of why people share information online.[9] His team found that among medium-to-heavy sharers, 94 percent carefully consider how information they share will be useful to the recipient(s). Furthermore:

- 84 percent share to *show support* for causes they care about
- 78 percent share in order to *stay connected* with people
- 73 percent share as it connects them to people with *shared interests*
- 69 percent share because it helps them *feel more involved* in the world
- 68 percent share to give people a better sense of *who they are*
- 49 percent share to *inform others of products* they care about and influence their opinions and/or actions

Notice how the sharing of product experiences has evolved from 1966 to today. Nearly half of the sharers (49 percent) surveyed still share to pro-mote or inform others about products, but they are almost 60 percent *more likely* to share content when it helps them stay connected with people or meet

*I have deduced the 23 percent figure from Dichter's research, as his original article omits this statistic without explanation.

others with common interests. As you consider how to inspire your own AMPLIFIER audience, keep in mind that AMPLIFIERS share when it is of *some personal benefit* to them.

Another obvious difference between Dichter's and *The New York Times's* research is the technology available to sharers of the day. When Dichter did his research in 1966, consumers only had a few ways to share content with others—the most important being their voices (a.k.a., big mouths). Today, however, the same social media and mobile technologies that companies use for their marketing also provide consumers with the ability to distribute their every opinion, thought, and observation about your brand—instantaneously and globally. For AMPLIFIERS, those technologies include:

- Blogs (including Tumblr)
- Email
- Facebook
- Foursquare
- Instagram and Vine
- Instant messaging
- Mobile apps
- Pinterest
- Quora
- SMS and Snapchat
- StumbleUpon
- Telephone
- Twitter
- Websites
- Yelp

Amplifiers share when it is of some personal benefit to them.

We focus much of our attention on the social media channels in the list above—Facebook and Twitter foremost among them—because of the public nature of likes, comments, shares, and retweets on each platform. Do not forget, however, that email is a critical channel for AMPLIFIERS. In fact, according to a number of recent studies, email remains the top channel through which people share content online.[10] It's just that much of that sharing is done on a private, one-to-one basis under cover of private email inboxes.

From Illustration to Amplification

Len Peralta (@LenPeralta) calls himself a freelance artist, but I know him for what he really is—an immensely talented and creative entrepreneur. With a self-proclaimed goal to make art affordable to everyone, he has set up numerous storefronts on the web. MonsterByMail.com offers buyer original, hand-drawn cartoon monsters for $50. FlipFace.me turns your boring social media avatar into a unique caricature for only $15.

But Len's most ambitious project to date, the Geek A Week Trading Card Series (@GeekAWeek) owes much of it success to his AMPLIFIERS. Launched as a labor of love in 2010, Len set out to interview one influential person from the realm of pop culture, meme culture, or general geeky fandom each week for a year—all the while turning those interviews into podcasts and immortalizing them in a hand-drawn trading card. Early cards featured "Internet rock star" Jonathan Coulton (@JonathanCoulton), nerdcore rapper MC Frontalot (@MCFrontalot), and film director Kevin Smith (@ThatKevinSmith).

As the series progressed, many of the "geeks" Len profiled turned into AMPLIFIERS, sharing news of the series (www.Geek AWeek.net) with friends around the world. The amplification helped Len not only land additional interviews with the legendary Stan Lee (@TheRealStanLee) and *Game of Thrones* author George R. R. Martin; it also helped him sign on partners to manufacture and sell actual Geek A Week card sets.

With the fourth set of Geek A Week cards now under his belt, Len has seen firsthand the power of AMPLIFIERS—and approaches every new project with the goal of ensuring that he produces something exciting for them to share.

The Double-Edged Sword of AMPLIFIERS

The primary value of AMPLIFIERS is clear: They extend your brand's reach and content distribution at no cost to you. They can also help drive SEEKERS to your website, blog, or mobile app, and encourage others to become JOINERS. We must not forget, however, that AMPLIFIERS can also be bad for business. As Andy Sernovitz (@sernovitz), author of *Word of Mouth Marketing*, puts it:

> Happy customers are your greatest advertisers.[11]

Unfortunately, the corollary is also true:

> Unhappy customers are your worst advertisers.

If you're going to engage AMPLIFIERS, you must prepare for the inevitable day that one of them turns on you by writing a bad review on Yelp, tweeting about poor customer service, or—God forbid—posting pictures of sewage flowing down the walls of their luxury cruise cabin.[12] Social media plays no favorites. It can turn any customer with a smartphone into a reporter and any consumer with an axe to grind—legitimate or not—into a cause célèbre.

As a result, your PR team has a huge stake in developing your company's proprietary audiences. It is not enough to just push consumers to amplify content about your brand. When a brand crisis hits and "it's all gone Pete Tong,"* you need audiences other than AMPLIFIERS and SEEKERS to help tell your side of the story. You need audiences that are just a push button away.

Enter the JOINERS.

JOINERS

Make no mistake about it; *JOINERS are the most valuable audiences you can build for your company.* They are the foundation of all *permission marketing*, because they are your *push-button* audiences (i.e., you initiate contact).

What JOINERS Want

JOINERS are the people who buy your products, work with your company, or put their hands up and say, "I want to hear from you!" They *like, follow,*

---

*As a fan of Cockney rhyming slang, I couldn't resist. "It's all gone Pete Tong" means "it's all gone wrong." I hope that clears things up such that "Bob's your uncle" (i.e., everything's good).

pin, register, and *subscribe* to receive information that is of interest to them; and in so doing, they selectively open the communication channels they use to your messaging. You may know JOINERS better by these familiar names:

- CUSTOMERS
- DINERS
- DONORS
- EMPLOYEES
- FANS
- FOLLOWERS
- PARTNERS
- SUBSCRIBERS

JOINERS are the most valuable audiences you can build for your company.

I have a particular affinity for JOINERS for three reasons:

1. They grant you permission to **send direct messages** to them.
2. They provide you with an individually addressable **means of contact**.
3. Their interactions with your brand provide you with **personal data** about each JOINER—data that you can use to better tailor messaging to their needs and serve them at point of sale.

CUSTOMERS are the be-all and end-all of JOINER audiences. They pay the bills and refer business your way when they're happy (thereby becoming AMPLIFIERS). EMPLOYEES and PARTNERS, on the other hand, are slightly different creatures.

Like AMPLIFIERS, EMPLOYEES and PARTNERS are audiences with audiences (friends, family, clients, etc.). The difference is that EMPLOYEES and PARTNERS work with you of their own volition, thereby giving you permission to message them in the regular course of business. If their business relationship with you ends, however, so may their desire to be a part of any of your proprietary audiences.

Obtaining Permission from JOINERS

Notice that the prerequisite to having any JOINER audience is first obtaining permission to message. This may come in the form of a subscription process or the *like* or *follow* button. In limited circumstances and channels—such as with certain emails to CUSTOMERS, EMPLOYEES, and PARTNERS—the permission may even be *implicit* based on a *preexisting business relationship.**

Absent some form of legitimate permission to message, you do not have a JOINER audience; you have a captive, unwilling group of individuals being force-fed your marketing. In his seminal work, *Permission Marketing*, Seth Godin (@ThisIsSethsBlog) called such marketing without permission "*interruption marketing.*" The alternative of *permission marketing* is superior because:

> [It] offers the consumer an opportunity to *volunteer* to be mar-
> keted to. By talking only to volunteers, Permission Marketing
> guarantees that consumers pay more attention to the marketing
> messages.[13]

When Seth wrote this, Facebook and Twitter didn't exist, and email was the primary permission marketing channel. Today, however, you can build SUBSCRIBERS, FANS, and FOLLOWERS through numerous channels. These push-button JOINERS grant you a greater measure of control over message content, design, timing, and frequency—control you lack with SEEKERS and AMPLIFIERS. And while the various channels you use to communicate with SUBSCRIBERS, FANS, and FOLLOWERS may limit you creatively (picture the difference between a highly visual email message and a 140-character tweet), the limitations play no favorites—they apply to all companies who message JOINERS.

SUBSCRIBERS, FANS, and FOLLOWERS are also unique because you *tailor* your content, products, and services to their needs thanks to their individually addressable means of contact (email address, Facebook profile, Twitter handle, etc.). Each individual address provides the foundation upon which you can add data to each JOINER'S profile, using the information they provide or you collect. This can include demographic, click-stream, search, amplification, and purchase data, and it fuels highly beneficial Customer

---

*Be sure to consult both the laws and prevailing customs of your country to determine what constitutes permission to message. While the U.S. CAN-SPAM law enables businesses to message customers with whom they have a "preexisting business relationship," it does not always mean you should.

Relationship Management (CRM), marketing automation, and remarketing efforts.

The holy grail, of course, is to build relationships of such quality that your JOINERS value each message from your brand. This not only increases response but also gives you an opportunity to turn JOINERS into AMPLIFIERS in ways that attract new SEEKERS. In essence, JOINERS supercharge all of your *Proprietary Audience Development* efforts.

If your messaging isn't personally useful, timely, or meaningful to your JOINERS, you will lose them.

The Four Rights of JOINERS

Of course, with great data comes great responsibility. There's an unspoken contract between JOINERS and companies built upon what I call *The Four Rights*:

1. The *right message*
2. To the *right person*
3. At the *right time*
4. Through the *right channel*

I first wrote about these rights back in October 2007 in the context of email and SMS.[14] *The Four Rights* remain amazingly relevant because Facebook, Twitter, and similar social channels are *consumer-controlled* (like email) instead of *marketer-controlled* (like direct mail). Consumers hold all the power; it takes only one click for them to turn off your messaging by *un-liking, unfollowing,* or *unsubscribing from* your content.

The Four Rights can actually be condensed into a single mandate for every marketer interested in *Proprietary Audience Development*: be relevant. You must constantly be working to meet or exceed JOINER expectations—because if your messaging isn't personally useful, timely, or meaningful to them, they will lose interest, and you will lose *them*.

With our understanding of permission and *The Four Rights* secured, it's now time for us to do a deeper dive into the key proprietary JOINER audiences: SUBSCRIBERS, FANS, and FOLLOWERS. They are, after all, a few of the most important marketing assets you can build for your company today.

Chapter 4

The VIP Joiners: Subscribers, Fans & Followers

I maintain that couchsurfing and crowdsurfing are basically the same thing. You're falling into the audience and you're trusting each other.[1]

—Amanda Palmer

Amanda Palmer (@AmandaPalmer) has a lot of SUBSCRIBERS, FANS, and FOLLOWERS due to her years as a solo artist, band member (one-half of The Dresden Dolls), and front woman of The Grand Theft Orchestra. She is also accessible to her FANS in more ways than most anyone with a modicum of fame. She "couchsurfs" in their homes when on tour, crowdsources items from them as needs appear, and interacts with them personally via her website, blog, email, Twitter, and Facebook.

In 2012, nearly four years since her last album and after an acrimonious breakup with her record label, Amanda decided to seek funding for her new album, *Theatre Is Evil*, from her FANS via Kickstarter (@Kickstarter), the crowdsourced funding phenomenon. The campaign sought to raise $100,000. It finished north of $1.2 million. And soon, Amanda Palmer had a new, very vocal audience.

Detractors.

With that kind of money in hand, people who never had any interest in Amanda began to scrutinize how she planned to use the money. They wondered out loud and in print if both Amanda and Kickstarter had an "accountability problem."[2]

Theatre Is Evil was released in September 2012, and five months later, Amanda delivered a TED Talk called "The Art of Asking." In it, she discussed her career, the Kickstarter controversy, and her plans to continue couchsurfing, crowdsourcing, and asking FANS for different types of support.[3]

Why would she do this when she had such a lucrative Kickstarter campaign? Because she didn't just *take* from her FANS in these exchanges; she *gave* as well: attention, conversation, free music, artwork, and more. To Amanda and her FANS—her *people*—she gave as much as she received. And it doesn't matter if her detractors roll their eyes at that notion; to Amanda's JOINERS—her SUBSCRIBERS, FANS, and FOLLOWERS—the value exchange is just fine.

I share Amanda's story because it highlights something every marketer needs to master: *the art of asking*. While it's necessary, it's not enough to obtain the permission we discussed in Chapter 3. You must also give your JOINERS something meaningful in return. When you do that, it doesn't matter what the occasional detractors say. All that matters is the strength of your SUBSCRIBER, FAN, and FOLLOWER relationships—because they're the engine that powers your business.

To put it in a more colloquial way: *Haters gonna hate*. So don't fixate on the people who will never be a part of your audience; concentrate on the ones who are or who could be.

Over the course of this chapter, we'll dig into what distinguishes the three JOINER audiences that are most important to marketers—SUBSCRIBERS, FANS, and FOLLOWERS—from one another. At the risk of putting the cart before the horse, here's how I would differentiate the expectations of each:

SUBSCRIBERS = Convenience delivered.

FANS = Passion empowered.

FOLLOWERS = Information shared.

The channels JOINERS use impact their expectations. Therefore, your success with SUBSCRIBERS, FANS, and FOLLOWERS depends on your ability to meet or exceed their channel and messaging expectations. Let's take a look at each JOINER audience to understand their differences better.

With More than a Little Help from a Friend

Back in late 2009 while we were colleagues at ExactTarget (@ExactTarget), Morgan Stewart (@mostew) and I first hatched the idea of studying the different core motivations of SUBSCRIBERS, FANS, and FOLLOWERS. That idea gave rise to our research series of the same name and planted the seed for this very book.

Morgan has since gone on to launch Trendline Interactive (@trendlinei), his own consultancy focused on helping companies maximize the value of their proprietary audiences—particularly email SUBSCRIBERS. While he's not listed as a co-author of *AUDIENCE*, he certainly contributed mightily to its existence. And for that, I'm forever grateful—and his #1 FAN.

SUBSCRIBERS

Well before there was an Internet, there were SUBSCRIBERS. They had newspapers on their front stoops, magazines in their mailboxes, and cable television networks on their TVs. Back then, SUBSCRIBERS were best defined as: *Consumers who provided something of value (money) in order to receive exclusive information delivered to their home or office.*

What SUBSCRIBERS Want

These traditional SUBSCRIBERS still exist today, and I'm proud to count myself among them. *The Cleveland Plain Dealer* (@PlainDealer) currently lies spread out on our kitchen table with my daughter's head in the comics. My son is busy reading a dog-eared copy of *FourFourTwo* (@FourFourTwo), our favorite world football (soccer) magazine. My latest copy of *Wired* (@Wired) is on my desk waiting for its usual cover-to-cover read. Oh, and there's also the two TVs with cable—mainly because of my addiction to the English Premier League (@PremierLeague) and HBO's *Game of Thrones* (@GameOfThrones).

You may be tempted to call me a Luddite due to my consumption of "old media." However, that misses the point. I keep each of my "old media" subscriptions because they're *convenient*. Yes, I could consume newspaper, magazine, and video content on my iPad or Kindle; however, I want them delivered in a fashion that is easy and useful for my lifestyle. That's the value of being a SUBSCRIBER; I get to choose because I've paid for the privilege.

The value exchange is similar for your company's SUBSCRIBER audiences:

> *Consumers provide something of value (such as an email address) to receive exclusive information delivered to the channel of their choosing.*

How SUBSCRIBERS Are Acquired

You can build SUBSCRIBERS online through these digital direct channels:

- Email
- Mobile apps*
- Online communities
- Podcasts
- RSS**
- SMS***
- YouTube

We'll delve into the specifics of the major SUBSCRIBER channels in Part II. The key point to understand right now is that SUBSCRIBER expectations are set *at the time of subscription.* Thus, if you promise that SUBSCRIBERS to your emails will receive exclusive offers, you had better provide exclusive offers—not just stuff that everybody gets. If you promise convenience to your mobile app SUBSCRIBERS, you absolutely must offer an experience that doesn't frustrate. Failing to meet SUBSCRIBER expectations will inevitably cause poor channel performance, negative brand experiences, and higher unsubscribe rates.

---

*While it's more accurate to refer mobile app audiences as "users" or "downloaders," I have included them as SUBSCRIBERS because our interest is in your company's ability to communicate with them in an exclusive fashion—something a mobile app affords both when opened and when push messaging is enabled.

**RSS stands for Really Simple Syndication as and is a means to distribute content online.

***SMS stands for Short Messaging Service and is better known as text messaging.

A Social Guy Catches Email Religion

I could barely contain my frustration a few years ago as marketers half my age waxed poetic about Facebook and Twitter, while disparaging email marketing. Email has been and remains the Internet's silent workhorse, directly accounting for a much higher volume of sales revenue than Facebook and Twitter combined.[4]

So imagine my delight when SocialTriggers founder Derek Halpern (@DerekHalpern) posted a video in which he proclaimed, "If you're not building an email list, you're an idiot."[5] Derek graduated from college in 2006 and came of age during the social media explosion. As a result, he focused many of his early, traffic-driving efforts for his websites on Facebook and Twitter. But then he caught religion in 2012 when he saw that an email to his neglected email SUBSCRIBER list generated 14 times the amount of traffic to his website as a tweet on the same day and topic did.

To watch Derek's impassioned endorsement of email on YouTube still warms my heart. We must remember—and help all our colleagues understand—that just because a channel is old by Internet standards doesn't mean it's not valuable. Just ask Derek and his email SUBSCRIBERS.

This is not to say that you can't *evolve* your communications with SUBSCRIBERS over time, but you must explain the changes when you do so, and always, *always*, give them the opportunity to opt-out of future communications. This is a legal requirement in email and SMS SUBSCRIBER channels. In other SUBSCRIBER channels, it's simply understood that consumers can delete your app or unsubscribe from a podcast at will. As with all of your JOINER audiences, the decision to stay or go is the consumer's alone.

To summarize, SUBSCRIBERS want content from your company that is:

- Convenient
- Useful
- Delivered through the channel they choose
- Consistent with expectations set at time of subscription (or after)

This is markedly different than what your FANS want.

FANS

We use the term *fan* so frequently these days that it's easy to forget that the word that really didn't originate until the late nineteenth century. Take a look at this definition:

> **fan:** *"devotee," 1889, American English, originally of baseball enthusiasts, probably a shortening of* fanatic, *but may be influenced by* the fancy, *a collective term for followers of a certain hobby or sport (especially boxing); see* fancy. *There is an isolated use from 1682, but the modern word is likely a late 19c. formation.* Fan club *attested by 1930.*[6]

If you've ever been to a football match of any kind—be it soccer, rugby, Aussie, Canadian, or American rules—you know that FAN is short for *fanatic* and little else. From the body paint to the vuvuzelas to the waving banners to the obscene chants to the words shaved into (or out of) chest hair, FANS often embody what Charles Mackay so rightly called "the madness of crowds."[7] There's just something about rooting your team on to victory that brings insanity to the surface and leaves common sense waiting at the door.

What FANS Want

This essence of fandom is *emotion*. Whereas SUBSCRIBERS want convenience, FANS want to express and share their passion for something they enjoy. They form emotional bonds with teams, entertainers, and products, and wearing their team colors or buying their favorite brand of shoes is as much an expression of their personal identity as it is their loyalty. FANS aren't relationships of convenience like SUBSCRIBERS. They have heart-pumping, pulse-racing relationships built on *passion*—the degree of which is dictated by the quality of their experiences with the person, team, or brand in question.

The rise of "brand FANS" significantly predates the Internet and probably owes much of its growth to the rise of pop culture. We're all *consumers* of soda pop, toilet paper, and automobiles; but we're *FANS* of Coke (@Coke), Charmin (@Charmin), and the Ford Mustang (@FordMustang). In moving from the generic to the brand-specific, businesses provided consumers with the means to literally wear their loyalty on their faces (Oakley® brand sunglasses—@Oakley), feet (Nike® brand shoes—@Nike), and sleeves (Threadless® brand T-shirts—@Threadless). But before the Internet came along, it was a challenge for brands—other than those in sports and entertainment—to gather their FANS together.

That's not to say it never happened. Consider:

- In 1949, the Pillsbury Bake-Off got its start by whittling thousands of FAN entrants to 100 competitors who used Pillsbury Best Flour to make creations that wowed the judges. The competition now runs every other year with a $1 million prize for the winner.[8]
- In 1976, 33 rabid FANS and collectors of Coca-Cola memorabilia met to form The Coca-Cola Collectors Club, sponsors of the annual "Springtime in Atlanta" convention for worldwide Coke collectors.[9]
- In 1978, FANS of the Mini brand automobile organized the inaugural International Mini Meeting (IMM), a three-day camping event in Germany. Today, the event rotates locations around Europe, with over 10,000 Mini FANS attending IMM 2013 in Italy.[10]

How FANS Are Acquired

Nowadays, the job of aggregating brand FANS together is made far easier by FAN-focused, online channels like Facebook and Myspace. Facebook is obviously the 800-lb. gorilla of these two, having displaced Myspace years ago as the preeminent, global social media channel.*

If there is one thing you must know about Facebook, however, it is this: Facebook never *created* a Cleveland Browns FAN. Not one. Browns FANS are created in the same way they have been since their last NFL Championship in 1964—by geography, bloodlines, and experiences. I'm cursed to walk the Earth as a Browns FAN because I hit the trifecta: I was born in Toledo, Ohio (just two hours from Cleveland), my father was a Browns FAN (clearly a form of abuse), and I attended what was one of the greatest games in Browns history (the 23–20 double-overtime playoff victory over the New York Jets on January 4, 1987).**

---

*As of this writing, Justin Timberlake (@JTimberlake) and his fellow Myspace investors are doing their utmost to breathe new life into the once-dominant social network. If they succeed, then those in entertainment industries may have a new/old place to build and engage FANS.

**Many thanks to Mark Gastineau for his roughing-the-passer penalty that enabled the Browns' 1987 playoff comeback. Also, my sincere apologies to Jets future owner, mega-FAN, and best-selling author Gary Vaynerchuk (@garyvee) for referencing the sordid tale at all. When you're a Browns FAN, you cling to ancient victories.

I share my curse because it highlights a very important point: Facebook doesn't create the vast majority of brand FANS; it provides *a place* for them to congregate online. In fact, a recent study found that 78 percent of a brand's FANS are already CUSTOMERS.[11] If your products and services stink and you have zero brand loyalty to see you through, then you aren't apt to have many FANS on Facebook. In fact, the people who *like* your page in such a scenario may just as easily be detractors looking to post complaints. To build Facebook FANS, you must have a product or service with passionate *offline* FANS. If you don't, don't even bother with this chapter; your time is better spent improving your products and services.

A Tasty Exception to the Facebook Customer-Before-FAN Rule

Chef Matt Fish is a rock star at heart. He grew up listening to KISS (@KISSOnline), Black Sabbath (@OfficialSabbath), and Rocket from the Crypt (@RFTCRFTC), and he's been playing in bands since he was a teen. It was no wonder, then, that when he opened Melt Bar & Grilled (@MeltBarGrilled) in 2006, he took a rock-and-roll approach to marketing.

Matt promoted his gourmet grilled cheese restaurant like a band and treated every new sandwich like a record release—complete with its own concert poster. In 2009, he launched an email club, a Facebook FAN page, and special Melt Tattoo Family promotion. The deal was simple—get a Melt-inspired, grilled cheese tattoo and receive 25 percent off food and alcohol for life. Four days after launching the Tattoo Family promotion, a regular walked in with a tattoo. Today, over 500 people display their FAN fervor for Melt via body ink.

But you want to know the craziest thing? Matt counts at least five Tattoo Family members who got their tattoos *before ever eating at Melt!* When asked why, one of the FANS said that he decided to get his tattoo after seeing raving reviews and pics from his Facebook friends. When Matt asked how he would feel if he didn't like the food, the FAN responded, "Not a chance, dude."

Melt's success has surprised Matt in many ways. He's been featured on the Food Network (@FoodNetwork), named Business Person of the Year, and expanded to five locations. But if you ask him what's most surprising about his success, he'll tell you about the FAN who got a grilled cheese sandwich tattoo before ever tasting his grilled cheese. Yes, Facebook can help you create FANS, but you had better deliver the goods if you want to keep them as paying CUSTOMERS.

Before 2010, a consumer became a FAN of a company on Facebook by clicking the *Become a Fan* button. While this button's purpose was as clear as day, Facebook came to view it as setting too high a bar for brand interaction. And when you're trying to increase FAN/brand interactions—and the advertising opportunities that go with them—you want as frictionless an experience as possible.

Enter the *Like button*. Introduced in a limited fashion on Facebook in 2009, it replaced *Become a Fan* entirely in 2010. Facebook explained its rationale for the change as follows:

> To improve your experience and promote consistency across the site, we've changed the language for Pages from "Fan" to "Like." We believe this change offers you a more light-weight and standard way to connect with people, things and topics in which you are interested.[12]

While there was some initial user backlash to this change, Facebook held firm, and the *Like* button is now as commonplace as *email, comment,* and *share* across the Web. The *Like* button does continue to raise an interesting question for all brands: Does one click truly create a brand FAN?

The answer is both yes and no. "Yes" in the sense that clicking *Like* on a brand page opens the door for direct communications between brands and consumers—the basis of any JOINER audience. "No" in the sense that the "light-weight" expression of positive sentiment that the *Like* button captures is not exactly the height of brand passion we'd expect from true FANS.

Still, Facebook, Myspace, and other FAN-focused social networks afford companies the opportunity to capture a broader spectrum of both new and veteran FANS. To put it another way: Think of the *Like* button as the "gateway click" that puts the burden on your company to deepen the FAN relationship over time. It's a tool that gives consumers the opportunity for more peer-to-peer discussions about your brand.

Think of the like button as the "gateway click" that puts the burden on your company to deepen the FAN relationship over time.

This is a critical point about your FAN audience: Their communications with *other FANS* are just as important—if not moreso—than *your* communications directly with them. Online FAN environments provide a virtual watercooler where FANS can discuss your products and services, share tips, and amplify stories about your brand. Remember how we discussed earlier that AMPLIFIERS are a *momentary* audience because they share your content one moment and are gone the next? Well, your online FANS often also transform into AMPLIFIERS when they want to share their passion with their networks. These AMPLIFIER/FAN hybrids are one of the most powerful dual audiences at your disposal—passionate people willing to share their love of your company with the world.

One final thought: FANS can be fickle. Every week in football, there's a team that's booed mercilessly off the field. Often, those aren't their enemies booing; those are their FANS. The double-edged sword of FANS is that they can turn on you just as quickly as they support you.

This is the risk you run when you chose to aggregate your FANS online. You are creating a public environment to share your successes just as easily as your failures. If your company doesn't have the stomach to deal with the inevitable emotional ups and downs of passionate FANS, then it may be best to avoid building your FAN audiences online altogether.

But those who do take the risk and weather the occasional crisis will reap one of the unexpected benefits of FAN audiences: free customer service.

Serenity Now: When FANS Attack

As an online purveyor of "stuff for smart masses," it's no surprise that online retailer ThinkGeek (@ThinkGeek) has over half a million Facebook FANS. When you sell hard-to-find items like bacon wallets, Chewbacca robes, and canned "unicorn meat," you tend to inspire deep loyalty from people with humorous sensibilities.

But all was not fun and games in April 2013 when ThinkGeek found itself the subject of sudden FAN outrage regarding a single product called Jayne's Hat.[13] The hat, a licensed version of one worn by tough-guy character Jayne Cobb on the short-lived, 20th Century Fox TV (@20CenturyFoxTV) series *Firefly*, was not unlike versions knitters had been selling on their own for a decade.

So, when unlicensed Jayne Hat knitters started getting cease and desist letters from 20th Century Fox in early 2013, many jumped to the false conclusion that ThinkGeek had something to do with it. The negative Facebook posts and tweets started rolling in, criticizing ThinkGeek for putting profits over FANS.

Fortunately, however, ThinkGeek had the facts—and its FANS— on its side. The company quickly clarified the situation on its blog and announced that all proceeds from sales of its Jayne Hat would go to benefit Equality Now (@EqualityNow), the preferred charity of *Firefly* FAN organization Can't Stop the Serenity (@CSTS).[14]

In the end, ThinkGeek found its serenity thanks to its FANS who helped the company combat misinformation in the marketplace and amplify their shared dislike of the license owner's actions.

FANS Serving FANS

When my team recently examined how the fastest-growing U.S. retailers interact with FANS online, we discovered something interesting. Fifty-one percent of the time, FANS answered questions on company Facebook pages before the company itself did.[15] That's right, engaged FANS *voluntarily* become an extension of your customer service department.

FANS can also play a critical role in PR and crisis management. When your brand is attacked—be it by outside critics, misinformed AMPLIFIERS, or angry CUSTOMERS—FANS will often rally to the defense of your brand on Facebook. They do so to correct perceived wrongs and to protect your brand. Unbound by rules, regulations, or lawyers, FANS can tell someone they're wrong to their face without worrying about the PR implications. They are your *social white blood cells* that help fight those who want to infect your brand with negativity. Accordingly, your company needs to build FANS online for *defensive* purposes as well as *offensive purposes*. In so doing, you capture their full potential.

To summarize, consumers join your FAN audiences to:

- Express their **passion** for your brand.
- Connect with **like-minded** individuals.
- Derive **benefits** from their fandom.
- **Protect** your brand when needed.

Now let's take a look at an audience that loves first-to-know information—as well as the prestige that comes with sharing it with others.

FOLLOWERS

In the pre-Internet world, a FOLLOWER had a pretty simple definition:

An adherent or devotee of a particular person, cause, or activity.

Yet when I ask people to give me examples of pre-Internet FOLLOWERS during my presentations, the answers don't flow so freely. Someone will whisper, "Disciples." Then someone with a bit more gumption will say, "Voters." And finally, the comedian of the bunch will yell, "Cult members!" or "Stalkers!" The laughter that usually greets those last answers points to a certain awkwardness many people have about the whole notion of "following." Perhaps it is today's Type A personality–driven culture or our desire to be in control, but many people don't want to be considered FOLLOWERS so much as leaders.

What FOLLOWERS Want

The key attribute of FOLLOWERS is that they're seeking *curated information*, straight from the source, and they often want the *social prestige* that comes from sharing it. FOLLOWERS may or may not have a passionate relationship with your brand; information is their currency. This not to say that FOLLOWERS can't be passionate; just look at the tweets from Justin Bieber's (@JustinBieber) rabid Twitter FOLLOWERS. But by and large, FOLLOWERS are there to be *the first to know* information from the companies, events, organizations, people, and teams that interest them.

Another interesting twist is that most FOLLOWERS don't follow just to follow; *they follow to be followed.* If your brand can provide its FOLLOWERS with interesting insights, information, or other content that not everyone has seen, you give them the opportunity to be the first person to bring that same content to *their* FOLLOWERS' attention.* That gives them a measure of prestige and, potentially, the opportunity to grow their own following by becoming a trusted source of interesting information.

Sounds circuitous, right?

How FOLLOWERS Are Acquired

But that's the power of FOLLOWERS. They are a type of JOINERS you can message directly and transform into AMPLIFIERS. And you can build them in a variety of channels today, including:

- Google+
- Facebook
- Instagram
- LinkedIn
- Pinterest
- SlideShare
- Twitter
- Vine

---

*This is the basis of Earned Media, which we'll explore in the next chapter.

What's fascinating about these FOLLOWER channels is the fact that each has materialized in just the past decade. We began following people's careers (LinkedIn), then their 140-character tweets (Twitter), and now our informational voyeurism also encompasses images (Pinterest), presentations (SlideShare), and photos and videos (Instagram and Vine). Moreover, look at the dizzying array of who, what, where we can follow just on Twitter:

- Actors (like @KevinBacon)
- Agencies (like @WeAreSocial)
- Airlines (like @United)
- Appliances (like @mytoaster)
- Athletes (like @GarethBale11)
- Authors (like, oh, I don't know . . . @jkrohrs)
- Bands (like @Hollerado)
- Charities (like @DonorsChoose)
- Cities (like @LakewoodOhio)
- Comedians (like @PattonOswalt)
- Companies (like @ExactTarget)
- Fictitious characters (like @HomerJSimpson)
- Financial Institutions (like @Chase)
- Food (like @mmsgreen)
- Games (@AngryBirds)
- Hotels (like the @NYHiltonMidtown)
- Journalists (like @AmberLyon)
- Leagues (like the @AFL)
- Magazines (like @TheEconomist)
- Mobile apps (like @VineApp)
- Movies and movie theaters (like @Avengers and @AMCTheaters)
- Museums (like @MuseumModernArt)
- Musicians (like cellist Zoe Keating, @ZoeCello)
- Newspapers (like @NYTimes)
- Pets (like @Sockington the cat)
- Places (like the Golden Gate Bridge—@GGBridge)
- Plants (via technology from companies like @Botanicalls)
- Political parties (like @GOP)
- Racing teams (like @FollowAndretti)
- Radio stations or podcast hosts (like @KQED and @MenInBlazers)
- Religious leaders (like @Pontifex)
- Restaurants (like @DeagansKitchen)
- Stores (like @CLEClothingCo)
- Teams (like @ManchesterUnited)
- TV networks, shows, and stations (like @AMC_TV, @WKYC, and @60 Minutes)
- Universities (like @MiamiUniversity)
- World Leaders (like @BarackObama)

Tired yet? I assure you that this list could go on and on and on. And this is a reason some use *not* to build FOLLOWERS; there's simply too much noise out there already. The fact is, however, that the consumers who want to follow your company will cut through the clutter to find you—if you let them.

A Peek Behind the Steel Curtain

When the 2012 Super Bowl came to Indianapolis, die-hard Pittsburgh Steelers (@Steelers) FAN Seth Paladin (@sdpaladin) was only moderately enthused. After all, a Patriots–Giants matchup left him rooting for the lesser of two evils.

All of that changed on the Tuesday before the game, however, when, as a FOLLOWER of Antonio Brown (@AntonioBrown84), he saw the Steelers wide receiver tweet that he was in Indianapolis for the week and looking for things to do. On a whim, Seth tweeted back: "I live in Indy! Let's get lunch! How's 12:30?"

Antonio not only took Seth upon on the offer; the two went on to hang out together multiple times that week. They lifted weights and shared stories about their families, and Antonio even joined a birthday dinner for one of Seth's friends at The Capital Grille (@CapitalGrille), where the NFL player graciously picked up the entire check. Antonio's generosity was repaid when he discovered he had left his dress shoes back home and Seth was able to buy a pair for him.

It's rare these days that an NFL (@NFL) football player can just "hang" with a FAN/FOLLOWER; but that's what Twitter afforded Antonio and Seth. One got to step behind the Steel Curtain—the other, from out behind it.[16]

In summary, your FOLLOWER audiences want:

- *Information* (that you've curated)
- *Access*
- *Unique insights*
- *Shareable content* with which they can build *their own* FOLLOWERS

So there you have it: the composition, motivations, and interests of the three JOINER audiences that are critical to marketing: SUBSCRIBERS, FANS, and FOLLOWERS. Our *SFF* research has determined that among U.S. adults, who are online and age 18 years and older:

- 93 percent are email SUBSCRIBERS to one or more brands.
- 58 percent (and growing) are Facebook FANS of one of more brands.
- 12 percent (and growing) are Twitter FOLLOWERS of one of or more brands.[17]

The growth of Facebook FANS and Twitter FOLLOWERS has not come at the expense of email SUBSCRIBERS. Thus, the marketing opportunity today is to grow all of your JOINER audiences. To do that, you're going to need to optimize your Paid, Owned, and Earned Media in ways that would make an old-school marketer's head spin.

Beyond Don Draper: Paid, Owned & Earned Media

Change is neither good [n]or bad, it simply is. It can be greeted with terror or joy. A tantrum that says, "I want it the way it was," or a dance that says, "Look, it's something new."[1]
—Don Draper, *Mad Men*

I owe a debt of gratitude to Don Draper. For the past few years, the stylish lead character of *Mad Men* (@MadMen_AMC) has starred in many of my presentations about marketing's changing landscape. Indeed, it's nearly impossible to watch the show about a 1960s Madison Avenue advertising agency without wondering how Don would fare in today's world. After all, he was a fossil fuel marketer, a creature of mass media whose only job was to generate great ideas while someone managed the design, layout, media buying, and ad trafficking.

But my, how times have changed. To understand this, all we need to do is to compare the marketing tactics around in Don's day to those available today. What the *Mad Men* had to contend with is shown in Table 5.1.

TABLE 5.1 The Marketing Tactics of Don Draper's Day

Direct Media Tactics	Mass Media Tactics
Events	Outdoor
Direct Mail	Signage
Catalogs	Print
Telemarketing	Radio
	Television

These were *stable* channels that allowed Don's creativity to flourish unhindered by the vagaries of technology. Sure, TV went from black and white to color, FM supplanted AM radio, and newspapers began printing in color, but these moves didn't result in wholesale changes to the mechanics of advertising or how consumers interacted with each medium. That made Don Draper's professional life pretty easy.

Now rest your eyes in wild amazement at the tactics available to marketers today (Table 5.2).

TABLE 5.2 Today's Ever-Expanding Universe of Marketing Tactics

Direct Media Tactics	Mass Media Tactics
Events	Signage
Direct Mail	OOH* (Outdoor)
Catalogs	Print
Telemarketing	Radio
Direct Fax	Television
Email	Infomercials
IM (Instant Messaging)	Video Games
SMS (Short Message Service)	Internet Relay Chat
MMS (Multimedia Messaging Service)	Websites
Automated Voice Messaging	Chat Rooms
RSS (Really Simple Syndication)	Organic Search
Social DM (Direct Messaging)	Online Display
Push Notifications (via Mobile Apps)	Paid Search
OTT Messaging Apps (i.e., Snapchat)	Landing Pages
	Microsites
	Webinars
	Affiliate Marketing
	Online Video
	Blogs
	Podcasts
	Contextual Advertising
	In-Game Advertising
	Wikis
	Social Networks
	Mobile Web
	DOOH (Digital Out of Home)
	Behavioral Advertising
	Social Advertising
	Virtual Worlds
	Widgets
	Twitter

(continued)

TABLE 5.2   *(continued)*

Direct Media Tactics	Mass Media Tactics
	Mobile Apps
	Location-Based Apps
	SlideShare
	Instagram
	Pinterest
	Vine

*OOH stands for Out-of-Home and is another way these days to refer to Outdoor. OTT stands for "Over The Top" and refers to messaging apps that circumvent carrier networks to enable free peer-to-peer messaging.

If you're keeping score, that's over 50 ways businesses can now connect with consumer audiences—up from just *nine* a few short decades ago. And we've barely had time to digest many of these tactics as consumers, let alone marketers. Indeed, the media landscape has changed radically—and that's why the first mandate of *The Audience Imperative* is so critical.

> *Use your* **Paid, Owned, and Earned Media not only to sell in the short term** *but also to increase the size, engagement, and value of your Proprietary Audiences over the long term.*

Paid, Owned, and Earned Media is literally such a broad topic that it is the subject of entire books today. Our interest for purposes of this book is how the different forms of media can help your *Proprietary Audience Development* efforts. In Don's era, it was enough for media to just sell; but in the *Hybrid Marketing Era*, that's no longer the case.

Paid Media

We've already discussed Paid Media (a.k.a. advertising) at great length. It is the fossil fuel of marketing and still one of the most effective ways you can make your cash register ring. The million-dollar question is whether your company is demanding enough—and receiving enough in return—from its advertising.

According to Google, 77 percent of adult U.S. television viewers watch TV with a mobile device in hand—a smartphone, tablet or laptop.[2] Today's viewers aren't passive; they're multitaskers waiting for some cue to take action. And yet, of the 83 paid commercial advertisements run during Super Bowl XLVII, only *two* asked viewers to join a brand's proprietary audience.[3]

Pizza chain Papa John's (@PapaJohns) is a brand that bucked this trend. While technically not a Super Bowl advertiser in that their spots didn't run *during* the Big Game, they were Super Bowl sponsors of one of the most watched parts of the game.

The coin toss.

The Super Bowl coin toss is the most watched coin toss in the world—yet few viewers care about it save for the occasional Vegas prop bettor. But in 2012, and again in 2013, Papa John's staked very big bets on the outcome.

In television and other advertising leading up to the Super Bowl, Papa John's encouraged VIEWERS to predict whether the coin would land on heads or tails. Once VIEWERS registered for the Papa Rewards program by providing their email address (thereby becoming SUBSCRIBERS), they could cast their vote. When the coin toss landed "heads" at Super Bowl XLVII, every correct voter received a code via email for a free, large, one-topping pizza. Consumers walked away with an untold number of free pizzas. Meanwhile, Papa John's built a proprietary SUBSCRIBER database on the back of its advertising—something none of its competitors did.

The Super Bowl is the biggest sales day for pizza restaurants in the United States.[4] Instead of using its Paid Media to sell commercials *for one day*, Papa John's set themselves up to sell pizzas *for the entire year*. With SUBSCRIBER permission in hand, they could now email all registrants—winners *and* losers—to promote new products, sales, and the Papa Rewards program in hopes of increasing CUSTOMER loyalty well after the Big Game. And by driving participation on Facebook and Twitter, they also picked up more FANS and FOLLOWERS capable of becoming AMPLIFIERS.

If I were Papa John's competition, I'd be asking my marketing team, "Why didn't we do that?" or "Why *don't* we do that now?!?"

Audience Exercise #4: Go Watch Some TV

Go watch an hour of uninterrupted, commercial-filled TV. Jot down every single call to action (CTA), whether they appear in the commercial breaks or the show itself (like a hashtag, Twitter handle, or in-show promo). How many did you find? What percentage built or engaged SEEKERS, AMPLIFIERS, or JOINERS? Did any of the brands embrace the power of hybrid marketing?

Now back to your regularly scheduled book . . .

Now you may be shaking your head and saying, "But I hardly have a Super Bowl advertising budget." That's okay; there are countless brands in the same position. But the call to use your Paid Media to grow your proprietary audiences is just as strong—if not stronger—when you have a limited marketing budget. The key is to make sure that you establish goals for sales and *Proprietary Audience Development* at the *outset* of your creative planning. Otherwise, you'll be adding in audience development as an afterthought. And while that may still help, it will never produce the same results it does when you make *Proprietary Audience Development* a primary objective along with sales.

Please Stop Advertising Facebook and Twitter for Free

One of my other pet peeves watching Super Bowl XLVII (other than the Baltimore Ravens' victory) was that it showcased an advertising practice that *must stop now:* free advertising for Facebook and Twitter.

A ridiculous number of Super Bowl commercials ended with a slate that prominently featured Facebook and Twitter icons without any explanation whatsoever. WHY ARE BRANDS PUTTING THOSE ON THEIR COMMERCIALS?!? It's not like VIEWERS can click on them. And it's not as if they're accompanied by any meaningful CTA. They are simply brand logos, and whether they're on your TV ads, your store window, or your website, they often do little more than provide free brand advertising for Facebook and Twitter.

If you really want your advertising to build your FANS and FOLLOWERS, ditch the icons in favor of a meaningful CTA that tells VIEWERS why they should engage you on Facebook and Twitter. Give them real reasons to engage with your brand. Other companies' logos should never be window dressing in your paid advertisements.

And if that's too much to ask, then please start billing Facebook, Twitter, Instagram, Pinterest, and so forth for all the free impressions you're giving their brands. After all, it's your Paid Media.

Google AdWords sit at the opposite end of the cost spectrum from Super Bowl commercials. Depending on the keyword, companies can spend as little as a penny per click (although it usually costs much more). Unbeknownst to many advertisers, Google's AdWords offers other means of conversion other than the almighty click. Take the following paid search ad that appears when I search for the company Brooks Brothers (Figure 5.1).[5]

FIGURE 5.1 A Brooks Brothers Paid Search Ad on Google AdWords That Incorporates an Email Opt-In Ad Extension

This ad from Brooks Brothers takes advantage of Google's "Ad Extensions" feature, which allows advertisers to include more than one CTA in their paid search ads.[6] The main and sale links drive SEEKERS, while the subscription form builds email SUBSCRIBERS. It's an extremely cost-effective way to build your proprietary audiences on the back of Paid Media.

No matter how big your Paid Media budget is, you can do more than just sell with it. You can also build proprietary audiences that put you on a path toward more cost-effective direct marketing options in the future.

Paid Media is not the only weapon at your disposal. You also probably have a website, blog, Facebook page, Twitter profile, and other digital assets just lying in wait to capture prospective customers' interest. We call these assets *Owned Media*, and they are driving the Content Marketing revolution.

Owned Media

Owned Media encompasses all of the marketing assets that belong to your company. These include your:

- Catalogs
- Direct mailers
- In-store circulars
- Product packaging
- Signage (fleet vehicles, in-store, etc.)
- Blog
- Email messages
- Facebook content
- Instagram content
- LinkedIn content
- Mobile apps
- Pinterest content
- Podcasts
- SMS messages
- Twitter content
- Videos
- Website
- Whitepapers
- YouTube channel

The lure of Owned Media is *control*. Because there's no network or middle-man with Owned Media, you can do exactly what you want with it. Outside of production and maintenance costs, you don't have to pay any third parties for distribution. You put a sign up in your store, and customers can see it. You publish a podcast, and it's available for the world to listen to. You launch a website, and someone halfway around the world can visit it to learn about your products and services.

Of course, the mere act of creating Owned Media does not ensure that there will be an audience for it. Look at the list of Owned Media again; the left column includes content that comes with some built-in audience based on physical corporate assets (stores, vehicles, etc.). However, you still need to buy or build a direct mail database for your catalogs and a distribution system for your circulars, products, and signage to reach SHOPPERS in store.

> *The mere act of creating Owned Media does not ensure that there will be an audience for it.*

By contrast, the right column lists Owned Media that first comes to the attention of SEEKERS via search engines or other online discovery tools. Owned Media's first opportunity, therefore, is to help you grow your proprietary SEEKER audience: the folks looking for the types of products, services, information, or entertainment you provide. This is why SEO and Content Marketing are kissin' cousins; they ensure your content is indexed by search engines, found by mobile device users, and browsed easily by visitors.

Search-engine-optimized Owned Media should deliver a steady stream of SEEKERS; however, these are people who come and go as they please. To get more value from Owned Media, you need to take every opportunity to convert each SEEKER into a JOINER. In so doing, you transform fleeting VISITORS into on-demand proprietary audiences of SUBSCRIBERS, FANS, and FOLLOWERS—audiences you can access in the future with the push of a button.

Chances are that you're already using your Owned Media to build SUBSCRIBERS, FANS, and FOLLOWERS through tactics like:

- An email opt-in form on your website or at point-of-sale
- Facebook, Twitter, and social media sharing buttons on your website
- Promotion of your mobile app(s) via your website or social media
- Social media widgets that expose SEEKERS to social content

- A lead capture form on a white paper or other downloadable resource
- SMS calls to action at events or in-store

While each of these definitely helps build your proprietary audiences, very few companies have maximized the full potential of their Owned Media. In fact, our SFF report *RETAIL TOUCHPOINTS EXPOSED* highlighted that of the 100 fastest-growing retailers in the United States, only 2 percent were using in-store signage to drive consumers to opt-in to email or SMS communications.[7]

Owned Media should provide a home field advantage. It's where you're supposed to play your A-game and engage consumers in ways that maximize their value to your organization. One of the folks who most fully understands the importance of building JOINER audiences is one of Owned Media's biggest advocates: Joe Pulizzi (@JoePulizzi). As founder of the Content Marketing Institute (@CMIContent), the Content Marketing World conference, and *Chief Content Marketer* magazine, many rightly refer to Joe as "The Godfather of Content Marketing." According to Joe:

> Content Marketing is *owning*—as opposed to renting—media. It's a marketing process to attract and retain customers by consistently creating and curating content in order to change or enhance a consumer behavior.[8]

If that sounds familiar, it should. The justification for Content Marketing is exactly the same as for *Proprietary Audience Development*: to own rather than rent attention. It's just that the focus with Content Marketing is on developing Owned Media, whereas our focus is to build proprietary audiences to consume and amplify your Owned Media.

Content Marketing and *Proprietary Audience Development* are really just opposite sides of the same coin. One provides the *content for consumption*, and one provides the *audience that consumes*. They are modern marketing's *Ouroboros*, interrelated jobs that never end. They just keep feeding each other— more content, more audiences—in order to serve the company's bottom line.*

Content Marketing and Proprietary Audience Development are sides of the same coin. One provides content for consumption, and one provides the audience that consumes.

---

*The Ouroboros represents cycles that continue without end. It is depicted the world around as a serpent eating its own tail.

The Truth About Your Home Field Advantage

Ever wonder if home field advantage is really a thing? Well, so did some researchers at Harvard University (@Harvard) back in 2007. After examining over 5,000 English Premier League games, they determined that for every additional 10,000 fans in the stands, the advantage for the home team increased by 0.1 goals.[9]

Home field advantage is real in sports—*and* in business. Your store, restaurant, office, or whatever other physical space you own isn't just meant to house your business; it must also *work for it*. Today, that means optimizing in-store signage to build your Proprietary Audiences. It means coaching your employees to inform customers of the myriad ways they can stay informed of upcoming sales, specials, or unique FAN opportunities. It means doing everything consistent with your brand to convert the feet on your floor to SUBSCRIBERS, FANS, and FOLLOWERS before they leave the store. *That's* how to beat the competition.

So if you don't know them already, go get to know the folks who build your website, develop your signage, manage your social media, and message your audiences. Each will play a critical role in ensuring that your Owned Media helps build your Proprietary Audiences—all while your Proprietary Audiences drive traffic to your Owned Media.

Earned Media

The last type of media to aid your *Proprietary Audience Development* efforts is *Earned Media*. But here's a bit of a curveball: Earned Media isn't really media at all. Whereas Paid Media is media you effectively rent and Owned Media consists of marketing assets you own, Earned Media is more a *process* whereby an audience member produces and distributes content beneficial to your brand. To better understand this, we need to go back to college.

How Earned Media Is Made

Back when I was a freshman at Miami University (@MiamiUniversity), I took a Communications 101 course taught by Professor Robert Vogel (@vogelrav)—a man with more energy for communications than any human being has a right to have. It was in his course that I was first introduced to the *Shannon-Weaver Model of Communications* (Figure 5.2).[10]

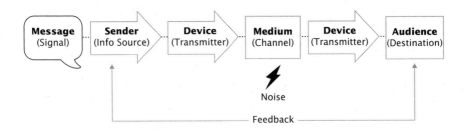

FIGURE 5.2 Shannon-Weaver Model

I can see more than a few of you out there with fleeting looks of recognition. But before you hurt yourself trying to recall specifics, let me jog your memory. Shannon-Weaver was first developed to explain the technical specifics of electronic communications to engineers, but over time, it evolved into one of the most popular theories to describe marketing communications as well.

In the Shannon-Weaver model, a *sender* transmits a *message* through a *medium* (i.e., a channel) to reach an *audience*. *Noise* (technical, environmental, or other interference) can negatively impact the message. And upon receipt, the audience can provide *feedback* to the sender regarding the message.

The Shannon-Weaver model contemplates a calm, linear process driven by a single sender, message, medium, and audience. Of course, this is a far cry from the world in which we live today. Our audiences have audiences of their own; and as AMPLIFIERS, they mold, shape, and add to our message as they pass it along via *social media*—a term we use so frequently that it's worth unpacking what *social media* actually is.

The temptation, of course, is to deliver your Charlton Heston impersonation and yell, "Social media is peeeeeeeeeeeople!!!"* However, social media isn't people; it is a catchall term for the *channels* people use to transmit their messages. These channels include the usual suspects of Facebook, Twitter, Google+, LinkedIn, Instagram, and Pinterest, but they also include channels we tend to forget are social—email, phone, and word of mouth. We

---

*An homage to Heston's famous line in the movie Soylent Green, when he discovers (spoiler alert!) that the dystopian food rations being served are actually made of human beings ("Soylent green is people!").

bundle all of these channels as *social media* because they facilitate two-way communications among real people.*

In his recent book, *Paid Owned Earned: Maximizing Marketing Returns in a Socially Connected World*, author Nick Burcher (@NickBurcher) does a great job updating the Shannon-Weaver Model for the social media age.[11] Building on Burcher's vision, Figure 5.3 shows my take on a Shannon-Weaver Model for the Hybrid Marketing Era.

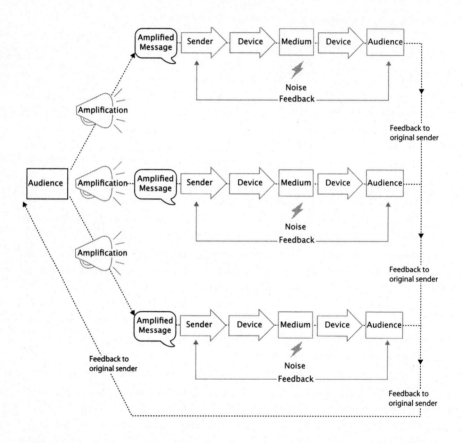

FIGURE 5.3 Modified Shannon-Weaver Model

---

*We marketers (present company included) constantly refer to people as consumers. It does us well to step back now and then and think of our mom, dad, friend, spouse, or someone else very real. That helps us focus on their needs instead of solely ours—a perspective that proves highly valuable in social media.

As you can see, each audience member—once a passive recipient of information or entertainment—now becomes a potential sender (AMPLIFIER) in their own right. The original sender only controls the initial message content, channel selection, and primary audience selection. Each point of amplification after that is our Earned Media; not media that we can buy or own, but rather a process by which audience members become AMPLIFIERS. Let's take another look at the other names for our AMPLIFIERS from Chapter 3:

- ADVOCATES
- ANALYSTS
- COMMENTERS
- CREATORS
- INFLUENCERS
- REPORTERS
- REVIEWERS
- SHARERS

Each of these AMPLIFIERS creates Earned Media for you. CREATORS blog, podcast, and make videos. INFLUENCERS post, tweet, and pontificate. REPORTERS write news stories about your company, and SHARERS take your message to the far corners of their personal networks. Earned Media is the *output* of AMPLIFIER actions; not an audience unto itself. To put it another way:

Just because you use generate Earned Media does not mean you've built lasting Proprietary Audiences for your company.

The AMPLIFIERS who generate your Earned Media are the most fleeting members of your proprietary audiences. They can like, share, or tweet—and then leave without a trace. That may not limit the impact of your Earned Media in the moment, but it requires you to pay for or build audiences from scratch the next time you need one.

For this reason, just as with Paid and Owned Media, it is imperative that you encourage AMPLIFIERS to also become SUBSCRIBERS, FANS, and FOLLOWERS. This allows you to message them directly whenever you want—and potentially set the dominoes of Earned Media in motion. If you fail to convert some of your momentary AMPLIFIER audience members into SUBSCRIBERS, FANS, and/or FOLLOWERS, you're leaving money on the table.

Converged Media

As you've undoubtedly determined by now, the lines between Paid, Owned, and Earned Media are blurring every day. Perhaps no one has documented this better than Rebecca Lieb (@lieblink) and Jeremiah Owyang (@jowyang) from Altimeter Group (@AltimeterGroup). Their research report, *The Converged Media Imperative: How Brands Must Combine Paid, Owned, and Earned Media*, is a must-read for anyone seeking to understand the changing media landscape.[12] In it, they visualize marketing's Paid, Owned, and Earned Media landscape as shown in Figure 5.4.

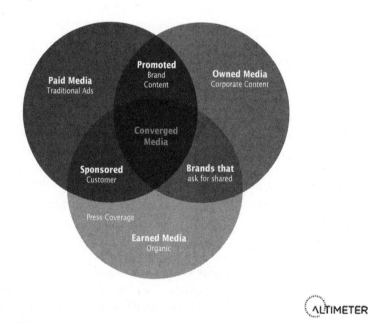

FIGURE 5.4   The Convergence of Paid, Owned, and Earned Media

Source: The Converged Media Imperative: How Brands Must Combine Paid, Owned, and Earned Media," Altimeter Group (July 19, 2012). Used with permission.

In describing this model, they explain that:

> As consumers become increasing mobile, paid/owned/earned convergence will intensify. Rapid journeys across multiple digital devices will increasingly blur the lines until almost all distinction between paid, owned, and earned media dissolve.[13]

Converged Media refers to those marketing efforts where a company uses two or more forms of media plus a consistent creative execution across multiple channels to achieve their desired results. As Rebecca and Jeremiah observe, media companies themselves are a driving force behind the rise of Converged Media. They offer products and services that merge the best of Paid Media with the control of Owned Media and the amplification of Earned Media. Examples include:

- *Facebook Sponsored Stories*, which allow advertisers to pay to promote consumer posts in ways that increase visibility, reach, engagement, and FAN audience size (via *likes*).[14]
- *Facebook Custom Audiences*, which allow advertisers to map email SUBSCRIBER addresses or CUSTOMER phone numbers to their existing Facebook FANS in order to facilitate highly targeted advertising within the Facebook platform.[15]
- *Twitter Promoted Accounts, Promoted Trends, and Promoted Tweets*, which allow brands to pay to increase their FOLLOWER count, increase visibility around relevant trending topics, and amplify the best stories about their products and services.[16]

A clear byproduct of Converged Media is proprietary audience growth. Our mission is to make sure it's not just an afterthought but rather a primary objective. If you aren't using your Paid, Owned, and Earned Media to increase the size, engagement, and value of your Proprietary Audiences, then your marketing isn't standing nearly as tall as it could.

Chapter

Increase What Matters: Size, Engagement & Value

Effective marketing now stands on your audience's shoulders.[1]
—Rebecca Lieb and Jeremiah Owyang

By now you know that marketers need *audiences*. All media—converged or otherwise—depends upon them as a destination for any message. In fact, marketer's livelihoods now depend on who can build bigger and better proprietary audiences than the competition.

But what does "bigger and better" really mean? Are we talking size only or is there something more at work? Let's revisit *The Audience Imperative:*

> **Use your Paid, Owned, and Earned Media not only to sell in the short term but also to increase the size, engagement, and value of your Proprietary Audiences over the long term.**

As it turns out, "bigger and better" is comprised of three elements today:

1. Size
2. Engagement
3. Value

I view each of these attributes as a leg on a stool. Fail to build one well, and you don't have a stool; you have kindling. To discover the reasons why, let's explore each at greater length.

Size

"Size doesn't matter." It's the most biting euphemism of all euphemisms to the chronically insecure. But the truth is that *size does matter* in three critical ways when building proprietary audiences:

1. *Relative size*: the size of your audiences compared to direct competitors
2. *Database size*: the volume and quality of the data you have gathered about your audiences to improve message relevance
3. *Reach*: the percentage of your audience that sees your message

Relative Size

This is the easiest to tackle because it's often the "box score" of marketing. How many email SUBSCRIBERS do you have? Facebook FANS? Twitter FOLLOWERS? We keep track of such things because they are either a sign of growth or decay—and we certainly know which of the two we want.

Your audience size doesn't convey much value, however, until you compare it with your head-to-head competitors. Take the case of two travel agents—a vocation under a ton of competitive pressures today if ever there was one. One travel agent—let's call him Steve—relies on offline relationships, traditional advertising, and referrals to bring in new business. Another agent, Sally, has those things working for her—plus she maintains a monthly email newsletter, Facebook page, and Twitter account. These give her loyal customers multiple ways to learn about the latest sales and share them with friends and family.

Which travel agent has the competitive advantage today? No contest, right? It's Sally because she's built a variety of proprietary audiences that can amplify her vacation travel offers to broader audiences. By contrast, Steve has only built a Rolodex of clients that he must call with every new vacation deal. Steve may be the nicest guy in the world, but if he has zero email SUBSCRIBERS, Facebook FANS, and Twitter FOLLOWERS, Sally's going beat him every quarter. She simply has more ways to reach her CUSTOMERS and generate new PROSPECTS.

Audience Exercise #5: How Do Your Audiences Stack Up?

Here's a quick exercise to help you focus on your relative proprietary audience size compared to the competition:

1. Grab a pen and paper. (Yes—those old-fashioned tools).

2. Write down your three most fearsome competitors.

3. Look up their number of Facebook FANS, Twitter FOLLOWERS, and YouTube SUBSCRIBERS.

4. Next, do the same thing for your own company.

5. Finally, tape the paper where you'll see it every day at work.

Where do you stand? Are your audiences bigger or smaller than your dear competitors? Who has the competitive advantage out of the gate when promoting a new product, service, piece of content, or event?

Whether you like it or not, your audience size relative to your direct competition *does matter*. What doesn't matter—unless you're Pepsi (@Pepsi) or RedBull (@RedBull)—is that Coke (@CocaCola) has over 72 million FANS on Facebook. Be inspired by brands outside of your industry, but make sure the yardstick by which you measure success contains data from direct competitors.

Another important point—don't forget the *email audience!* Email SUBSCRIBERS are the hidden, bigger part of the audience iceberg, adding buoyancy to both sales and social media via messages that only SUBSCRIBERS see. As a result, it's a good idea to at least get *some* idea of the size of your key competitors' email SUBSCRIBER audiences. If you're looking for a very rough approximation (and I do mean *very rough*), you can do the following:

- Add up a selected competitor's number of Facebook FANS and Twitter FOLLOWERS; let's say the total is 36,000.

- Divide that number by *your* company's total number of Facebook FANS and Twitter FOLLOWERS (with your total at 25,000).

- Multiply the result (1.44, with our figures) by the number of active email SUBSCRIBERS in your company's database (let's say 80,000).

- The resulting—again, *very* rough—estimate is that your competitor has 115,200 email SUBSCRIBERS to your 80,000.

This guesstimate makes a huge leap of faith; namely, that the gap between your social media audiences will be of a similar percentage to your email SUBSCRIBERS. Admittedly, you could be killing it in email while your competitor is putting all their eggs into social media channels. Still, in cases where you need a quick, cost-free visual to explain to leadership why your company needs to focus on email acquisition, this method may help get their competitive juices flowing in your favor.

If you have both the need and budget for something more precise, a number of companies have email competition tools that may be of use. Inbox Insight from Return Path (@ReturnPath) is particularly helpful, as it tracks a panel of users to help approximate the size of your competitor's email SUBSCRIBERS database as well as what percentage of your email SUBSCRIBERS may overlap.

Take, for instance, the real-life example from two competitors in the Financial Services industry, shown in Figure 6.1.

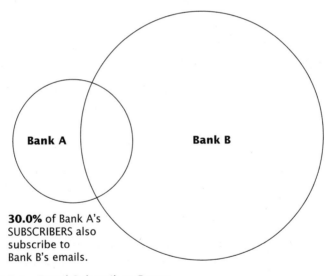

30.0% of Bank A's SUBSCRIBERS also subscribe to Bank B's emails.

FIGURE 6.1 Email Subscriber Group
Source: Return Path Inbox Insight. Used with permission.

Wouldn't you rather be Bank B? And if you're in charge of Bank A, wouldn't you hate to explain why your audience is so small compared to the competition's? I know, I know . . . these are obvious answers. So *why*, then, are so many companies failing to emphasize proprietary audience growth as a key marketing objective? It boggles the mind.

Database Size

We hear a lot these days about the importance of "Big Data" and the revolution it will bring to all aspects of our lives. After paging through the awe-inspiring book *The Human Face of Big Data* from author and photographer Rick Smolan (@RickSmolan), I have no doubt that Big Data will transform much of our knowledge of the world and our own hidden behaviors. I also know three simple facts:

1. There's no Big Data *if you don't collect it*.
2. Big Data isn't big *if it's wrong*.
3. There's nothing big about data *if you don't use it*.

For marketers, this means that both the *quality and quantity* of data you collect about JOINERS (SUBSCRIBERS, FANS, and FOLLOWERS) matter. Size isn't just a factor of how many *people* you can communicate with; it's also a factor of how *well* you can communicate with them—and that all ties back to data such as:

- Demographics (gender, age, ethnicity, language, employment, etc.)
- Location (past and present)
- Mobile behaviors (app usage, interactions, channel preferences, etc.)
- Online behaviors (content interaction, clicks, abandoned carts, etc.)
- Offline behaviors (favorite stores, waking hours, etc.)
- Psychographics (personality, values, lifestyle, etc.)
- Purchase behaviors (online, offline, history, brands, etc.)

Today's marketing organizations may have access to some of this information about your JOINERS thanks to your CRM, e-commerce, email marketing, marketing automation, mobile, and website teams. If you're active in social media, the channels themselves—such as Facebook, Google+, LinkedIn, Pinterest, and Twitter—also maintain a lot of data about your FANS and FOLLOWERS. Your company can't usually access such data directly, but you can use it to increase the relevance and targeting of your ads through each of those channels.* This can be a frustrating scenario, to help Facebook and others acquire data about your consumers that you can only access by advertising with Facebook; however, social media's Big Data is dictated by the

---

*There is one notable exception. Social Login options from Facebook, Google, Twitter, and others will pass limited social media data with consumer permission; more on this in Chapter 23.

channels, not marketers. The only way to combat this is to grow the quality of data you acquire directly from your JOINERS and use it through channels that *you* control—like email, mobile apps, SMS, and your website.

Audience Reach

The third and final dimension of size that impacts *Proprietary Audience Development* is *reach*. Most often associated with paid advertising, *reach is simply the percentage of a target audience that was exposed to your advertising within a given period*. In today's world of email, mobile, and social media, it can also be defined as the percentage of your SUBSCRIBERS, FANS, or FOLLOWERS who viewed your message. Facebook defines the term as follows:

> Reach measures the number of people who received impressions of a Page post. The reach number might be less than the impressions number since one person can see multiple impressions.[2]

Within Facebook, reach is the percentage of your audience that was on a page where your post was displayed. It is not a metric of *interaction*—a click, read, or view. Reach defines your *effective audience*. It also highlights that audience size and attention are not the same thing. Just because you have 100,000 Facebook FANS does not mean they're hanging on your every word.

In fact, Facebook disclosed in 2012 that on average, any given post reaches only 16 percent of a company's Facebook FANS.[3] This angered a number of marketers who felt they were owed 100 percent distribution and didn't want to pay for *Sponsored Stories* to get it.* But the number reflected a fundamental reality about Facebook and social media in general: they're virtual *waterfalls* of information that consumers dip into and engage as they see fit. Whether we're talking posts (Facebook, LinkedIn, and Google+), tweets (Twitter), photos (Instagram), or pins (Pinterest), social media channels produce *streaming content* akin to television; that is, it's your choice to tune in when and where you want. More importantly, the consumer does not feel the obligation to retroactively check every update from every connection since their last login.

Reach defines your effective audience and also highlights that audience size and attention are not the same thing.

---

*Sponsored Stories are Facebook posts that a company pays to promote to broader audiences on Facebook.

By contrast, email and SMS are channels where consumers are more conditioned to check every last message either out of:

- Fear of missing something important
- Visual cues within the channel (e.g., unread-message bolding)
- Physical cues of their devices (e.g., noise or vibrations)

Far from the waterfalls of social media feeds, email and SMS inboxes are more akin to "to-do" lists that consumers check off, one message at a time. Your email and SMS messages tend to have far greater reach than social media, because every message the user receives creates an impression through its FROM and SUBJECT lines—even if they never open it. That's vastly different than Facebook posts and tweets that your audience members might never even see.

Of course, the big asterisk next to the email channel is whether the message is received by SUBSCRIBERS. Aggressive spam filters have always been the bane of the permission-based email marketer's existence, but the new challenge is from newer features, like Inbox Tabs and Priority Inbox from Gmail. Released over the summer of 2013, Gmail's Inbox Tabs automatically sort unread messages into tabs of Gmail's choosing (Primary, Social, Promotions, and Updates).[4] Priority Inbox, on the other hand, allows the inbox owner to sort messages based on the importance they assign to the sender.[5] Should more consumers adopt such features, then we may see the average email's reach drop because it's automatically being placed in "nonpriority" folders.

Whatever the channel, reach—in combination with your audience size—helps you determine the *potential visibility* of your message. Here's how it may play out when comparing a fictitious company's same sized audiences of email SUBSCRIBERS, Facebook FANS, and Twitter FOLLOWERS:

	Email SUBSCRIBERS	Facebook FANS	Twitter FOLLOWERS
Audience Size	100,000	100,000	100,000
Reach*	96%	16%	2%
Effective Audience	96,000	16,000	2,000

*Reach in an email sense refers only to emails delivered, not necessarily read. This is the same leap of faith taken in other channels such as Facebook, where reach refers only to the percentage of Fans to whom a post was displayed without regard for whether it was read.

Which channel would you prioritize? Based solely on the data above, you'd have to say email. But there's a lot more that goes into determining the right audience for the job—factors that may shift your channel priorities to Facebook, Twitter, or elsewhere. That's why we need to answer *The Audience Imperative's* call to increase audience *engagement and value*, too.

Engagement

If I had a nickel for every time some marketing type uttered the word *engagement* over the past few years, I'd be a very rich man. Unfortunately, marketers who are "all hat and no cattle" often use the word as a cover. They're big on talk, but light on metrics that *actually document* the revenue impact of specific marketing activities.

However, *engagement* is a critical metric in *Proprietary Audience Development*. An engaged audience is an *attentive* audience. An engaged audience is a *responsive* audience. And an engaged audience is a *profitable* audience.

So how the heck do you get an engaged audience? You nurture them. You interact with them personally. You amplify their content, even if there's no direct or immediate benefit to you.

And it's just as important to know what NOT to do. You don't aggravate them. You don't inundate them with irrelevant—or worse yet, unrequested—messages. You don't hard-sell them in channels where they don't welcome the hard sell.

The reasons for these dos and don'ts are very clear. Ignore them, and you not only may lose your audience's attention; you may lose them as audience members altogether. That's because engagement:

1. Increases **social media visibility**
2. Improves **email deliverability**
3. Increases **mobile app usage**

Engagement for Social Media Visibility

Social media doesn't exist without engagement. Indeed, the fundamental unit of social media is a connection between two people who share content that is meaningful to them. Not to get all "Maslow-y" on you, but people socialize to fulfill some hole in their hierarchy of needs—be it love, belonging, esteem, or self-actualization. People engage with brands via social media for the same reasons—to serve *their* needs.

Facebook gets this. It's why they use an algorithm with over 100,000 different factors to determine what posts are displayed and prioritized in their users' News Feeds.[6] This algorithm (once known as EdgeRank[7]) looks at the affinity between people, the type of content posted, and the time the content was posted to determine if the content should show up in someone's News Feed. The net effect is to suppress posts from people who aren't strong connections or limit the distribution of stale or uninteresting content.

And this is how brands only reach an average of 16 percent of their total Facebook FANS.* Whether by Facebook's algorithm or by the user's own hand (choosing to hide content or *dislike* a brand altogether), your wonderful posts meet an ignominious end, unseen by the vast majority of your FANS.

There is a solution, however; it's called engagement. With *better content*—content that inspires *likes, comments* and *shares*—you grow your affinity with your FANS. This, in turn, increases the likelihood that your FANS will see your next post. Other ways to enhance engagement on Facebook include:

- *Interacting with FANS*: Facebook excels when it connects people with people. So why not act like a real person and congratulate a FAN on an accomplishment, or share their content? It both humanizes your brand and boosts future post visibility when it resonates.

- *Serving customers*: Like it or not, Facebook sometimes turns into an open forum for customer service issues. Rather than approach these fearfully, embrace them as a chance to resolve a customer issue while increasing your EdgeRank-worthy engagement.

- *Posting pictures*: By one estimate, photos on Facebook receive 53 percent more "Likes," 104 percent more comments, and 84 percent more clicks than posts with just text and links.[8] There's a reason Facebook bought Instagram: Pictures drive engagement across desktops, smartphones, and tablets.

- *Asking for open-ended questions*: Whether asking for FAN opinions on a new product or simply helping them waste time with a humorous question, posts that ask for input tend to receive it.

While Facebook is currently the only social network to boost and lower posts based on engagement metrics, the others won't be far behind. As they scale and add members, there's simply too great a signal-to-noise ratio and too great a risk of inundating users to the point they tune out. So, the next

---

*More recent analysis places the average reach of a brand Facebook post at 10 percent, but your company's reach will vary greatly on the size of your FAN audience, industry, and degree of engagement.

time you see your company's social media person "just Facebooking" or "just tweeting," remember that they're helping to keep your social audience attention for the next time you really need it.

Audience Exercise #6: Find the Narcissistic Brands!

Narcissism is a personality disorder characterized by an excessive sense of self and a lack of empathy for others. The last thing you want to be on social media is narcissistic, because nothing kills engagement faster than a stream filled with self-absorbed, self-promotional posts.

For this exercise, I'd like you to go on the hunt for narcissistic brands on Facebook.

Step 1: Pick three competitive brands not in your industry.

Step 2: Visit the Facebook page of each.

Step 3: Log each of their posts for the past month based on whether they were self-promotional, FAN interactions, or shares of others' content.

Step 4: Determine the percentage of Facebook posts attributable to each type.

Step 5: Log the average likes, comments, and shares for each type of post.

Find any narcissistic brands that only talk about themselves and never interact with any FANS? Better yet, did you find any correlation between unselfish interaction or sharing and the volume of engagement a post received? Social media rewards brands that engage their FANS and FOLLOWERS like real human beings—just like we reward friends who care enough to ask us how we're doing. Emphasize the *me* in social media at risk to your own engagement.

Engagement for Email Delivery

Speaking of feeling inundated, welcome to today's email inbox! In reality, most consumers today *don't* feel overwhelmed by email. That's just a bias that we marketers who live in our inboxes for a living bring to the table. Gmail, Microsoft's Outlook.com, and Yahoo! Mail have been honing their filters to catch and delete most spam before consumers see it. So for most users, an inbox is a comfortable, stable environment.

For marketers, however, the story is a bit different. Because today's inbox providers have stepped up their efforts beyond mere spam filtering, having a consumer's permission to send email is just a starting point. Increasingly, inbox providers are weighing a variety of factors when determining whether your email goes to the inbox, spam folder, or straight to the trash. These include:

- *Prior engagement*: Has the recipient read and clicked on links in your prior emails, or sent them all straight to the trash?
- *Time spent*: Time spent viewing prior emails.
- *Current email activity*: How others engage with emails.
- *User markings*: When other users mark emails as "spam."
- *Priority designation*: Whether you are designated by recipients as a priority-sender or a trusted-sender IP address.
- *Address familiarity*: Whether or not your sender email address in the recipient's address book.

While not anywhere as *public* as social media engagement, email engagement carries the same importance; that is, it can determine whether or not your intended audience sees your messages. As a result, it's never been more critical for marketers to increase their email SUBSCRIBERS' engagement with each message they send. This means:

- Making each email more relevant by better leveraging SUBSCRIBER preferences and data to personalize content
- Testing content, subject lines, and design to improve performance
- Designing emails to render properly across PC, smartphone, and tablet devices—especially since more U.S. consumers now open emails on mobile devices than either desktop or webmail clients[9]
- Initiating reengagement campaigns for dormant SUBSCRIBERS
- Purging your email SUBSCRIBER database of unresponsive recipients

That last step is a difficult one for many marketers to take, especially when you're also trying to grow the size of your email SUBSCRIBER audience. However, in my experience, scrubbing inactive SUBSCRIBERS from your email database can help overall deliverability and increase audience *profitability*.

Money Can't Buy You Love

In July 2013, the U.S. Inspector General's office released the results of its audit of the State Department's Bureau of Information Programs. Among its findings was the little gem that the State Department spent $630,000 buying Facebook FANS via ad campaigns over the prior two years. Unfortunately, the FANS they obtained delivered very little engagement after their campaigns ended.[10]

Now you could go ballistic about government waste, but I'm going to suggest you first look in the mirror. Countless companies have fallen for scams promising to sell them high-quality email SUBSCRIBERS, Facebook FANS, and Twitter FOLLOWERS. Indeed, if you Google "buying Facebook FANS" right now, you'll see all sorts of social snake-oil salesmen trying to separate your company from its hard-earned cash.

Buying SUBSCRIBERS, FANS, and FOLLOWERS isn't just bad business; it's illegal in many countries. And while incentives are a great way to get consumers to *like, follow*, and *subscribe to* your brand, incentives that have nothing to do with your products or services do little but attract the wrong crowd. Size matters, but engagement is what actually pays the bills. Don't be fooled.

Engagement for Increased Mobile App Usage

If a mobile app is central to your business or marketing strategy, then increasing SUBSCRIBER engagement is critical to your success. Consider that:

- Wireless data traffic is set to grow 66 percent a year through 2017.[11]
- Over four times as many smartphones were sold in 2012 as PCs.[12]
- Smartphone users check their devices an average of 150 times daily.[13]

The problem with many companies' mobile app strategies, however, is the same problem they had with websites in the mid-1990s: they have a "build it and they will come" mentality. Neither websites nor mobile apps are a "Field of Dreams" where millions of users walk out of the cornfields mindlessly to download your app.

Both the Apple AppStore and Google Play have over *one million apps* available to consumers. To stand out among that crowd, you need to promote your app to your proprietary audiences (and you probably need paid advertising). Even assuming you do get SUBSCRIBERS to download your app, you still need them to *use it* in order to derive any benefit from your investment.

And that's where mobile engagement rears its ugly head. We've all downloaded apps with the intention to use them, only to use them once or twice. Slowly, those once shiny new apps get pushed to some buried screen on our smartphones or tablets, never to be opened again—victims of a condition known as *disuse apptrophy*.

It doesn't have to be that way, however. If your company has produced or is planning on developing a mobile app, remember that it is really just a gateway to a different sort of proprietary audience. As such, you must launch your app with a mobile engagement strategy in mind. Smart app developers now do a few things to boost app engagement, including:

- Acquire mobile app SUBSCRIBER email addresses to enable direct updates and other communications from the developer.
- Encourage activation of the app's *push notifications* (on-screen messages that appear within the device) to foster reengagement.

Whether we're talking email, mobile or social media, engagement isn't just a fluffy marketing term providing cover for those afraid of performance measurement. It's a critical activity that helps ensure broader visibility/distribution of social media posts, increase email deliverability, and boost mobile app engagement.

Value

The final attribute we must seek to increase with our proprietary audiences is their *value*. If beauty is in the eye of the beholder, then value is in the wallet of its owner. Your company's leadership rightfully expects proprietary audiences to deliver measurable ROI. But when it comes to audiences, what is the "Return" in "Return on Investment"? It is a value that we can measure in many different ways:

1. Lifetime CUSTOMER Value (LCV)
2. Lifetime Incremental Value (LIV)
3. Campaign Conversion Value (CCV)
4. Net Equivalent Value (NEV)

5. Direct Comparative Value (DCV)
6. Comparative Incentive Value (CIV)

Lifetime CUSTOMER Value (LCV)

Of all the ways you can measure a CUSTOMER's value, Lifetime CUSTOMER Value (LCV) is probably the most important.[14] LCV is best stated as:

The net present value of the future stream of cash flow a company expects to generate from a CUSTOMER.[15]

The easiest way to calculate LCV is the following equation:

LCV = (Average Value of a Sale) × (Number of Repeat Transactions) × (Average Length of Customer Retention)

Thus, if on average your CUSTOMERS make purchases of $50 per month, and you retain CUSTOMERS for five years, your LCV is $3,000 ($50 × 12 × 5) or $600/year.

LCV helps determine what you should be willing to spend on CUSTOMER acquisition. Some companies will spend up to, but not over, the value of the first sale ($50 in our example). Others may be willing to spend more depending on their ability to absorb the initial marketing expense and upsell CUSTOMERS over and above the projected LCV. Whatever the case, the LCV provides a clear line around which you can make marketing investments.

To use LCV to determine the value of a proprietary audience, you need to be able to *identify* which of your audience members are CUSTOMERS and which are not. Such efforts are easiest in industries where email addresses, loyalty program member numbers, or phone numbers are associated with CUSTOMER accounts (B2B, online retail, etc.). In such cases, you can use the following equation to derive the value of your audience:

LCV for Proprietary Audience = LCV × (Number of CUSTOMERS in Your Proprietary Audience)

Thus, if we have an email SUBSCRIBER base of 100,000 people, of which 10,000 are CUSTOMERS, the value of that proprietary audience to our organization is $30 million (LCV of $3,000 × 10,000 SUBSCRIBER CUSTOMERS) or $6 million per year (since our original LCV was calculated over a five-year period).

Put a figure like that in front of management and you're bound to convince some folks that audiences are assets! After all, you don't just want *anyone* being a push button away from $30 million in future revenue. You'd want your *best* people, and you'd want them happy and healthy.

While using LCV can turn heads in the C-suite, it can also lead your *Proprietary Audience Development* efforts horribly astray. That's because LCV is not solely attributable to your proprietary audience communications. Advertising, experience with products, the quality of your service, and many other factors contribute to a CUSTOMER's LCV. Thus, when we use it to express our proprietary audiences' value, we must recognize that while LCV tells *how* valuable the people in our audiences are, it doesn't indicate *how much more* valuable they are than any other group of CUSTOMERS.

Fortunately, there IS another measurement that does.

Lifetime Incremental Value (LIV)

To get to that deeper appreciation of the value our *Proprietary Audience Development* efforts adds, we must modify the LCV calculation to help derive a given audience member's Lifetime Incremental Value (LIV):

$$LIV = LCV \text{ of average SUBSCRIBER/CUSTOMER} - LCV \text{ of average NON-SUBSCRIBER/CUSTOMER}$$

Thus, using our prior example, we separate our CUSTOMERS into two groups—SUBSCRIBERS and NON-SUBSCRIBERS. We then calculate the LCV for each. To determine the LIV, we subtract the LCV of NON-SUBSCRIBER CUSTOMERS from the LCV of SUBSCRIBER CUSTOMERS. For example:

$4,000 LCV of average CUSTOMER who's also an email SUBSCRIBER
$2,000 LCV of average CUSTOMER who's not an email SUBSCRIBER
= $2,000 LIV

If you can document that your email SUBSCRIBERS (or FANS or FOLLOWERS) generate twice the revenue of NON-SUBSCRIBERS, you'd be a fool not to invest more acquiring them across all forms of media.

Your LIV number documents the incremental value that a JOINER audience delivers. From a statistical standpoint, it's a pretty unassailable figure as it isolates the true impact of a CUSTOMER becoming a SUBSCRIBER, FAN, or FOLLOWER. The trick, however, is being able to isolate those relationships—something that's easily done with email but a bit trickier with social networks.

If your company lacks the data necessary to get to your LIV figure, there are still a variety of other proprietary audience valuation methods that require less effort and yet may yield attractive outcomes to discuss with management.

No, Facebook FANS Are Not Worth $174.17 (Unless They Are to You)

The value of a Facebook FAN is $174.17. It has to be true, right? After all, I read it in *The New York Times*.[16] Ugh. I was tired of this meme with email SUBSCRIBERS, and I'm even more tired of it now that it has jumped over to Facebook FANS. Can we *please* get a couple of things straight?

1. ***To determine the value of a Facebook FAN, you must compare the value of your Facebook FANS to your FANS who aren't on Facebook.*** Yes, Facebook may be the biggest social media site in the world, but it has not cornered the market on your FANS. In fact, you probably have many, many more FANS offline than online. Thus, when you compare LCV of your Facebook FANS and your FANS not on Facebook, you actually see the incremental value (the LIV) that Facebook brings to the table.

   Comparing your Facebook FANS to *non-FANS*, however, reveals jack squat about the value you derive from Facebook. It only tells you the value of a brand FAN generally. Guess where the $174.17 figure came from—that's right, a study that compared Facebook FANS and non-FANS instead of Facebook FANS and *FANS not on Facebook*. Bad data make for great headlines, but they are a horrible foundation upon which to build your marketing priorities.

2. ***There's no universal average value of a Facebook FAN; there's only the value of your Facebook FANS to your***

(continued)

(*continued*)

organization. I know math is hard, and it's easier to copy off of other people's homework. But if you want to know the value of a Facebook FAN, you have to calculate yours. There are simply too many variables of brand, communication, promotion, and service that influence whether Facebook adds incremental value to your bottom line.

So sorry to be Captain Buzzkill, but Facebook FANS aren't worth $174.17 each. Unless, of course, *your own* research into *your own* FANS demonstrates that they are.

Campaign Conversion Value (CCV)

In this valuation method, you offer a specific discount or promotion with one or more of your proprietary audiences in order to determine their value. The key is that you must be able to track:

1. Which channel drove purchase
2. That a CUSTOMER redeemed the offer
3. The total transaction value

With that information in hand, your audience's total Campaign Conversion Value (CCV) is simply the difference between the revenue driven by CUSTOMERS who redeemed your offer and those who did not. For example:

- For one week, you tweet out a 2 for 1 dinner offer.
- Customers receive individual identifiable coupons for redemption.
- The offer requires all redemptions be made in a specific week.
- You then track redemptions and total purchase amount.
- Next, you add up your total purchases during the promotional week, subtract out-of-pocket costs for the promotion, and compare that final figure with an average, non-promotional week.

The resulting difference is your proprietary audience's CCV—the value over and above your average weekly sales delivered via the promotion to your proprietary audience. You can measure CCV for any length of time so long as you have a comparable control period.

You can also use CCV to compare the relative worth of your different proprietary audiences to one another. Do your email SUBSCRIBERS lift sales more than Facebook FANS or Twitter FOLLOWERS? If you track them with different redemption coupons or codes, a CCV analysis should tell you. Of course, to increase your accuracy, you would be wise to run the analysis several times a year to avoid seasonal bias.

Net Equivalent Value (NEV)

As the old saying goes, there are many ways to skin a cat. Admittedly, it is not a pleasant saying, but it is apropos here. When you can't get at the *actual* value of your audiences, another way to appeal to management's bottom line is to document how much it would cost you to reach the same audience via paid advertising—the Net Equivalent Value (NEV) of your proprietary audience. To calculate your NEV:

- Pick one of your proprietary audiences.
- Identify the paid advertising unit closest to the same type of attention you command when you interact with your proprietary audience.
- Determine the CPM, CPC, CPA (cost per acquisition), or other billing method.
- Multiply the appropriate ad cost by logical subset of your audience or its activities (for instance, if you've identified the CPC for a paid ad unit, you would multiply that figure by the number of clicks your proprietary audience generates).

The NEV method makes management more fully aware of the market value of your social audiences. Take Facebook FANS, for instance:

- If you have 100,000 Facebook FANS
- And your average organic (free) reach is 16 percent
- Your average post reaches 16,000 FANS
- Now, if Facebook charges a CPM of $10 for a Sponsored Post
- Your NEV is $160 for every 1,000 FANS reached

As you apply this valuation model over time, you'll soon be able to demonstrate to management that your proprietary audiences are delivering *real value* that you would have otherwise had to purchase via paid media.*

---

*As my colleague Joel Book (@JoelBook) rightfully notes, don't forget to also capture any amplification by FANS or FOLLOWERS in your NEV calculations. AMPLIFIERS can dramatically boost your reach.

Direct Comparative Value (DCV)

With Direct Comparative Value (DCV), you extrapolate the value of one proprietary audience channel from the cost to message another. Friend and author Jay Baer (@JayBaer) developed a DCV methodology to value Facebook impressions based on cost per email open.[17] His logic is that a Facebook post impression is akin to an email open since both FANS and SUBSCRIBERS are JOINERS who have opted into your company's messaging. Accordingly, the cost to reach email SUBSCRIBERS can be used to approximate the cost to reach Facebook FANS.

Jay's methodology is as follows:

1. Multiply your total number of email SUBSCRIBERS by your open rate.
2. Add up the cost to produce and send a single email to your SUBSCRIBERS (design, development, per email send fees, etc.).
3. Multiply #2 by #1 to get your Cost per email Opened.
4. Multiply the result of #3 by your Total Facebook Post Views from the past month (available in your Facebook Insights reporting).

Using Jay's methodology, let's say you have a $0.0175 cost per email opened and had 50,000 post impressions the past month. The DCV you're generating on Facebook would be $875 ($0.0175 × 50,000). Again, it's not a *precise* measurement of value; however, it is a justifiable comparative one based on what you already know you're paying to have an email reach a SUBSCRIBER.

Comparative Incentive Value (CIV)

Our final valuation model, Comparative Incentive Value (CIV), is useful in industries where competitors provide consumers with incentives to *subscribe, like,* or *follow*—such as fast food or retail. To calculate your CIV:

- Anonymously shop/visit your competitors (online or offline).
- Document what incentives, if any, they provide to consumers to become SUBSCRIBERS, FANS, or FOLLOWERS.
- Chart each incentive's retail value and divide each by half (or whatever is an appropriate value for your industry) to get to the out-of-pocket cost for the incentive.

- Add up the out-of-pocket incentive costs and divide by the number competitors offering them.
- And *poof*! You have your CIV.

CIV provides a shorthand way to understand your audience members' potential value, and gives you an idea of what type of incentive you might use to acquire new JOINERS. If you want to try a quick CIV analysis, just visit some of the fast food restaurants in your area. When I did just that, here's what the different chains were offering me to become an email SUBSCRIBER:

Arby's:	$2.89 (free Regular Roast Beef with drink purchase)
Boston Market:	$3.00 off next purchase to join "The V.I.P. Club"
Burger King:	No incentive (but email offers provided throughout year)
Chipotle:	No incentive (but email offers provided throughout year)
Jack in the Box:	No incentive (but email offers provided throughout year)
Jimmy John's:	No incentive (but email offers provided throughout year)
KFC:	No incentive (but email offers provided throughout year)
McDonald's:	No incentive
Qdoba:	$1.99 (free chips & salsa or large drink)
Quizno's:	$2 off next purchase to join "The Q Club"
Penn Station:	$4.49 (free 6″ sub)
Popeyes:	No incentive (but email offers provided throughout year)
Subway:	No incentive (but email offers provided throughout year)
Taco Bell:	No incentive (but email offers provided throughout year)
Wendy's:	No incentive (but email offers provided throughout year)
White Castle:	$2.64 (4 Free Sliders to join "The Craver Nation")

Using a CIV analysis, you add up the incentives offered and divide by the number of companies offering them. You then divide result ($2.83) in half and get a CIV of $1.42. If you're in the fast food or quick-service restaurant (QSR) space, you can use that figure to convey to management both the initial value of email SUBSCRIBERS and the potential level of incentive that you may want to use to acquire new email SUBSCRIBERS.

It's worth noting that even those fast food restaurants that did not promote email opt-in incentives do provide SUBSCRIBERS with discounts *once they join*. Thus, if you truly wanted to get a sense of the value that your competitors placed on SUBSCRIBERS, you should monitor and track the value of their offers over time—adjusting your CIV analysis accordingly. Such an ongoing CIV analysis is particularly important in social media channels like Facebook and Twitter where up-front incentives to *like* or *follow* have largely dried up.

Organizational Value

There is one other value to keep in mind as you seek to build your proprietary audiences: the value they command *in the eyes of your company*. To ensure that you continue to hold your audiences in high regard, you must regularly communicate their financial value to management—both in terms of real revenue and advertising cost savings. Only then will your C-suite and the people who manage your proprietary audiences fully appreciate their value as business assets.

Chapter

A Larger Font: Our Long-Term Responsibilities

The audience is the most revered member of the theater. Without an audience there is no theater.[1]

—Viola Spolin

In *Improvisation for the Theater*, known by actors around the world as "the bible of improvisational theater," the late Viola Spolin imparts the above bit of knowledge to her readers. With hundreds of thousands of copies of her book now circulating around the globe, Ms. Spolin's legacy is clear. She ensured that each new acting generation would embrace the theater as an audience-driven medium.

Can we say the same thing about marketing? Do we fully appreciate the long-term importance of the audience to our companies?

Based on my experience and without reservation, I'd say "no." Proprietary audiences are a corporate afterthought, and nothing illustrates this more clearly than the word cloud in Figure 7.1. Created by Econsultancy (@Econsultancy) and Adobe (@Adobe) as part of their *2013 Quarterly Digital Intelligence Briefing*, it captures responses to the question, "What do you consider to be the most important marketing opportunity today?"[2] The most popular answers appear in larger, bolder fonts.

What jumps out at you first? My eye is immediately drawn to how the words *content*, *mobile*, and *social* are among the biggest—just as content

FIGURE 7.1 The Word Cloud Formed from Answers to the Question "What do you consider the most important marketing opportunity today?"

marketing, mobile marketing, and social media garner the biggest headlines in marketing today.

Notice what's missing from the word cloud? If you answered "audience," you get a gold star for effort. The truth is, however, that "audience" is not technically *missing* from the word cloud; it's just so darn small that you need a magnifying glass to see it. Let's zoom in a bit—400 percent, to be exact (see Figure 7.2).

FIGURE 7.2 With the help of 400% zoom (and great eyesight), we find "Audience" in the word cloud of today's marketing opportunities

Thar she blows! A blurry, 1-point Arial needle in a haystack, but at least "audience" made it in there somewhere—illegible though it might be.

Of course, the barely visible size of the word underscores how little marketers prioritize *Proprietary Audience Development* today. Instead, they are focused on content development within specific channels, which, while entirely understandable, leaves a giant hole in their marketing efforts. Why? Because the biggest practice areas in the cloud—*content, social*, and *mobile marketing*—all need that tiny word, *audience*, in order to succeed.

If we are to deliver on the final mandate of *The Audience Imperative* and embrace *Proprietary Audience Development* over the long term, we cannot have a quick-fix mentality. Ours is not a one-and-done job. It requires vision, commitment, and execution as long as our company is in business.

Clearly, there are a lot of forces working against us. We live in a fast-paced, youth-dominated culture where it's often difficult to think beyond this week, let alone next quarter, next year, or the next decade. We are siloed into teams that foster "us" versus "them" battles while we keep our customers waiting. Moreover, we work in a field—marketing—with fancy awards for finite, creative campaigns, but little pomp and circumstance for those who build lasting audience assets.

If you're going to overcome these forces, you must be prepared to:

1. Embrace change permanently.
2. Ditch any "not my job" attitude.
3. Retrain your agencies.
4. Respond to results, not headlines.
5. Never stop learning.

It's a tall order, for sure. Let's look at each in more detail.

Embrace Change Permanently

We've already seen that today's marketer has to deal with over 50 different ways of reaching consumers versus just nine when Don Draper roamed the Earth. Adding to that complexity are the Converged Media options available within each channel. Facebook alone has over 10 different types of advertising units to offer—a number that seems tame when you consider that until recently, they had over 27.[3] As mobile devices become even more ubiquitous around the globe over the next decade, even more tactics—and perhaps entirely new channels—will emerge.

If there is one thing you must embrace to lead the charge on *Proprietary Audience Development* within your company, it is this: *Change is marketing's only constant today.* As channels morph and grow and partner and merge, those who can embrace and adapt to change will rise above those who cannot. For *Proprietary Audience Development* to succeed, it must be championed by individuals who don't fear change, because they stay focused on the goal that matters: generating sales in as cost-effective a manner as possible.

Change is marketing's only constant today.

Ditch The "Not My Job" Atttitude

On his average work day, Don Draper:

- Arrived at work when he wanted to
- Sat around thinking deep, creative thoughts
- Gave orders to a dedicated creative team that executed his ideas
- Slipped away for three-martini lunches
- Engaged in extramarital activities. *Frequently*

Don Draper never had to run a printing press, read ad copy on air, or build a television from parts in order to run a commercial. Once his team had the creative together, the traffic department shot it over to the newspaper, radio station, or television network du jour and the ad ran. Nationwide readers read, listeners listened, and viewers watched. Then, as if by magic, cash registers began ringing all over America. Don Draper's America. Paid Media America.

If anyone had asked Don to type, tweet, or blog, he'd have punched them in the nose. It wasn't that he didn't have time to do such things. It was just that such work was beneath him. He was a *partner*. It wasn't his job.

In today's marketing environment, anyone who cops a "not my job" attitude deserves to be fired. Thanks to social and mobile, we're all in a boat that's taking on the weight of additional consumer channels and expectations, and it's going to take all hands on deck to stay afloat. Accordingly, to advance your *Proprietary Audience Development* mandate, you need to be prepared to give a little to get a little, collaborate whenever possible, and stray from the hard lines dictated by your company's org chart. This is already happening in the world of CRM, where an acronym that used to be synonymous only with *sales* is now being unpacked for what it is—*Customer Relationship Management*—a discipline that requires collaboration among your *Sales, Service*, and *Marketing Teams*.

In short, your job is to do whatever is necessary to help your company succeed. If ever something is "not your job," be prepared not to have one for long.

Retrain Your Agencies

Secretly, a lot of marketers still want to be Don Draper.* And who can blame them? He's suave, confident, and the smartest guy in the room. He has one job: creative. He's the magic man, the storyteller, the person to whom everyone turns to pull inspirational advertising campaigns out of thin air armed with nothing more than his imagination.

There are lots of these creative minds still in marketing today—as well there must be. At a time of unprecedented competition for consumer attention, you need people who can produce breakthrough campaign ideas for your brand. Today, however, those ideas must span the full breadth of Converged Media—consider marketing's fundamental goals:

1. Make the sale
2. Serve the customer
3. Build the brand
4. Optimize your Paid, Owned, and Earned Media
5. Build proprietary audiences

Of these goals, Don Draper really only cared about numbers 1 and 3. He was an agency guy who pitched business, and if he won it, he cranked out one creative campaign after another in hopes of padding his billings. And if any client got too demanding, he was only too happy to show them the door—because there was always new business to be had.

This agency model still pervades much of today's marketing thinking and structures. The inherent problem is that it allows agencies to work towards *short-term sales goals* without considering *long-term objectives*. That may have been fine when companies didn't have proprietary audiences; however, it's a recipe for disaster today. Repeat it with me: If you're not focused on developing proprietary audiences, you may be threatening their very existence.

---

*Save for the self-loathing, existential ennui, and Faustian death spiral, of course.

This is why it's imperative for you to retrain your agency (or agencies) so they share your *Proprietary Audience Development* goals. I'm not suggesting that every campaign has to be driven by a desperate mantra of "Subscribe! Like! Follow!" But you do need to keep your agency apprised of the revenue that proprietary audiences deliver to your bottom line. Armed with that knowledge, they can help make certain your Paid Media campaigns build your audiences—rather than drive them away.

Respond to Results, Not Headlines

If you're going to commit your company and your career to the practice of *Proprietary Audience Development*, you need to steel yourself against a force that is driving far too many marketing priorities today.

Misinformation.

If someone wanted to build a machine to do nothing but spread falsehoods, they probably could do no better than the Internet. Anyone with a connection can publish erroneous facts, make unsubstantiated claims, and post doctored photos for the entire world to see. The Internet is an information network, not a lie detector. It relies on human beings to separate truth from fiction, and we aren't always so great in that role.

Perhaps you remember these recent internet hoaxes*:

- The pic of Bill Gates offering $5,000 to anyone who shared the photo on Facebook—a riff on a similar 1999 chain email.[4]

- The tweet from the official Associated Press Twitter account (@AP) that sent stocks plunging more than $200 billion in mere minutes—only to be exposed as a hacker's hoax.[5]

- The video of a "golden eagle" flying off with a toddler in a Montreal park.[6] It was exposed later as student's viral video project.

Despite the occasional fake-out, marketers are usually pretty good at sniffing out such hoaxes. Our online lifestyles have forced us to develop a healthy skepticism toward easy money, too-good-to-be-true stories, and all-too-convenient explanations. However, we marketers do have a significant blind spot in our B.S. detectors: the "next big thing."

---

*Of these three, this was the only one that fooled me. Clearly, there is something particularly dark in my soul that wants to believe in a world where giant raptors are flying off with French-Canadian children.

The blessing and curse of our marketing generation is that if you wait long enough, a "next big thing" will appear. First, it was email. Then banner ads. Then Google. Then Google AdWords. Then LinkedIn. Then Friendster, Myspace, and Second Life. Then Facebook. Then Twitter. Then the iPhone. Then Instagram. Then the iPad. Then Google+. Then Pinterest. Then Vine. Then Snapchat. Then Google Glass. And so on, and so on, and so on . . .

The net effect of this nonstop flood of "next big things" is that we fall prey to marketing pundits and headlines proclaiming that the channel we love so dearly today is "dead"—killed by some shiny, new channel. Just check out this hit parade of headlines since 2010:

- "Haven't You Heard? Email Is Dead" (June 2010)[7]
- "The Web Is Dead" (August 2010)[8]
- "Twitter Is Dying—and It's All Your Fault" (October 2011)[9]
- "Facebook Is Dead for Gen Y" (November 2011)[10]
- "Blogging Is Dead" (December 2011)[11]
- "The Death of SEO" (July 2012)[12]
- "Marketing Is Dead" (August 2012)[13]
- "The CMO Is Dead" (November 2012)[14]
- "Advertising Is Dead" (March 2013)[15]

I know popular culture today is fascinated with zombies, but this is a bit ridiculous. CMOs are still alive and kicking in marketing departments all over the globe. I'm also pleased to tell you that not one of the channels mentioned above is dead or dying. In fact, not one of those 50-plus channels listed earlier in this book have disappeared. There are even still people marketing via broadcast faxes. *Broadcast faxes*, people!!!

Marketing's "dead and dying" headlines are a byproduct of two factors—*link-baiting* and *shiny object syndrome*. Authors and editors know that declaring any channel "dead" is bound to get a rise out of the professionals who work in that field—and therefore generate more inbound links, traffic, and discussion. That's called link-baiting. But here's the funny thing: If you read any of those articles previously listed, you'll see that a number state the opposite of what their headlines proclaim. Truth, you see, is quite malleable when referral traffic is on the line.

We humans also love chasing shiny, new objects. In the Internet era, countless folks have built entire careers on the early adopter status of new channels as opposed to genuine, ROI-driven expertise. These pied pipers touted quick and easy traffic and fed into the deep-seated desire in many of us to be on the cutting edge instead of the cutting room floor.

In so doing, however, these gurus helped fuel marketing's "hype culture" in which every new social network or mobile app is touted as a "killer" of something else. Let me put an end to this once and for all. "Dead" is dead. Facebook isn't going to "kill" email, and Twitter isn't going to "kill" Facebook. Instead of reading headlines, we must focus on and use *our actual marketing results* to guide our hand.

"Dead" is dead. Facebook isn't going to "kill" email, and Twitter isn't going to "kill" Facebook.

If you're serious about *Proprietary Audience Development*, then you should be leading the charge in your marketing department to track, measure, analyze, and test everything you can. The more data we can process, the better equipped we become to:

- Prioritize our investments based on performance rather than "gut feel."
- Personalize messaging based on insights as opposed to convenience.
- Demonstrate the value of our proprietary audiences.

Now, it's one thing for me to convince you that "dead" headlines are dead, but it's another thing altogether for *you* to convince your management when they forward the next "_____ Is Dead" article to you. If and when this happens, I want you to:

1. Mark this page for easy future reference.
2. Read the article they present carefully—not just the headline.
3. Highlight where the article doesn't actually support the headline.
4. Pull up the latest stats on how the channel in question performs for you.
5. Drop this book like a hot mic and walk off like Jay-Z after his final encore.

The fact is that you're never going to stop marketing misinformation from causing you the occasional headache. All you can do is focus on what matters—the *Proprietary Audience Development* channels that work for you.

Never Stop Learning

The mere fact that you've reached this point in the book is an indication that you're committed to the kind of lifelong learning that today's marketing requires. It was unfathomable to me when I graduated college in 1991 that a marketer would have to know anything about HTML, responsive design, or mobile app development. And yet, that's exactly where we are.

We deal with a dizzying array of consumer technologies that would make Don Draper's head spin. Print, radio, and television are now consumed through their original channels as well as on laptops, smartphones, tablets, and even game consoles. Marketers cannot just "run a commercial" any longer; they must run ads that accommodate device form factors in ways that take full advantage of the unique points of consumer interaction for each device—at least, if they want to maximize response.

The only way to remain relevant as a marketer is to *never stop learning*. As you progress, however, do more than just focus on *what's new*; focus on *what delivers results* and *what is lasting*. There's a reason I'm so passionate about *Proprietary Audience Development*. I firmly believe that it is now part of the bedrock of marketing responsibilities that include advertising, branding, content marketing, customer service, demand generation, product development, and sales. Figure out how to deliver the audiences that fuel these initiatives, and you will truly help define *The Hybrid Marketing Era*.

Part

The Audience Channels

Before you can build the best proprietary audiences for your business, you must fully appreciate the strengths, weaknesses, and breadth of channels available to you today. For some readers, this part may feel like review. Trust me, however—everyone from CEOs to new hires to the most seasoned social media professionals will benefit from reviewing each channel with fresh eyes. That is because we are examining them not for what they *have meant* to your company but rather for what they *could mean* as part of a far more coordinated Proprietary Audience Development effort.

A book can only contain so much information, so I have opted to present snapshots of the channels that I feel are the most important today (based on my highly subjective opinion). In reality, your channel priorities will vary greatly based on your brand strategy, industry competition, marketing objectives, and available staffing. Later, in Part III, you'll have the opportunity to express that mix as part of your *Proprietary Audience Development* strategy. And for a discussion of even more proprietary audience channels, join the conversation over at www.AudiencePro.com.

Website: Marketing's Magnetic Center

A bad website is like a grumpy salesperson.[1]

—Jakob Nielsen

Jakob Nielsen (@NNgroup) knows a thing or two about websites. Thanks to his numerous books and tireless work with global companies on improving their websites for consumers, his name has become synonymous with website usability. For all his efforts, however, one thing is clear: There are still a lot of abominable company websites on the World Wide Web.

Jakob's certainly not to blame for this state of affairs. He's done more than his fair share to educate marketers that a bad website is often worse than no website at all. The real fault lies with companies that fail to see their website for what it is—the magnetic center of all their marketing efforts. Whether you're a sole proprietor or the world's biggest online retailer, your website is your primary Owned Media asset and the first place you should look to build your company's proprietary audiences.

> *Your website is the magnetic center of your marketing efforts, your primary Owned Media asset, and the first place you should look to build your company's proprietary audiences.*

There are entire books, courses, and online services that will teach you how to build a website. However, the goal of anyone focused on *Proprietary Audience Development* is how best to *optimize* a website to:

- Attract SEEKERS from mobile apps, online maps, and search engines.
- Convert those SEEKERS into JOINERS by becoming:
  - Paying CUSTOMERS
  - SUBSCRIBERS, FANS, and/or FOLLOWERS
  - AMPLIFIERS of positive sentiment or experiences

The two disciplines that focus on getting SEEKERS to your website are:

1. *Content Marketing*: The practice of publishing content to your website on an ongoing basis that appeals to SEEKERS looking for your products or services and aids SEO efforts
2. *SEO*: The process of optimizing website content, structure, and technology in order to obtain better search engine rankings on keyword searches that capture more qualified SEEKERS

Once you're driving a steady flow of SEEKERS to your website, you can turn your attention to optimizing their experience on the site through the additional disciplines of:

- *Conversion Optimization*: The practice of streamlining data collection, opt-in, and purchase processes to eliminate friction, maximize conversions of SEEKERS to CUSTOMERS, and boost ROI
- *Responsive Design*: The process of designing a website such that it's optimized for increasingly mobile means of consumption by SEEKERS (smartphones, tablets, etc.)
- *Usability Design*: The process of optimizing a website's usability by eliminating points of friction and frustration for SEEKERS that negatively impact both experience and conversion opportunities
- *Website Analytics*: The process of analyzing how SEEKERS interact with your site in order to identify opportunities to optimize conversions, interactions, and time on site
- *Website Optimization*: The process of improving all aspects of site performance through continuous testing

Ultimately, your number one goal with all of these efforts is to convert SEEKERS to CUSTOMERS. However, in the new tradition of *hybrid marketing*, we're also interested in converting them into other proprietary audiences through:

- Comment forms (COMMENTER/AMPLIFIERS)
- Email and SMS opt-in forms (SUBSCRIBERS)
- *Like* and *follow* buttons (FANS and FOLLOWERS)
- *Comment, pin, tweet*, and *share* buttons (AMPLIFIERS)

It is not enough to optimize your home page for *Proprietary Audience Development*. You must optimize every aspect of your site to encourage SEEKERS to amplify your messaging and join your audiences. None of this, however, should be done to the detriment of:

- The ultimate sale
- Your brand
- Your existing proprietary audience relationships

In other words, if your brand is upscale, you may want to be far more discreet with the *Proprietary Audience Development* efforts on your website than a daily deal site where SEEKERS arrive with a clear understanding that an aggressive email opt-in request is par for the course. However, this not to say that brands shouldn't experiment with new ideas. The real-time nature of social media presents tremendous opportunities to transform company websites from dusty site maps into living, breathing visualizations of proprietary audience engagement.

For example, take the fast food burger chain Wendy's (@Wendys). As part of their 2013 brand refresh, they redesigned www.wendys.com so that its homepage features:

- A responsive design that accommodates any desktop or mobile device
- A clear CTA to join *My Wendy's*, their email loyalty program
- Constantly updated social posts from Facebook, Instagram, and Twitter
- GPS-friendly store and job opportunity locators[2]

The net effect of Wendy's new site is to project the brand and its restaurants as a place where something is always happening (Figure 8.1). SEEKERS

FIGURE 8.1   A Sampling of the Social Elements on Wendys.com That Help Build Proprietary Audiences

not only find the information they need; they also find themselves intrigued by what Wendy's offers to its SUBSCRIBER, FAN, and FOLLOWER audiences. And ultimately, that's what every website should do: attract interested SEEKERS and give them every reason to become AMPLIFIERS and JOINERS as well.

Don't Overlook Your Landing Pages

Landing pages are one of the more interesting creatures in our marketing bag of tricks, and according to landing page optimization expert Tim Ash (@Tim_Ash):

> *Landing page testing is the best accelerator available to your business.*[3]

Marketers created landing pages to circumvent website development bottlenecks and support quick-turnaround advertising campaigns. Today, they remain an indispensable part of most companies' online marketing efforts. Unfortunately, most landing pages are also a mess.

Unlike a website, which usually has a principal owner, landing pages are a virtual Wild West of branding, content, and ownership. As a result, they probably aren't aiding your *Proprietary Audience Development* efforts as much as they could. Since you're often using Paid Media to drive SEEKERS to your landing pages, the potential downside is twofold—lost advertising dollars and lost proprietary audiences.

Accordingly, as you look to optimize your website for *Proprietary Audience Development*, don't forget to review your landing pages as well. Chances are that they could be helping to generate far more SEEKERS, AMPLIFIERS, and JOINERS with only modest effort.

SNAPSHOT:	WEBSITE
FIRST WEBSITE:	1991[4]
INTERNET USERS:	Est. 2.56 billion (36.1% of world population)[5]
PROPRIETARY AUDIENCES:	SEEKERS (SEARCHERS, READERS, VIEWERS, and VISITORS) Also key driver of all types of SEEKER, AMPLIFIER, and JOINER growth via e-commerce, SEO, social sharing, and opt-in forms.
SKILLS REQUIRED:	HTML and other code development, design, copywriting, ongoing management.
EFFORT REQUIRED:	Moderate to high depending on website complexity, e-commerce integration, and content publishing requirements.
WHO OWNS THE DATA:	Your company owns its website data; although, use of "free" analytics software (e.g., Google Analytics) or social widgets may grant third parties the ability to access or aggregate select data.
GATEKEEPERS:	Your company controls its website content governed only by relevant, prevailing laws.
STRENGTHS:	Instantaneous, worldwide distribution of content, design, and features that you control.
	Websites, microsites, and landing pages provide ability to publish content that serves very specific organizational needs or campaigns.
	Extraordinarily flexible medium (simple informational sites to sophisticated interaction and online retail operations).
	Drives "free" traffic (SEARCHERS) through SEO.
	Crucial point in SUBSCRIBER, FAN, and FOLLOWER acquisition efforts through embedded email opt-in, social widgets, and data collection forms.
	Website analytics provide performance and behavioral data that you can use to optimize website performance and tailor personalized messaging to SEEKERS and JOINERS.
CHALLENGES:	Depending on your website's complexity, it can require a significant investment to build and maintain with proper technical, design, content, analytics, and other staff.
	Search engine visibility is at the mercy of Google and other search engines as they evolve their indexing methodology and search algorithms.
	Requires investment of time, people, and money (advertising, branding, promotion, etc.) to build direct SEEKER traffic (those who bookmark or type in website URL versus searching).
	Competing organization priorities can lead to websites that serve too many masters and, in so doing, serve none of them well.

Chapter

8

Email: The Bedrock Audience

In an ironic twist of fate, it turns out that email is social media's secret weapon . . . [I]f you want to drive retention and repeat usage, there isn't a better way to do it than email.[1]
— Fred Wilson

Fred Wilson (@FredWilson) is one of the most social media savvy VCs (venture capitalists) you'll ever meet. He was an early-stage investor in Twitter, Tumblr, Foursquare, and Etsy, and he has been blogging about the VC life since 2003.[2] As a result, when Fred speaks, entrepreneurs, investors, marketers, and social media managers tend to listen. And that is what made his above statement such a bolt from the blue.

It was May 2011 and headlines were proclaiming that email was "dead," killed by the rise of Facebook and Twitter. As someone who understands the inner workings of online marketing, Fred knew the truth: Email remains the hidden engine driving much of the engagement, reengagement,

---

Email remains the hidden engine driving much of the engagement, reengagement, and e-commerce activity on the web.

---

and e-commerce activity on the Web. But email doesn't get the public adulation because:

- Email marketing requires more effort to create and send messages than it takes to post or tweet.

- Email marketing's financial impact lies hidden from public view because companies are under no obligation to disclose it.

- Email's cost-effective nature means that it commands a smaller portion of marketing budgets than Paid Media. Less budget = less attention.

- Email SUBSCRIBERS are private assets to whom companies send personal messages through private systems to individual inboxes. It is therefore impossible to compare SUBSCRIBER counts or engagement among competitors as directly as one can with Facebook FANS.

- Many people don't think of transactional messages such as receipts or friend alerts as email marketing.

So Fred—with his behind-the-scenes startup insight—blogged about the continued power and relevance of email, dubbing it *social media's secret weapon*. Suddenly, a lot of folks stopped suggesting email was dead. And a lot of "social media gurus" started email newsletters.

The Origin of Email

The ubiquity of *electronic mail* (i.e., *email)* today makes it hard to believe there was ever a time before email, but there was.* In 1971, prior to the debut of the Internet, engineer Ray Tomlinson invented the "@" structure of email addresses (user@hostdomain) and sent the first email (which he characterized as "completely forgettable").[3] Fortunately, someone remembered that email; and in 2012, the Internet Society inducted Ray as part of its inaugural Hall of Fame class.[4]

The date of the first permission-based commercial email is probably an unascertainable bit of trivia, since only God, Chuck Barris,

---

*It took until March 2011 for the AP Stylebook to shorten e-mail to just email. While hyphen-loving netizens mourned, social media praised the move—mainly because it was announced by the AP via Twitter.

and the CIA know what government scientists were up to in the 1970s.[5] However, legend has it that in 1978 Gary Thurek, a marketing manager for Digital Equipment Corp. (DEC), sent the first unsolicited commercial email (a.k.a. "spam").[6] While he was chastised by many recipients, DEC went on to sell 20 of the $1 million systems. The Pandora's box of email spam had been opened.[7]

In 1988, Vint Cerf (@vgcerf), "Father of the Internet" and himself an Internet Hall of Fame inductee, helped arrange for the first commercial connection of email systems to the Internet.[8] This paved the way for email to become the foundation of online communications today.

Email Is a Must-Have

Email remains an incredibly productive and profitable channel for those who invest the time to build their *permission-based email SUBSCRIBERS*. Consider:

- Email is ranked as the "Most Effective Marketing Tactic" by a majority of both B2C (63 percent) and B2B (58 percent) marketers.[9]
- Email drives 20 percent or more of the revenues for nearly half of companies recently surveyed by the DMA.[10]
- In a recent survey of online retailers, email SUBSCRIBERS were found to be 11 percent more valuable than average CUSTOMERS.[11]

Email is also an incredibly flexible medium, used for:

- Alerts
- Content syndication
- Customer service communications
- Lead nurturing
- Order communications
- Receipts
- Service notifications
- Tickets
- Boarding passes
- Coupons
- Event notifications
- Newsletters
- Promotions
- Reminders
- Shipping communications

Here are just a few of the millions of companies benefitting from email:

- The Denver Center for the Performing Arts (@DenverCenter) realized a 738 percent ROI from a single email marketing campaign targeting 40,000 lapsed PATRONS.[12]
- eBags (@eBags) estimates that the acquisition of 28,000 email SUBSCRIBERS and 46,000 Facebook FANS via a recent cross-channel campaign netted over $400,000 in revenue and an average value per email SUBSCRIBER of $15.[13]
- The Thomas Cook Group (@ThomasCookUK) leveraged its data to create a personalized email experience with localized deals for each of its customers. Open rates shot up to over 50 percent, and a single email generated over $10,000 in sales from just one corporate client.[14]

It's a fool's errand to try to capture all the ways email is contributing to the bottom lines of recognizable brands. Accordingly, if you're in need of some great case studies regarding email SUBSCRIBER profitability, I highly recommend checking out www.MarketingSherpa.com (@MarketingSherpa).

Email works in large part because it is familiar, predictable, and linear. Email inbox visitors are rarely subjected to the kind of wholesale design changes found annually on Facebook, and bold fonts make it clear where their new email messages begin and end. Mobile devices have further conditioned consumers to check their new messages regularly—if nothing else than to make the bold font (or "little red dot" on the iPhone email app) disappear.

Even as email volume increases and competition for consumer attention continues to grow, email marketing will continue to thrive and survive. Why? Because despite all of the "death of email" predictions over the years, no new proprietary audience channel commands the consumer adoption, message flexibility, and direct-to-consumer control that email does. In short, if you aren't building an email SUBSCRIBER audience, you're likely missing out on what could be a primary revenue and reengagement driver for your company.

SNAPSHOT:	*EMAIL*
FIRST CONSUMER EMAIL SERVICE:	Early 1980s (CompuServe)[15]
PROPRIETARY AUDIENCES:	JOINERS (SUBSCRIBERS). Capable of influencing all other proprietary audience types—SEEKERS, AMPLIFIERS, FANS, and FOLLOWERS.
EFFORT REQUIRED:	Varies depending on program complexity and automation efforts.
WHO OWNS THE DATA:	You own SUBSCRIBER data whether it resides in your servers or that of your Email Service Provider (ESP).
USERS WORLDWIDE:	As of 2013, there are an estimated 2.317 billion email users and 4.657 billion email accounts worldwide.[16]
SKILLS REQUIRED:	Coding, copywriting, data integration, design, strategy, and performance analysis.
GATEKEEPERS:	Internet/Mail Service Providers (ISPs/MSPs: Gmail, Outlook, Yahoo! Mail, etc.); corporate mail clients/IT departments; spam filtering software; industry watchdogs (Spamhaus, etc.)
STRENGTHS:	Channel ubiquity, stability, flexibility, measurability (via click tracking), and cost-effectiveness.
	Highest ROI of any direct messaging channel and preferred consumer channel for permission-based alerts, receipts, and marketing messages.[17]
	Top channel for social sharing (Facebook is second).
	High degree of personalization and testing optimization possible using demographic, performance, and behavioral data.
	Factory-installed app on all smartphones and tablets, and a top smartphone activity among 18–44-year-olds.[18]
	Email address is near-ubiquitous requirement for nearly all types of online registration (e-commerce, social networks, etc.). This reinforces the use of email even among younger consumers.
CHALLENGES:	More staff effort required to create, send, and track emails than posts on Facebook at tweets via Twitter.
	Consumer migration of personal messages to SMS, Facebook, Twitter, and other social media channels may impact channel engagement over time.
	Channel noise due to spam (unsolicited commercial email), personal, business, and other commercial emails.

Chapter 10

Facebook: Making It Personal

Facebook was not originally created to be a company. It was built to accomplish a social mission to make the world more open and connected.[1]

—Mark Zuckerberg

If there is one thing you must know about Facebook, it is this: Users are not there for the advertising. The social network has grown into the giant it is because it connects people to the individuals, organizations, causes, and things that matter most in their lives. It has reunited mothers and sons, long-lost loves, and families after natural disasters.[2] At its core, two basic, human needs drive most Facebook usage: the need to belong and the need to present oneself to others.[3]

You may therefore ask why any company should maintain a presence on Facebook. The answer is clear to those who spend just a few minutes on the site. First and foremost, Facebook has critical mass. As of this writing, Facebook is used by over 51 percent of all Internet users, making it the largest social network in the world.[4] Second, personal associations with brands, causes, and organizations are one way that many people express who they are to others online. As a result, the businesses that are most successful on

Facebook are those that build communities and amplify their FANS' stories, as opposed to just shilling for a product or service.

The businesses that are most successful on Facebook are those that build communities and amplify their FANS stories, as opposed to just shilling for a product or service.

When you were a brand FAN in Facebook's early days, their logo would appear on your profile—a sort of virtual badging akin to having a Nike "swoosh" on your hat or shoes. Today, however, the virtual badging takes place in the News Feeds and advertising of your FANS and their connections. Figure 10.1 shows one that just popped up in my Facebook News Feed while writing today.

 Evan D. Rossio likes BookBub.

———— RELATED POST ————

BB **BookBub**   👍 **Like Page**

Free Bestselling eBooks for Kindle, Nook, iPad, and more.

Get BookBub's Free Daily Email → http://bub.to/YogQo7

Like · Comment · Share · 👍 2,174 💬 146 📄 882 · 🌐 · Sponsored

FIGURE 10.1   A Facebook Sponsored Post from BookBub

I haven't seen my former colleague Evan Rossio (@EvanRossio) in years, but we stay connected thanks to Facebook. BookBub (@BookBub) is a service offering free and bargain books for e-readers. I've never used it; however, because Evan has *liked* their Facebook Fan page, they can use his endorsement ("Evan D. Rossio likes BookBub") as part of their advertisement. Since Evan is someone I know and respect, it makes me more likely to respond to this paid advertisement in a dizzying number of ways:

- I can *like* BookBub's Facebook Page (building their FAN audience).
- I can visit their website (feeding their SEEKER audience).
- I can subscribe to their free daily email (building SUBSCRIBERS).
- I can *like* their ad (feeding their AMPLIFIER audience).
- I can *comment* on their ad (also feeding their AMPLIFIERS).
- I can *share* their ad with my friends (also feeding their AMPLIFIERS).

This single example demonstrates why Facebook is perhaps the most multifaceted audience development and engagement platform out there today. Within its walls, you can:

- Build FANS by getting users to *like* your brand page via free posts or paid advertising.
  - EXAMPLE: DonorsChoose.org (@DonorsChoose), which includes your Facebook friends who like the organization in their website header
- Communicate with FANS via posts on your page, their News Feed, and direct messages where permission is granted.
  - EXAMPLE: Crocs (@Crocs), which publicly responds to feedback and CUSTOMER or FAN questions posted to Facebook
- Encourage FANS to also become SUBSCRIBERS or FOLLOWERS through cross-promotion of email, Twitter, and other channels.
  - EXAMPLE: Half Price Books (@HalfPriceBooks), which uses its Facebook Timeline and Pages to promote the value of email subscription to FANS
- Capture attention from SEEKERS who are searching Facebook or browsing it for entertainment purposes.

- EXAMPLE: Oreo (@Oreo), which entertains SEEKERS—as well as over 34 million Facebook FANS with humorous questions, photos, and videos featuring the cookie as the star
- Inspire AMPLIFIERS to *like, comment,* and *share* content with their own proprietary audiences—both inside and outside of Facebook (via organic/free posts or Sponsored Posts in Facebook's desktop and mobile environments).
    - EXAMPLE: Mobile app developers who have discovered Facebook mobile ads to be a great way to not only get new SUBSCRIBERS but also AMPLIFIERS who tell others about their apps

If we view marketing as a game of football, each of these efforts on Facebook takes place on the *offensive side* of the ball. Each uses Facebook in positive ways that get SEEKERS, AMPLIFIERS, and FANS to:

- Interact with your brand.
- Share comments and stories about your brand, products, or services.
- Share pictures, videos, and other visual content related to your brand.
- Share ideas for new products or feedback about existing ones.
- Visit your website or other Owned Media.
- Buy your products or services.

Undoubtedly, the key reason to develop proprietary Facebook FANS is to enable these types of "offensive plays" on Facebook. However, Facebook FANS also provide you with protection on the ***defensive side*** of the ball. As many brands have discovered unexpectedly, Facebook is a very public forum in which:

- Consumers can vent about negative experiences with your brand.
- Executive and employee stupidity can be amplified exponentially.
- Activists can attack your company's policies, investments, or activities.

The presence of negative commentary on a brand's Facebook page can be difficult for some companies to manage—which is what makes Facebook

FANS an audience asset with a higher risk profile than, say, an email SUBSCRIBER. Email SUBSCRIBERS can certainly choose to share negative brand experiences with friends via email; however, such stories are not publicly visible or instantly shared to one's entire social network as they are on Facebook.

Thus, if you're going to embrace Facebook as a proprietary audience channel for your business, you must be prepared to not just build FANS but also serve loyal customers. Fortunately, you're not alone in this mission. Our research found that 51 percent of the time, retail brand FANS answer questions before the brands themselves.[5] A quick review of consumer packaged goods (CPG), restaurant, travel, and other brands similarly finds FANS answering questions on behalf of their favorite brands.

Facebook has enabled a form of *FAN-to-FAN Customer Service* where knowledgeable, engaged FANS—through no prompting of the brand itself— supplement the capacity of corporate social media and customer service teams. While this may seem like sacrilege to corporate command and control structures, it is a tremendous asset—especially when the volume of Facebook comments and questions may outpace your team's ability to respond.

Facebook FANS also can take their responses a step further and challenge negative comments or assertions about your brand. I call this the "white blood cell effect" because FANS rush in to defend your brand from attack. FANS can do this because they are not bound by your internal rules or in-house lawyers. Yes, you will still need to weigh in to ensure that they don't perpetuate falsehoods or devolve into a war of words. However, FANS' ability to speak their minds is a great asset to have at the ready if and when trouble arises.

Facebook's unique ability to provide marketers with options *on both sides of the ball* means that every part of your marketing department has a stake in the ongoing development of your company's Facebook FAN audience.

The DNA of Facebook

I think it's fair to say that no social network has been subjected to the kind of media scrutiny that Facebook has. It certainly is the only one with a major motion picture about its origin (*The Social Network*)—let alone one that won three Academy Awards.[6]

So, rather than rehash the various origin stories, let's focus on something inherent in Facebook's DNA: sharing. As stated in the company's S-1 filing, Facebook CEO Mark Zuckerberg believes that "personal relationships are the fundamental unit of our society," and that "people sharing more—even if just with their close friends or families—creates a more open culture and leads to a better understanding of the lives and perspectives of others."

Sharing is the social currency of your AMPLIFIER audience. If your company can inspire the consumer's need to share, it can extend the reach of your brand, message, and products to people and places you never could have imagined. Which is why Facebook is so important in your AMPLIFIER development efforts; it aims to corner the market on sharing.

But don't take my word for it; listen to Mark explain sharing:

> We talk about the Moore's law of sharing, but we never meant that all this will happen on Facebook—it will happen in the world. Our challenge is to make that happen on Facebook. I draw an analogy to Intel. Moore's law was great for them, because they could point at the world and say, "Okay, in 18 months, someone's going to fit this many transistors on a circuit board—we'd better be the ones to do it or else someone is gonna eat our lunch!" I look at this the same way. Three years from now, people are going to be sharing 8 to 10 times as much stuff. We'd better be there, because if we're not, some other service will be.

"Zuckerberg's Law," as it has come to be known, states that sharing will double or more every two or so years—and Facebook *obsesses every single day* about what this means to their business. It's why they bought Instagram, launched apps for Facebook Messages, and introduced Facebook Home, an app that effectively takes over your Android smartphone to encourage more social interaction. And it's why they'll do a lot more things in the coming years.

Now the question is, what is your business doing to benefit from increased consumer sharing? Is sharing in your DNA? It certainly is for Facebook and your potential AMPLIFIERS.

SNAPSHOT:	*FACEBOOK*
FOUNDED:	February 2004
PROPRIETARY AUDIENCES:	FANS but also SEEKERS and AMPLIFIERS. Also a place to acquire SUBSCRIBERS and FOLLOWERS.
EFFORT REQUIRED:	Variable depending on volume of content and FAN engagement.
WHO OWNS THE DATA:	You own your content but grant Facebook an unlimited license to use it. FANS are yours, but not directly portable to other channels.
USERS WORLDWIDE:	1.15 billion users with 669 million Daily Active Users (DAUs) and 819 million Mobile Active Users (MAUs) and 469 million Mobile DAUs as of June 2013.[7]
DAILY "LIKES" WORLDWIDE:	4.5 billion likes per day as of May 2013.[8]
SKILLS REQUIRED:	Copywriting, authenticity, responsiveness, modest coding/design.
GATEKEEPERS:	Facebook and its users.
STRENGTHS:	World's largest social network with multiple ways to build proprietary audiences through free activities and paid advertising.
	Free to create company page, post updates, or build and interact with consumers. Near-frictionless sharing through ubiquity of *like, comment,* and *share* buttons both within Facebook and via social widgets installed on websites across the web.
	Strong mobile app with high level of mobile user engagement.
	Incredibly diverse ways for consumers to interact with companies: messaging, reading posts, like/comment/share, follow posts, check-ins for physical locations.
	Facebook FANS can amplify your marketing, answer questions from CUSTOMERS, and correct negative statements about your brand.
CHALLENGES:	Facebook's evolution results in frequent changes to the site, pages, and features. This can frustrate both users and social media managers and add unexpected work or costs to marketing plans.
	Facebook's algorithm (previously known as EdgeRank) ensures that only a small percentage of all FANS see your posts.
	39 percent of FANS who "like" brands do not believe that "like" gives the brand the right to post messages to their News Feed.[9]
	Without proper management, negative comments can overwhelm a company's Facebook page, rendering it a liability.
	Organic posts reach only a fraction of Facebook FANS, thereby increasing the need for Paid Media (advertising) via Facebook to reach all FANS.
	Privacy concerns continue to flare up among users.

11

Chapter

Twitter: Real-Time Characters

We're in the media business. We're a distributor of content, and we're one of the largest distributors of traffic. We're trying to build a decades-long lasting business.[1]

—Dick Costolo

I haven't conducted an official survey, but my guess is that most CEOs do not have background in improvisational comedy. Thankfully for Twitter, Dick Costolo (@DickC) is not like most CEOs. His Second City (@SecondCity) and stand-up comedy background are perfectly suited for Twitter, a channel that seems to evolve like the classic improv game *YES AND*.

If you're not familiar with *YES AND*, its rules are simple. Never deny a fellow improvisational actor. If your partner begins a scene in a spaceship, you don't suddenly say that you're actually in a coal mine. Instead, you add to the scene by saying something like, "Yes, we're in this spaceship, and . . . we're under attack from a Flying Spaghetti Monster!!!"

Twitter's *YES AND* evolution goes a little something like this:

Can you publish 140-character tweets to FOLLOWERS?
Yes, and . . .
Can you retweet or "favorite" the tweets of others?
Yes, and . . .
Can you search tweets via words or hashtags you use?

Yes, and . . .

Can you link to people, websites, pictures, and videos?

Yes, and . . .

Can you view embedded pictures and videos without leaving Twitter?

Yes, and . . .

Can you pay to promote tweets and profiles via paid advertising?

Yes, and . . .

Can you enable payments via hashtags on Twitter?

Yes, and . . .

Can you leverage *Twitter Cards* to embed pre-filled forms in tweets?

Yes, and . . .

Can you use *Twitter Cards* for lead generation, sales, and audience-building?

Yes, and . . .

Can you use Twitter to view and share television highlights from partners?

Yes, and . . .

I think you get the point. Twitter has evolved *far beyond* its original 140 characters into a real-time reflection of the brands, content, events, ideas, music, news, and people shaping cultures around the world. Its website and mobile app now accommodate audio and video, making the 140-character tweet more of a springboard to rich content than a destination itself.

While smaller than Facebook in terms of total users, Twitter can often be *more influential* because:

- Twitter handles (ex. @jkrohrs) have become the de facto shorthand for public identity online. Facebook has no similar shorthand.
- Twitter is viewed as a fully *public, broadcast medium*, whereas Facebook is viewed more as a *semi-private, personal medium*.
- Twitter's public platform attracts INFLUENCERS who gravitate to Twitter in hopes of gaining more FOLLOWERS and, therefore, more influence.

If nothing else, your company should be on Twitter to enable Twitter users to link to your profile. Without a Twitter handle, CUSTOMERS who want to express positive sentiment about your brand do so by just mentioning

FIGURE 11.1   A Twitter Handle Provides One-Click Access to Your Profile so That SEEKERS, AMPLIFIERS, and FOLLOWERS Can Quickly Learn Who You Are via Your Profile or Linked Website

your name. When you have a Twitter handle, they can link to your Twitter profile, and the FOLLOWERS who see their tweet can learn more information about your company. (See Figure 11.1.)

Of course, Twitter's real value isn't found in merely maintaining a profile. The real value comes from building proprietary audiences of FOLLOWERS and AMPLIFIERS that extend your brand's reach at zero cost. To do this, however, you must use Twitter to do more than just *promote* your company—you must serve CUSTOMERS, engage FOLLOWERS, and celebrate AMPLIFIERS. Let's take a look at the reasons for each.

Serve CUSTOMERS

If you need a reason to monitor your brand mentions on Twitter, just Google: "customer service nightmares on Twitter." The results will curl your hair (or straighten it, as the case may be). Failure to monitor and respond to customer service complaints on Twitter is akin to not going to the doctor to deal with a greenstick fracture of your leg; it isn't gonna get better on its own.

The good news, however, is that most Twitter users view the channel as a last resort—that is, they only vent on Twitter if they've either exhausted all other official channels or it's the only one available in the moment. However, once consumers do turn to Twitter with an issue, 42 percent of them expect a response from your company within one hour.[2] Thus, to keep Twitter a viable channel for *Proprietary Audience Development*, you must first make sure that your CUSTOMERS are well-served—and that means proactively monitoring and responding to customer service issues on Twitter as you would anywhere else.

BRAND TO EMULATE: JetBlue (@JetBlue), which has the fastest Twitter response time of a brand with over 1 million FOLLOWERS (13 minutes or less).[3]

Engage FOLLOWERS

As of this writing, Twitter does not have anything comparable to Facebook's algorithm to filter the tweets FOLLOWERS see based on the degree of prior engagement with the sender's content. However, Twitter is rumored to be considering such a move. This isn't at all surprising, since just following a few hundred people can quickly turn your Twitter feed into a waterfall of information that few people have the time to fully read.

Regardless of how Twitter evolves, your objective must be to stand out from the crowd by being a brand that engages FOLLOWERS. Whether within the desktop app, mobile app, or via email, Twitter notifies users when they are mentioned by others. This not only raises your profile; it gives that individual FOLLOWER a reason to reengage with you and potentially amplify your message now and in the future.

AGNECY TO EMULATE: NASA (@NASA), which engages all manner of FOLLOWERS, PARTNERS, and AMPLIFIERS via its Twitter account—something surprising for a governmental agency.

Celebrate AMPLIFIERS

The greatest compliment you can pay anyone on Twitter is to *retweet* them. That single action transforms you from a mere FOLLOWER or SEEKER into an AMPLIFIER—while also generating Earned Media for the person you retweet. This may seem counterintuitive; after all, it is your company that is hoping to create AMPLIFIERS and gain Earned Media. However, one must never forget that Twitter is a *social medium*. As such, it rewards *human behaviors* that would similarly be rewarded offline.

Think of it this way: Are you more likely to loan money to the friend who helped you yesterday or the one who asks you for money every week? Unless you're a fiscal sadist, you reward the first friend. Similarly, AMPLIFIERS are more inclined to amplify those brands that amplify them. There's a sort of unspoken *digital prestige* in having a brand retweet you—a strange shiver of excitement that a company values something you created. So, if you want to inspire more AMPLIFIERS on Twitter, make sure your company becomes one itself.

GENTS TO EMULATE: The Men in Blazers (@MenInBlazers) radio/podcast duo, who not only bring humor to world football but also retweet FOLLOWERS in ways that bring a genuine sense of community to their Twitter stream.

It's in the Twitter Cards

One of the more interesting developments in Twitter's evolution away from its 140-character limitation is the creation of *Twitter Cards*. These hidden bits of content can be expanded with a single click and provide far more context and interaction than a tweet alone. Aside from photos and videos, marketers can embed lead capture and sales forms that streamline the tweet-to-conversion process far more easily than directing traffic to a landing page.[4]

With the pace of Twitter's evolution, no one can predict whether Twitter Cards are built to last. For now, however, they are the perfect example of Converged Media—Paid Media (an ad unit) that can drive engagement (via Owned Media) and sharing (Earned Media).

SNAPSHOT:	*TWITTER*
YEAR FOUNDED:	March 2006. The first tweet came from cofounder Jack Dorsey (@jack) and said simply "inviting coworkers."[5]
PROPRIETARY AUDIENCES:	FOLLOWERS but also SEEKERS and AMPLIFIERS. Also can be used to drive SUBSCRIBER and FAN growth.
EFFORT REQUIRED:	Low to moderate depending on content and customer service volume.
WHO OWNS THE DATA:	Users own their content, but grant Twitter an unlimited license to use it. FOLLOWERS are yours, but not directly portable to other channels.
ACTIVE USERS (WORLD):	Est. 288 million monthly active users (and over 485 million accounts worldwide as of end of 2012).[6]
TWEETS PER DAY:	Over 400 million as of March 2013.[7]
SKILLS REQUIRED:	Copywriting, common sense, and a broadcast mentality.
GATEKEEPERS:	Twitter and its users.
STRENGTHS:	Instant, worldwide distribution of content to FOLLOWERS and SEEKERS via twitter.com and searching indexed tweets.
	Low effort and zero cost required to create 140-character tweets.
	Huge channel adoption by AMPLIFIERS (particularly ADVOCATES and INFLUENCERS) in every industry.
	Twitter handle (e.g., @jkrohrs) has become a "social nametag" for everyone from television personalities to industry experts.
	New features make link, video, and audio content more robust—really expanding Twitter's capabilities well beyond 140 characters.
	New advertising options like "Twitter cards" provide brands Converged Media options by including lead generation, email capture, and other valuable elements into their tweets.
CHALLENGES:	Forum for venting about bad brand, product, or customer service experiences means that negative stories can go viral before you have an opportunity to contain them.
	Consumers increasingly using the channel as a means to ask questions, vet customer service issues, and otherwise engage companies in ways that demand responses from across the entire organization. This increases need for cross-functional team management of Twitter.
	Very public hacks and takeovers of corporate Twitter accounts illustrate need for companies to guard account access.

Chapter

Blogs: A Website by Another Name

Your audience is one single reader. I have found that sometimes it helps to pick out one person—a real person you know, or an imagined person—and write to that one.

—John Steinbeck

Blogs. Bloggy, blog, blogs. The word itself doesn't exactly inspire confidence, but it's what you get with a portmanteau derived from the term *web log*.* Perhaps the name is what kept businesses from embracing blogs earlier as a quick, low-cost means of instant Web publishing.

If you're still a bit unclear about what a blog is, here's the skinny:

- A blog is a type of website
- With an easy-to-use content management system
- That allows you to instantly publish *posts* to the Web
- And that presents them from most to least recent

---

*A portmanteau is a word formed by combining two words to form a single word that works in place of the two. By using it in this book, I receive both a triple-word score and the undying gratitude of the Portmanteau Preservation Society of America.

Blog software also enables you to create static pages for "About Us" or other important content. The way blogs structure content makes them very search-engine friendly and enables users to browse by date, category, or content tags. Most blog software also allows for the easy integration of widgets that enable social sharing, traffic analytics, and advertising.

The first professionals to jump into the blogging revolution were, not too surprisingly, writers and journalists. At first, many made fun of blogging pioneers as nothing more than "guys in pajamas who live in their parents' basement." However, a growing professional class of bloggers helped establish the channel's relevance and viability.

Andrew Sullivan (@SullyDish) is one such early adopter who built his blog, *The Daily Dish* (now just *The Dish*), into one of the most well read and respected political blogs on the Web. In reflecting on what initially excited him about blogging, Andrew recalled:

> The simple experience of being able to directly broadcast my own words to readers was an exhilarating literary liberation. Unlike the current generation of writers, who have only ever blogged, I knew firsthand what the alternative meant. I'd edited a weekly print magazine, *The New Republic*, for five years, and written countless columns and essays for a variety of traditional outlets. And in all this, I'd often chafed, as most writers do, at the endless delays, revisions, office politics, editorial fights, and last-minute cuts for space that dead-tree publishing entails. Blogging—even to an audience of a few hundred in the early days—was intoxicatingly free in comparison. Like taking a narcotic.[1]

Interestingly, most marketers could empathize with Andrew's publishing pains in the early 2000s because their creativity was often stonewalled by IT gatekeepers who guarded corporate websites like Fort Knox. This Marketing vs. IT struggle remains alive and well in some organizations; but it was particularly pronounced back then due to the lack of easy-to-use website content management systems. As a result, websites were often stale, inhuman affairs that seldom let a company's personality—and its most passionate employees—shine through.

The arrival of blogging platforms like Blogger (@Blogger) and WordPress (@WordPress) empowered those passionate, expert voices within companies to step up and publish their thoughts in ways that connected personally with consumers. One of the first companies to jump into the fray was Macromedia (later acquired by Adobe), which used its blogs to provide a forum for "community managers" to discuss new products with developers, show off new features, and answer questions. The blog's independence from Macromedia.com made it feel more independent, less corporate, and far more human.[2]

The primary audience that blogs served then and still do now are your SEEKERS—people looking for information about your company, products, and services. As anyone who has blogged will tell you, however, relying solely on direct and search engine traffic to sustain your blog is a recipe for failure, as memories of your site fade and Google ranking algorithms change.

Blogs built for the long haul drive SEEKERS to become SUBSCRIBERS via email and RSS. Instead of having to rely on SEEKERS to remember to visit your blog, you can push SUBSCRIBERS there with automated notifications of new posts. Social media channels now serve a similar purpose, turning SEEKERS into AMPLIFIERS with a click of a *like, share, comment, tweet, pin, plus,* or *stumble* button. Blogs can also build a direct audience of FANS and FOLLOWERS. In fact, as I write this, Andrew Sullivan's *The Dish* has 97,379 Twitter FOLLOWERS and 20,911 Facebook FANS—both proprietary JOINER audiences that Andrew can drive to revisit *The Dish* with a quick status update or well-timed tweet.

Tumblr: The Billion-Dollar Social Blog Mash-Up

Tumblr is a hard service to pin down. Yes, it's a cloud-based blog software provider. Yes, it's a social network in that it lets you connect and interact with fellow Tumblr users. And yes, it was acquired by Yahoo! in May 2013 for a reported $1.1 billion.

Tumblr was an attractive acquisition target in early 2013 because its users had created over 112.4 million blogs and 52 billion posts while spending over 24 billion minutes per month on the site.[3] Tumblr could be an appealing addition to your *Proprietary Audience Development* strategy if you're looking for something that offers a mash-up of the best that blogging and social media. As Tumblr itself states:

> *Tumblr lets you effortlessly share anything. Post text, photos, quotes, links, music, and videos from your browser, photo, desktop, email or wherever you happen to be.*

(continued)

(continued)

Tumblr ushered blogging into the mobile age by developing easy-to-use smartphone and tablet apps that enable blogging on the go—and by allowing fellow Tumblr users to follow each other. This, combined with the ability to both push Tumblr content to other channels (via Facebook, Twitter, and other sharing) and pull content into Tumblr from other channels (such Twitter and Instagram), frees creators to both blog and promote their blog any way they see fit.

Tumblr's major unknown is how its users will react to Yahoo!'s efforts to monetize the service. If they embrace it, Tumblr could emerge as a do-it-all environment to build SEEKERS, AMPLIFIERS, and JOINERS via both free and paid advertising. If not, it could become the next GeoCities—a $3.57 billion acquisition that Yahoo! made in 1999, only to shutter it in 2009.[4] Only time will tell.

If you, your teammates, or executives have any trepidation about "the right way to blog," rest assured that there is no single right way. Just take a quick look at these blogs and you'll see that they are as different as can be:

Consumer Goods

Fiskars Fiskateers Blog (http://www.fiskateers.com/blog/)

Tesla Blog (http://www.teslamotors.com/blog)

Financial

American Express Open Forum (www.openforum.com)

MintLife (https://www.mint.com/blog/)

Food

Butterball Blog (http://butterballblog.wordpress.com/)

McDonald's Let's Talk (http://community.aboutmcdonalds.com/)

Industrial

Caterpillar On the Level (https://caterpillar.lithium.com/caterpillar/)

GE Reports (http://www.gereports.com/)

Publishing

BBC News Editors Blog (www.bbc.co.uk/news/blogs/the_editors/)

BoingBoing (www.boingboing.net)

Real Estate

Realtor.com Blog (www.realtor.com/blogs/)

The Zillow Blog (www.zillowblog.com)

Retail

The Apron from Home Depot (http://ext.homedepot.com/
  community/blog/)

The Bass Pro Shops Blog (http://blogs.basspro.com/)

Software

Google Official Blog (http://googleblog.blogspot.com/)

The ExactTarget Blog (www.exacttarget.com/blog)

Travel

The Disney Parks Blog (http://disneyparks.disney.go.com/blog/)

Nuts About Southwest (http://www.blogsouthwest.com/)

Blogging can be a great way to build SEEKERS, AMPLIFIERS, and JOINERS via content that you create and control. But be warned: It takes commitment. It is preferable to have no blog at all than one you haven't updated in years—and that may scare off SEEKERS of current information.

SNAPSHOT:	*BLOGS*
FIRST APPEARANCE:	Justin Hall (@jah) is credited as creating the first blog (Links. net) in 1993; however, the term *web log* would not be coined until 1997 or shortened to *blog* until 1999.
PPOPRIETARY AUDIENCES:	SEEKERS as well as AMPLIFIERS and JOINERS. Very effective means to build SUBSCRIBERS, FANS, and FOLLOWERS.
EFFORT REQUIRED:	Moderate to high depending on volume of content production.
WHO OWNS THE DATA:	You own all the content you post unless your blog software terms of service state otherwise.
BLOG SERVICES:	Blogger (owned by Google), Compendium, LiveJournal, TypePad, Tumblr (owned by Yahoo!), Weebly, WordPress, and others.
USERS WORLDWIDE:	Difficult, if not impossible, to quantify number of bloggers and blog readers. Suffice it to say that blogs have the same potential reach of any website—any and all Internet users.
SKILLS REQUIRED:	Basic coding, copywriting, design, and SEO.
GATEKEEPERS:	Search engines (primarily Google)
STRENGTHS:	Blogs provide instantaneous, worldwide distribution of any content including text, images, audio, and video.
	Easy-to-use blog software makes it feasible for anyone—technical or not—to blog.
	Linear post structure (most recent to least recent with post title, tags, and links) makes content very search-engine friendly.
	Easy to integrate email and RSS opt-in forms as well as social media widgets to enable likes, tweets, and shares.
CHALLENGES:	While anyone can blog, not many do with the frequency and quality necessary to grow their SEEKER audience.
	Absent your development of blog JOINERS (particularly email and RSS SUBSCRIBERS), your blog is dependent on the whims and interests of direct, search, and social SEEKERS.

Chapter

Mobile Apps: Audiences on the Go

We are witnessing a seismic change in consumer behavior. That change is being brought about by technology and the access people have to information.[1]

—Howard Schultz

As CEO of Starbucks (@Starbucks), Howard Schultz is busy evolving his business to accommodate the seismic changes introduced by mobile Internet-powered consumers. He is not alone. Fueled by the great migration of global consumers from "dumbphones" to Internet-enabled smartphones, marketers are busy filling whiteboards with ideas for mobile apps. Perhaps they'll be inspired by . . .

- Chase Bank (@Chase), whose app lets CUSTOMERS scan and deposit checks any place, any time
- HBO GO (@HBOGO), whose app lets SUBSCRIBERS stream HBO's entire content library on their desktop and mobile devices
- Nike Fuel Band (@NikeFuel), whose app syncs with CUSTOMER Fuel Bands to track and share workout accomplishments with friends

- Starbucks (@Starbucks), whose app enables CUSTOMERS' mobile app payments that account for well over 10 percent of its U.S. transactions[2]
- *The Walking Dead* (@WalkingDead_AMC), whose Dead Yourself app lets FANS become AMPLIFIERS by creating and sharing personalized zombie photos that keep the show front of mind—even in the off-season
- Walgreens (@Walgreens), whose mobile app lets CUSTOMERS scan-to-reorder prescriptions and order Instagram photo prints
- Weber Grills (@WeberGrills), whose app builds CUSTOMER loyalty through free recipes, tutorials, and advice on selecting cuts of meat

Whatever the inspiration, the key question you must ask when developing your company's mobile app strategy is this: *Why?*

Answering the Why

You might assume that any company would answer this fundamental question before building a mobile app. Unfortunately, far too many companies build apps first, then determine the market demand later. This approach has the potential to waste precious marketing resources on an initiative that may amount to nothing more than a vanity project instead of a useful part of your *Proprietary Audience Development* efforts.

So what are some good reasons to develop a mobile app? How about:

- To engage AMPLIFIER/FANS with content that entertains and informs
- To provide on-demand viewing to CUSTOMERS far beyond what you can via traditional cable
- To provide secure and offline account access to CUSTOMERS
- To communicate with SUBSCRIBERS via push and in-app messaging
- To turn CUSTOMERS into AMPLIFIER/FANS
- To better serve existing CUSTOMERS with tools a mobile-optimized website cannot provide
- To increase CUSTOMER loyalty while also turning some SEEKERS into AMPLIFIERS and/or CUSTOMERS

The best mobile apps tend to share some common features:

1. They *provide a value or service* to consumers that a mobile website cannot serve.

2. The companies that build them *have already optimized their websites for mobile* to ensure they provide essential information and online services to SEEKERS and CUSTOMERS who do not have mobile devices.

3. The companies that build them **promote their apps via Paid, Owned, and Earned Media** to prospective SUBSCRIBERS.*

If your app does nothing more than your website, isn't optimized for mobile or can't be promoted effectively to its target audience, you may be well advised to invest your marketing dollars elsewhere. If, however, your app meets these criteria, then you need to build it for long-term success—and that means cooking in a *Proprietary Audience Development* strategy.

Build Mobile App SUBSCRIBERS

The first thing any mobile app needs is a base of SUBSCRIBERS. This requires you to "market your marketing." It is not enough to distribute your app via the various app stores. You must *promote its existence and value* to your CUSTOMERS and PROSPECTS at every turn—which you do through your Paid, Owned, and Earned Media and by leveraging your proprietary audiences like SUBSCRIBERS, FANS, and FOLLOWERS. You also do this because there's a lot of competition for attention from mobile app users. Consider:

- The average U.S. smartphone user has over 7 communications apps and 40 total apps installed.
- Those same users spend 87 minutes per weekday (Monday–Thursday) and 163 minutes each weekend day (Friday–Sunday) using apps.[3]

Vegas.com (@VegasCom) is a great example of a brand that understands their responsibility to market their mobile app. They use their Facebook

---

*Quick reminder: I refer to Mobile App users as SUBSCRIBERS because installation of the app opens up a direct, permission-based, push-button communication channel.

Timeline cover photo to promote their app to FANS—a smart tactic, considering many FANS use Facebook to share vacation ideas, experiences, and photos. See Figure 13.1.

FIGURE 13.1   Vegas.com's Facebook Timeline Image (July 2013)

Build Email and Push Reengagement Channels

Assuming you get the download, the next thing you need to do is *get permission to message SUBSCRIBERS via email and/or push messaging.* As far too many app developers continue to discover, getting the download is not enough; you also need an external means to drive SUBSCRIBER engagement with your app. That's where email and push messaging enter the picture. Both allow you to build messaging strategies that optimize both the use of your app and offline engagement with your company as needed.

Optimize Your Mobile Audience Experience

Mobile apps should not be static creatures; they must evolve with the needs of your SUBSCRIBERS. As they do, be sure to look for ways to increase your mobile app's contribution to your *Proprietary Audience Development* goals. Ask yourself:

- Are we serving CUSTOMERS as best we can?
- Are we giving SUBSCRIBERS frictionless opportunities to share content or experiences *inside the app* with audiences *outside the app*?

- Are we sufficiently cross-promoting our other proprietary audience channels to SUBSCRIBERS?
- Are we leveraging SUBSCRIBER data to fully personalize experiences inside the app and better personalize messaging outside of the app?

Just like a website, a successful mobile app demands a keen eye for optimization to ensure that you're not leaving money on the table or sending SUBSCRIBERS running for the DELETE button. Mobile app development in your company also deserves a champion who understands that your mobile audience is a company asset that's not to be squandered.

Mobile First and Responsive Design

Mobile First is a development philosophy championed by Luke Wroblewski (@LukeW)—an author, designer, entrepreneur, and former bigwig at Yahoo! and eBay. Luke believes brands should design websites and applications for mobile devices first and then adapt them to desktop PCs. In February 2012, he posted a simple infographic in support of his philosophy that compared the 317,124 live births worldwide each day to the 1.45 million mobile devices sold each day.[4] That's right—nearly five mobile devices are "born" each day for every human birth.

As that ratio has widened, Luke's work has helped spawn the *Responsive Design* movement and has inspired a host of startups that launch apps instead of websites. Instagram and Vine are prime examples, as are Everlapse (@Everlapse), a collaborative flipbook app, and Urturn (@UrturnOfficial), a social expressions platform. In these cases, the apps are the product; therefore, their modest websites serve more to initially support hiring and investment needs than CUSTOMERS.

However, for most companies, the need for a mobile-friendly website is only getting more pronounced. Mobile web browsers are installed on every smartphone and tablet—your app is not. Prioritize accordingly.

SNAPSHOT:	*MOBILE APPS*
ORIGIN:	Apple launched its mobile AppStore on July 10, 2008, ushering in the modern mobile app era with over 500 apps.[5]
PRIMARY CONTENT:	Any type of content (text, audio, video, interactive) to serve the account, communications, entertainment, financial, gaming, payment, service, shopping, social, and other needs of users.
PROPRIETARY AUDIENCES:	SUBSCRIBERS (app users). Mobile apps can also drive SEEKER, AMPLIFIER, and JOINER audience growth for other channels.
EFFORT REQUIRED:	High to create, maintain, and evolve app(s).
WHO OWNS THE DATA:	You own data generated by your proprietary mobile app, but it is shared/known by mobile OS provider (Apple, Google Android) and potentially the wireless provider (AT&T, Verizon, etc.).
POTENTIAL REACH:	As of December 2012, there were an estimated 1.5 billion smartphone users worldwide (there are 5 billion total cell phone users worldwide).[6] By September 2012, over 306 million iPads had been sold by Apple alone.[7] Factoring other manufacturers, there were likely a total of over 600 million tablets in use by end of 2012.
APPS DOWNLOADED:	Estimated that over 56 billion smartphone and 14 billion tablet apps will be downloaded in 2013.[8] In May 2013, the fifty-billionth app was purchased from Apple.[9]
SKILLS REQUIRED:	Mobile app development, programming, design, copywriting, additional skills specific to type of app developed.
GATEKEEPERS:	App store operators (Apple, Google, Microsoft, Blackberry, etc.).
STRENGTHS:	Fully controlled environment with experience optimized to increase usability of mobile environment (smartphone or tablet).
	Incredibly flexible medium that can be used to advise, entertain, inform, promote, and sell.
	Ability to provide online and offline content for use when there's no Internet connection. Can also provide location-based information and interactivity.
	Ability to communicate directly with SUBSCRIBERS in app, via push messaging and via email (both only with permission).
	Can monetize both apps and activities within apps.
CHALLENGES:	Getting and sustaining an audience. The volume of apps produced monthly can drown out new entrants.
	Cost to build, market, and maintain both the app and engaged SUBSCRIBERS across multiple mobile operating systems.
	Potentially onerous approval process to publish and update.

Chapter

14

LinkedIn: The Professional Audience

*We're focused on creating value by helping [enterprises] trans-
form the way they hire, market, and sell... [while also] enabling
companies to eliminate cold calls in favor of warm prospects.[1]*
—Jeff Weiner

LinkedIn CEO Jeff Weiner (@JeffWeiner) wants you to know a few things:

1. LinkedIn is much more than a jobs site.
2. LinkedIn is much more than a digital Rolodex.
3. LinkedIn is the world's largest professional network.

Don't feel bad if you didn't know one or two of these; after all, the
world has been a bit more fixated on social networks like Facebook and
Twitter the past few years. While LinkedIn has remained outside the glare of
the spotlight, it has grown its user base and diversified its business model to
place more emphasis on high-quality content and community development.
In so doing, the service has evolved from a place where individuals post their
online résumés to one in which individuals and companies curate their professional identities.

Content and Influence

This transformation means that LinkedIn will likely play a far more important role in your *Proprietary Audience Development* efforts than it may have just a few years ago. Indeed, if you're a B2B company, LinkedIn may emerge as one of your most important channels.

That's certainly the case for MedCity Media (@MedCityNews), a company founded in 2009 to provide events, news, and information to professionals in the growing healthcare and life sciences industries. According to CEO and cofounder Chris Seper (@ChrisSeper), LinkedIn was initially just a source for potential EMPLOYEES wanting to write for the company's primary publication, www.medcitynews.com. Today, however, LinkedIn also provides MedCity with:

- Access to healthcare INFLUENCERS
- Introductions to potential advertising and distribution PARTNERS
- Distribution of MedCity News content to SEEKERS and AMPLIFIERS
- A way to build FOLLOWERS

That last point is particularly interesting as Chris is part of an invitation-only content program called *LinkedIn Influencers*. Launched in October 2012, it gives selected industry thought leaders the ability to publish content directly to LinkedIn and build direct FOLLOWERS for that content.[2]

Titans of industry like Sir Richard Branson (@SirRichardBranson), Bill Gates (@BillGates), and Jack Welch (@Jack_Welch) all write for LinkedIn Influencers. And as of September 2013, Chris from MedCity had 20,165 FOLLOWERS via LinkedIn Influencers with his most popular post—"Why I Cheer When My Employees Leave"—amassing over 400,000 views.[3] While it may be invitation-only at present, the initiative points to LinkedIn's long-term strategy to become a hub for professional content from INFLUENCERS.

FOLLOWERS and Amplification

While LinkedIn Influencers can't message their FOLLOWERS directly at present, the site has long provided every member the ability to post content that your company's FOLLOWERS can read via their *LinkedIn Today* feed. Just like Facebook, each post lets your FOLLOWERS *like, comment*, and *share*; however, the signal-to-noise ratio is far better than on Facebook since only professionals see your posts.

HP (@HP) was one of the first to fully grasp the power of LinkedIn to its business, as it became the first company to surpass 1 million FOLLOWERS in February 2013.[4] At that time, those 1 million FOLLOWERS put HP just one degree of separation away from 43 million LinkedIn CONNECTIONS and just two degrees away from 138 million CONNECTIONS—well over half of LinkedIn's entire membership! Thus, much like Facebook and Twitter, LinkedIn is now a place where SEEKERS can become FOLLOWERS who quickly transform into AMPLIFIERS for your business.

Community

One last reason to include LinkedIn in your *Proprietary Audience Development* plans is its ability to build *LinkedIn Groups*, where like-minded professionals can discuss topics of interest. Veteran LinkedIn users may roll their eyes when they hear Groups mentioned because they are a long-time feature often dominated by more noise than signal. However, as with any community on LinkedIn, Facebook, or elsewhere, the Groups that succeed have:

- A singular focus
- Active MEMBERS
- Strong moderation from subject matter experts
- Value to offer all MEMBERS (not just promotion for the sponsor)

Any LinkedIn user—individual or company—can start a LinkedIn Group, and MEMBER updates are automated by LinkedIn via email and distribution to MEMBER feeds. Prime examples of LinkedIn Groups include the wide array of B2B software USER groups where MEMBERS share tips and tricks regarding specific providers. Then there's healthcare technology manufacturer Philips (@Philips), which maintains an "Innovations in Health" group to foster conversation around health technology issues.[5] Frankly, the opportunities with LinkedIn Groups are governed by the same principals of *Proprietary Audience Development*: your company's ability to attract, engage, and retain a vibrant audience.

LinkedIn has also recently begun building *Sponsored Communities* such as *Connect: The Professional Women's Network*.[6] With over 150,000 MEMBERS as of July 2013, the group serves as a virtual watercooler where professional women can share advice, insights, and business opportunities. Moderated by LinkedIn staff, the group affords its sponsor, Citi (@Citi), the ability to reach a highly desirable, upwardly mobile audience.

If this sounds familiar, it should. LinkedIn is building a Convergent Media machine that enables companies to buy Paid Media, leverage Owned Media, and create Earned Media in highly targeted, measurable ways.

Companies of all types would be wise to build LinkedIn FOLLOWERS so they can better:

- Capture and convert SEEKERS.
- Engage industry INFLUENCERS.
- Source and engage EMPLOYEES and PARTNERS.
- Tap EMPLOYEES and PARNTERS as AMPLIFIERS.
- Create communities of MEMBERS around relevant topics.
- Cross-promote other SUBSCRIBER, FAN, and FOLLOWER audiences.

In short, if your company's LinkedIn profile page looks a lot like it did last year, it's time to reexamine how the channel fits in your *Proprietary Audience Development* plans today.

Slideshare: Putting the Point in PowerPoint

In May 2012, LinkedIn acquired the professional content sharing platform SlideShare (@SlideShare) for $119 million.[7] A sort of "YouTube for PDFs and PowerPoints," SlideShare has emerged as *the* place to share presentations with a global audience. As of June 2013, that audience consisted of 60 million VISITORS generating over 130 million page views per month.[8]

SlideShare's primary appeal is the ability to attract SEEKERS, inspire AMPLIFIERS, and build FOLLOWERS. Much like LinkedIn itself, you can follow individual or company members, share content to any social network, and comment on presentations. Moreover, users can embed presentations on websites and blog posts just like YouTube videos—a feature that greatly expands reach through AMPLIFIERS. And while PowerPoints may not sound like the stuff that traffic is made of, the top presentations on SlideShare generate millions upon millions of views.[9]

With the recent ability to integrate lead-capture forms into presentations, SlideShare is now a channel that allows companies to convert SEEKERS into PROSPECTS seamlessly. In addition, with LinkedIn's launch of *SlideShare Content Ads*, you can now turn your presentations into ads that run within LinkedIn's pages.[10]

Who woulda thunk it? *Proprietary Audience Development* by PowerPoint. May the wonders never cease.

SNAPSHOT:	LINKEDIN
YEAR FOUNDED:	2002
PROPRIETARY AUDIENCES:	SEEKERS as well as AMPLIFIERS and FOLLOWERS.
EFFORT REQUIRED:	Low to moderate depending on investment in content creation and sharing.
WHO OWNS THE DATA:	Users own their content, but grant LinkedIn an unlimited license to use it. FOLLOWERS are yours, and LinkedIn allows you to export your Connections.[11]
USERS WORLDWIDE:	238 million as of July 2013.[12]
SKILLS REQUIRED:	Copywriting, page management.
GATEKEEPERS:	LinkedIn and its users.
STRENGTHS:	LinkedIn is the de facto global B2B social network where professionals connect directly with other professionals.
	Professional nature offers better signal-to-noise ratio than general social networks.
	Ability to build and participate in proprietary Communities and Groups that enable group sharing, conversation, and direct communication.
	Growing content creation and distribution options helping company pages on LinkedIn become Owned Media properties.
	Use of LinkedIn increasingly as a living résumé provides insights that power very precise ad targeting capabilities.
	Search capabilities allow for identification of sales targets, industry influencers, and a variety of other competitive intelligence relevant to *Proprietary Audience Development* efforts.
CHALLENGES:	Rapid feature expansion has created some user confusion.
	Recruiting and job-hunting features may suppress usage from those who see LinkedIn only in that context.
	Invite-only programs (such as *LinkedIn Influencers)* provide some users with content publication, distribution, and promotional advantages.

Chapter 15

YouTube: Internet Built the Video Star

TV means reach. YouTube means engagement.[1]

—Robert Kyncl

As the world's largest video-sharing website and the second largest search engine, one might think that YouTube (@YouTube) would have the full attention of marketers today. And certainly, from a Paid Media standpoint, you might be right. Analysts estimate that YouTube accounts for roughly 10 percent of Google's overall ad revenue—some $350 million in Q1 of 2013 alone.[2] YouTube courts advertisers annually each spring in New York City in the rite of passage known as the as the television "upfronts." Clearly, today's marketers grasp the Paid Media value of YouTube.

They also appear to grasp YouTube's Owned and Earned Media aspects as well. Longtime television advertisers like Dove (@Dove), Old Spice (@OldSpice), and Nike (@Nike) each boast well-established YouTube channels offering a mix of long-form content and television commercials. Brand channels help companies attract SEEKERS via YouTube, Google, and other search engines. They also engage AMPLIFIERS through *likes, shares, comments*, and embedding functionality that extends YouTube's reach to AMPLIFIER blogs and social media.

What a majority of marketers don't seem to grasp, however, is that YouTube also affords you the opportunity to build SUBSCRIBERS who are automatically notified by YouTube via email and in-site messaging whenever you post a new video. Consider these head-to-head competitors' stats as of September 2013:

Brand	YouTube SUBSCRIBERS
RedBull (@RedBull)	2,835,338
Monster Energy (@MonsterEnergy)	321,217
Old Spice (@OldSpice)	370,861
AXE (@AXE)	23,384
Orabrush (@Orabrush)	191,919
Oral-B (@OralB)	1,371

Measured on YouTube SUBSCRIBERS alone, there's no question of which competitor you'd rather be. Red Bull, Old Spice, and Orabrush have developed push-button, proprietary audiences for their video content. As a result, they immediately generate VIEWERS who may become AMPLIFIERS of that content every time they post a new video. Talk about audience as asset.

SUBSCRIBERS on the Tip of Their Tongue

If your leadership still needs convincing about the power of proprietary YouTube VIEWERS and SUBSCRIBERS, look no further than the story of Orabrush—the little tongue cleaner that could. The brainchild of Dr. Bob Wagstaff, the Orabrush offered consumers an innovative way to fight bad breath. His problem? After spending over $40,000 on an infomercial, Dr. Bob received only 100 orders for Orabrush.

After consulting then college student Jeffrey Harmon (@JeffreyHarmon), Dr. Bob tried something radical. He paid $500 to create a humorous video explaining how Orabrush fights bad breath and posted it to YouTube on September 10, 2009.[3] The rest, as they say, is history:

- The original "Bad Breath Test" video has generated over 18 million views to date.
- Orabrush landed shelf space in Walmart (@Walmart) as well as the major retail pharmacies.
- Orabrush has sold millions of units to customers around the world.
- Dr. Bob promoted that student, Jeffrey Harmon, to CMO of Orabrush.

Today, Orabrush has amassed over 42 million views of all its YouTube videos and has used that platform to help it launch a product line for dogs (@Orapup). Oh, and it still has more VIEWERS and SUBSCRIBERS than its next three biggest oral care competitors *combined*. Yes, YouTube should be on the tip of every marketer's tongue.

Ask for the SUBSCRIBE

There are a number of reasons for the great disparity in YouTube SUBSCRIBERS among competitive brands. First, some brands have emphasized YouTube growth over other channels like Facebook or Twitter. Second, up until recently, YouTube didn't do a great job presenting the subscription option to VIEWERS. In fact, according to Alex Carloss, YouTube's head of entertainment partnerships, SUBSCRIBERS were a big reason for the site's recent design.

When speaking to *Entertainment Weekly* (@EW) in March 2013, Alex said:

> We know that when people subscribe, they'll watch twice as much. The rearchitecture of the site has resulted in subscriptions doubling in a very short period of time.[4]

While YouTube's redesign has boosted the prominence of the subscription option, your company cannot rely on organic SUBSCRIBER acquisition only. *You must proactively ask YouTube VIEWERS to become SUBSCRIBERS* via:

- In-video CTAs
- Video "Click to Subscribe" overlays
- Inclusion of a YouTube SUBSCRIBE button on your Owned Media
- Creating and promoting a video devoted solely to promoting the benefit of subscribing to your YouTube channel (for example, search YouTube for "Red Bull Subscribers Have Wings")

As video engagement becomes increasingly mobile, YouTube's importance to marketers will only increase. Wouldn't you rather be there with a bigger on-demand, proprietary audience of VIEWERS and SUBSCRIBERS than your competition? That's what I thought.

Judson Laipply and the Evolution of Proprietary Audiences

Before the "Harlem Shake," "Gangnam Style," and "Charlie Bit My Finger," there was one video that ruled them all: "The Evolution of Dance" by Judson Laipply (@JudsonLaipply). A professional speaker and inspirational comedian, Judson had little idea that the video he uploaded to YouTube on April 6, 2006, would change his life forever.[5]

Within days, however, the video of his humorous mash-up of dance moves traveled the world around, and within eight months, it had garnered over 70 million views. Judson went from local stages to national ones like *Ellen, Oprah, The Today Show, America's Got Talent, Tosh.0,* and even the Weezer (@Weezer) video for "Pork and Beans." Today, "The Evolution of Dance" and its sequel have been viewed over 300 million times.

To say that YouTube was a blessing to Judson would be an understatement. But Judson would be the first to tell you he could have done even more with his YouTube celebrity. He could have built and engaged more SUBSCRIBERS, developed more Facebook FANS, and attracted more FOLLOWERS. Judson gives himself a pass on those efforts because he continues to have more work than he can handle. As his own boss, he can make that decision. To paraphrase Bobby Brown (@KingBobbyBrown), "It's his prerogative."

However, if you're not your own boss, there's no amount of dancing that will get you out of answering why your proprietary audiences are smaller than the competition's.

SNAPSHOT:	*YOUTUBE*
YEAR FOUNDED:	February 2005[6] (purchased by Google for $1.65 billion in October 2006).[7]
PROPRIETARY AUDIENCES:	VIEWERS as well as AMPLIFIERS, and SUBSCRIBERS. Videos themselves can drive SEEKER, AMPLIFIER, and JOINER audience growth in any number of ways.
EFFORT REQUIRED:	Moderate to high depending on volume and complexity of video production.
WHO OWNS THE DATA:	You own your video, but you grant YouTube a nonexclusive, perpetual, worldwide license to do what they want with your video. SUBSCRIBERS are yours, but not portable to other channels.
USERS WORLDWIDE:	1 billion unique users/month (as of August 2013).[8]
VIDEO VIEWS/ UPLOADS:	As of August 2013, more than 100 hours of video were uploaded to YouTube every minute, and over 6 billion hours of video were watched each month.
SKILLS REQUIRED:	Video production, content creation.
GATEKEEPERS:	YouTube/Google and users.
STRENGTHS:	Free hosting, and instant worldwide distribution of video content that's indexed as part of Google (world's most popular search engine) and YouTube (world's most popular video viewing site and second most popular search engine).
	YouTube mobilizes the video content for you so it can be viewed on most any device (laptop, smartphone, tablet, Web-enabled TV, etc.)
	A wealth of free, how-to video production and YouTube optimization content available on demand.[9]
	Ability to brand your channel and videos as well as annotate your videos with embedded links that can drive VIEWERS to subscribe, click, or comment.
	Ability to monetize video content through Google advertising.
	Free, easy-to-use video analytics tell you how many viewers and SUBSCRIBERS you have as well as the average viewing time of your video content.
CHALLENGES:	All built on YouTube/Google's land—except for the largest video producers, everyone has very little negotiating power.
	Ad revenue splits weighted heavily in favor of YouTube/ Google. No direct relationships with advertisers.[10]
	Comments section can become a virtual Wild West of profane, sexist, and racist statements if not moderated.[11]

Chapter

Google+: The Great Unknown

*What's he building in there? What's he building in there? We
have a right to know . . .*[1]
—Tom Waits

On his 1999 album *Mule Variations*, musical raconteur Tom Waits performs
a haunting spoken-word piece titled "What's He Building?" As metal clanks
in the background, Waits assumes the persona of a paranoid homeowner
contemplating his mysterious neighbor's dead lawn, frequent deliveries, and
late-night activities in the basement. The nervous observations build to a cli-
max in which Waits asks the penultimate question—"What's he building
in there?"—before ending the song with a dose of righteous indignation by
stating, "We have a right to know!"

For the past few years, marketers peering over Google's fence have been
wondering the exact same thing about *Google+*, the search giant's high-profile
entry into the social networking space. What is it? What are they doing? *What
are they building in there?*

The confusion stems from the fact that several years into its existence,
Google+ has yet to establish a clear identity—a killer value proposition—
that a majority of marketers (or users for that matter) can understand. Yes, it
has a nice design. Yes, it is exceedingly cool that you can host no-cost video
chats with multiple people thanks to its *Google Hangouts* feature. But seeing

as Facebook has exponentially more users and engagement, we can legitimately ask:

Why do we need another social network in our lives?

Google's SVP of Engineering, Vic Gundotra (@VicGundotra), answers this question by stating simply:

"Google+ is Google."[2]

Vic's point is that Google+ is not a standalone social network, but rather the next stage in Google's evolution as a whole—Google 2.0, if you will. Viewed in this fashion, Google+ is important to marketers in a number of ways that are significantly different than Facebook:

1. ***Search influence.*** As search industry veteran Danny Sullivan (@DannySullivan) states, "Being on Google+ means you'll rank better on Google."[3] Google+ avatars appear next to search results from authors with linked Google+ accounts. This makes such listings more prominent and boosts CTR. Also, when you are logged into a Google product, your Google+ connections influence the order of the results displayed.

2. ***Google+ Sign-In.*** Facebook pioneered social sign-in as a convenience for consumers sick of remembering different passwords. Google+ takes things further, rewarding sites that offer its social sign-in option with greater search visibility.[4]

3. ***Content Recommendations.*** Google uses +1s and shares to determine content recommendations for users across multiple devices and platforms (Google, Google+, YouTube, etc.).[5]

4. ***Community Building.*** With its strong adoption among developers, Google+ is a valuable source of interaction within tech communities. In fact, open source technology provider Red Hat (@RedHatNews), counts Google+ as its most important social network.[6]

5. ***Google+ Hangouts.*** This free, multi-user video chat feature was made famous by its commercial featuring The Muppets (@MuppetsStudio), but marketers are using it as a way to create video interviews, online coaching, launch presentations, and more.[7]

If you're sensing a trend here, you're not alone. Google is using is market power in search (Google), video (YouTube), and mobile (Android) to increase Google+ adoption. This is why your company may not be able to ignore Google+, even though it adds "one more thing" to your list of responsibilities. While the proprietary FOLLOWERS you can build with Google+ right now may be of limited value, their value as AMPLIFIERS who help you capture more SEEKERS is undeniable.

If for nothing else than the potential growth in SEEKERS, Google+ is a *Proprietary Audience Development* channel worth evaluating for your company. It may not sound fair to players like Facebook that built their user base without benefit of the world's biggest search engine, video streaming site, webmail client, and mobile operating system—but all's fair in love and marketing.

A Search Insider's Take on Google+

Rand Fishkin (@randfish) knows a thing or two about Google. As CEO and founder of Moz (@Moz), he has been analyzing the search giant for years in order to provide advice to marketers on how to improve content, links, and overall SEO.

When it comes to Google+, he's active—but in a manner more akin to LinkedIn than Facebook. Because Google+ draws a tech-savvy audience, Rand finds it a great place to find AMPLIFIERS for Moz content as well as direct access to INFLUENCERS. Moreover, because of the high signal-to-noise ratio, he sees a CTR on Google+ around two times that of his Twitter FOLLOWERS.[8]

At present, Rand's top five marketing tactics for Moz are: website, blog, email, Twitter, and Google+ (with Facebook narrowly missing the cut). As for whether Google+ will move up in importance in the coming years, Rand just smiles. He knows better than to bet against Google.

SNAPSHOT:	GOOGLE+
LAUNCHED:	June 28, 2011
PROPRIETARY AUDIENCES:	FOLLOWERS as well as SEEKERS and AMPLIFIERS.
EFFORT REQUIRED:	Moderate to high depending on volume of content production.
WHO OWNS THE DATA:	Users own their content, but grant Google an unlimited license to use it. FOLLOWERS are yours, but not directly portable to other channels.
USERS WORLDWIDE:	Est. 343 million active users as of December 2012.[9] However, other stats suggest only 135 million active users out of 500 million accounts.[10]
SKILLS REQUIRED:	Copywriting, authenticity, responsiveness, modest coding/design.
GATEKEEPERS:	Google and users.
STRENGTHS:	Free to create company page, post updates, build audiences, and interact with consumers. Near frictionless sharing through ubiquity of "+1s," *Comment* and *share* features both within Google properties and via social widgets installed on websites across the Web.
	Google+ popularity (+1s) beginning to influence Google search rankings and display.[11] Authors can associate their profiles with their content so that their Google+ avatars appear next to content, which boosts click-through rates (CTRs).
	Many of the same amplification benefits as Facebook, just with a smaller audience.
	Great for tech and other brands targeting male audiences due to gender disparity (users are 70 percent men, 30 percent women as of June 2013).[12]
CHALLENGES:	Questions about usefulness and true user adoption rate. Lingering question as to whether users have truly joined or just been forced to due to Google's use of market power in other channels.
	No truly new features or "killer app" save for Google Hangouts. Consumers therefore continue to question why they should use it.
	Much lower engagement among women (antithesis of Pinterest).
	On average, far less engagement (*+1s, comments*, and *shares*) per post than on Facebook.
	Site rapidly evolving to capture market share which could cut both for and against marketers.

Chapter

Pinterest: A Collection of Beautiful Followers

The whole reason Pinterest exists is to help people discover the things that they love and then go take action on them.[1]
—Ben Silbermann

If ever there was a social media site that came out of marketing left field, it was Pinterest (@Pinterest). Founded by former Google employee Ben Silbermann (@Ben), the site is unique among its peers because its user base is over 70 percent female.[2] Indeed, if you ask most male marketers where they first heard of Pinterest, it was probably from a very wise woman in their life.*

Pinterest's feminine magnetism owes a lot to its mission: to help users curate beautiful collections of people, places, or things that inspire them. For artists, architects, crafters, and designers, the site is a godsend that enables the virtual aggregation, organization, and sharing of images. The act of "pinning" is akin to sticking an image on a corkboard—only this corkboard is digital, searchable, and available to anyone via the Pinterest website

---

*A loving hat tip to mine, @CraftTestDummy.

and mobile app. Within Pinterest, companies can create their own pin boards and:

- *Pin* images (and add descriptions) that attract SEEKERS.
- Inspire AMPLIFIERS to *repin* images to their own pinboards (akin to the *share* button on Facebook) as well as *like* and *comment* on pins.
- Attract FOLLOWERS who receive updates when you *pin* something new.

Since images are at the heart of Pinterest, it's a great channel to promote anything with a high degree of visual appeal, including:

- Automobiles
- Fashion
- Food
- Home Decor
- Travel

Retailers have quickly become some of the fastest Pinterest adopters as the "Pin It" button is easy to add to product pages, thereby allowing AMPLIFIERS to share objects of desire with their own FOLLOWERS. Because of this rapid adoption, Pinterest has surpassed Twitter as a referral source for many retailers.[3] Some companies are even converting Pinterest-sourced SEEKERS at higher rates and purchase amounts than SEEKERS from Facebook.[4]

However, Pinterest is just like any other social channel: The number of FOLLOWERS you have doesn't matter much if they don't engage with your content. You want FOLLOWERS who become AMPLIFIERS by *commenting, liking,* and *repining.* For instance, L.L. Bean (@LLBean) is one of the top brands on Pinterest with millions of FOLLOWERS. But a recent study found that they have one-seventeenth the number of brand mentions on Pinterest as Anthropologie (@Anthropologie) which has about one-seventeenth the FOLLOWERS as L.L. Bean.[5] Having a ton of Pinterest FOLLOWERS without any resulting amplification is like pinning a tree falling in the forest (nobody hears it).

Speaking of pinning trees, don't go thinking that Pinterest is only for big brands. One of the most followed Pinterest users is Nick McCullough (@NickGardenGuy on Pinterest and @McGardens on Twitter) (Figure 17.1).

Nick is the founder of a small, award-winning landscape design company in Columbus, Ohio (www.mccland.com). And as of this writing, he has nearly 3.7 million Pinterest FOLLOWERS. That's more than 99.9 percent of all companies on Pinterest.

FIGURE 17.1 Pinterest Profile Where Nick Curates Images to Inspire His Landscape Design Efforts

So what's Nick's secret? Well, first of all, he married well.* Second, he was an early Pinterest adopter—something that's hard to repeat. Third— and this is the part you *can* repeat—Nick sticks to pinning the things that inspire him: beautiful plants, landscaping, and outdoor amenities of every type. Instead of pinning a mix of things from across his various interests, he kept his pin board focused on plants, products, and people that inspire his landscape designs. This singular focus is what attracted his FOLLOWERS and keeps them engaging with Nick.

What Nick did not do was roll over at the first sign of Pinterest success. He's been approached numerous times by brands looking to pay him to pin things, promote contests, or otherwise water down the focus of his pin

---

*Nick's married to my cousin, Allison. Another sign of Nick's good taste.

boards, but he's always turned them away. As a result, as his audience has grown, so have his Pinterest-fueled business opportunities, including:

- Out-of-state jobs
- Overseas partners looking for distribution
- The opportunity to develop a product line of his own
- The opportunity to write a book of his own

Much like YouTube did for Orabrush, Pinterest is presenting opportunities to Nick that he never would have had otherwise. The key has been to be true to himself, valuable to his FOLLOWERS, and never too promotional. It's a lesson that many marketers could stand to learn about social media of every stripe. It's not about what you need; it's about what your FANS and FOLLOWERS want. And sometimes, they just want pretty pictures of beautiful things.

Pinterest for B2B?

Pinterest can even help B2B companies—you just may have to be more creative to find the value. Our content marketing team at ExactTarget (@ExactTarget) discovered that Pinterest is a great location to post images of the emails that we find innovative or interesting. The brainchild of Chad White (@ChadSWhite), Dawn DeVirgilio (@DawnDeVirgilio), Kristina Huffman (@krudz), and our entire design team (@ETDesign), *The Email Swipe File*, is a Pinterest board that captures email design ideas you can "swipe." In short order, the board has become a resource to our clients, consultants, and salespeople alike as the look for ideas to inspire better email marketing performance.

Don't have those kinds of visuals in your business? Then what about pinning images of people using your products? Or pictures of your EMPLOYEES? Pinterest won't punish you for trying new ideas; so if you have the bandwidth, stick a pin in it.

SNAPSHOT:	PINTEREST
FOUNDED:	2009 (First "pin," January 2010).[6]
PROPRIETARY AUDIENCES:	FOLLOWERS as well as SEEKERS and AMPLIFIERS.
EFFORT REQUIRED:	Low to moderate depending on effort for asset creation.
WHO OWNS THE DATA:	Intellectual property belongs to copyright holders, but you grant Pinterest a nonexclusive, royalty-free license relative to content you create or pin. Your FOLLOWERS are yours, but not portable to other channels.
USERS WORLDWIDE:	70 million (as of July 2013).[7]
SKILLS TO LEVERAGE:	Coding (to embed "Pin It" button), creative, copywriting, and visual mindset to make "pinable" content attractive and inspire action.
GATEKEEPERS:	Pinterest and its community of users.
STRENGTHS:	Visual medium that appeals to aspirational desires and aesthetic personality of users.
	Ability to control visual and explanatory content.
	One of only social channels where women outnumber men 2 to 1.[8]
	Has quickly evolved into one of the top referral sites for brands—particularly those with goods to sell.
	Content-specific pin formats (product, recipe, and movie) allow for the inclusion of more specific information, which increases potential for user interaction (if not also purchase).
	High degree of usefulness as consumer *wish list* tool; and, as a result, very appealing to retailers and those selling tangible goods.
CHALLENGES:	Young channel; will be in state of continuous evolution as it looks to grow, better serve users, and monetize its traffic to satisfy investors.
	While it is growing quickly, and is a top referrer for many consumer product brands, its overall adoption is a fraction of that of Facebook, Twitter, and other, more mature social media channels.
	User growth may lead to the need for comment moderation.
	Lower appeal to less creative or visual consumers.

Chapter 18

SMS: Cutting through the Clutter

[SMS] is really the most cost-effective way to reach consumers. It is low cost, easy to execute and it reaches a wide variety of people.[1]
—Ever Santana

Ever Santana is a bit different than most of the other folks I've quoted thus far. He didn't start a social media company, sell a million records, or play any of the leads in *Mad Men*. Instead, Ever is the President and Founder of Heritage Restaurant Group, an IHOP (@IHOP) franchise owner in the New York City area. In this role, he discovered something far too many marketers forget.

SMS works.

In the case of Ever's IHOP, a direct mail piece instructed recipients to text in *IHOPFREE* to receive a coupon for a free short stack of pancakes. In the first month of the program, participants redeemed over 105 coupons—far more than any other marketing promotion. The program also allowed the franchisee to build a proprietary SMS SUBSCRIBER database that enabled future SMS communications with less than 10 percent attrition.[2]

The key to the SMS channel is its ubiquity. While over 50 percent of U.S. cell phone owners have smartphones, nearly 100 percent of those same owners have cell phones capable of sending and receiving text messages. The increase in all-you-can-text plans have made consumers far more willing to engage with brands via SMS than they were just a few short years ago.

At the same time, the cost and effort to create SMS programs have dropped sharply. Campaigns that once took days or weeks to set up (thanks to the labyrinth of mobile carriers) now takes mere minutes to create due to send-side innovations. As a result, SMS is no longer only a channel for brands with deep pockets; it's one that any company, regardless of size, can consider for its marketing mix. You may want to consider SMS if you:

- Want a way to build mobile SUBSCRIBERS
- Who may or may not have smartphones
- And who may not have Internet access

I know it's hard for some to believe, but yes, there are still places without Wi-Fi. And those are locations where SMS becomes a creative option to:

- Alert event ATTENDEES of agenda changes and weather conditions.
- Connect with trade show ATTENDEES.
- Convert BROWSERS, SHOPPERS, and VISITORS with cell phones into SMS SUBSCRIBERS and/or EMAIL SUBSCRIBERS via SMS opt-in.*
- Engage with FANS/ATTENDEES via SMS on arena/stadium screens.
- Inform DONORS and VOLUNTEERS of community needs.
- Inform STUDENTS and PARENTS of cancellations and emergencies.
- Provide in-game updates to FANS.

SMS also does very well when used in combination with other media like:

- Direct mail (Paid Media)
- Facebook pages (Owned Media)
- In-store signage (Owned Media)
- OOH advertising (Paid Media like billboards and placards)
- Television commercials (Paid Media)

---

*Mobile email opt-in via SMS is where a consumer texts their email address to a designated number. The integrated SMS/email provider then adds the email SUBSCRIBER while automatically texting and emailing back the opt-in confirmation.

Examples of such combinations include:

- Men's Warehouse (@MensWarehouse) putting SMS calls to action on changing room signage to encourage SHOPPERS to save $5 off their purchase by texting in and becoming an SMS SUBSCRIBER
- Pei Wei Asian Diners (@PeiWei) using in-store signage and social media promotion to get VISITORS and FANS to text-in to become email SUBSCRIBERS and receive a buy-one, get-one meal offer[3]
- Redbox (@Redbox) promoting SMS opt-in on its physical kiosks as well as all of their digital channels to gain SMS SUBSCRIBERS who can be reached on the go[4]
- The Wounded Warrior Project (@WWPInc) asking TV viewers to donate $10 during their Super Bowl XLVII commercial by texting into their short code

SMS works because nearly every consumer uses or has access to the channel and 98 percent of messages received are viewed by recipients—something email, Facebook, Twitter, and any other channel can't say.[5] The difference, of course, is that consumers are more guarded about the brands they'll invite into SMS communications, and mobile carriers are notoriously punitive in dealing with any brand that sends unwanted messages to consumers. Accordingly, if you do want to integrate SMS into your *Proprietary Audience Development* efforts, be sure to work with a reputable partner and never, ever send unsolicited SMS messages to consumers. That's the surest way to turn the SMS channel from an asset into a liability.

You Down with OTT?

As if marketers didn't have enough acronyms to contend with, a new one has emerged with significant implications for the SMS channel. OTT stands for "Over the Top," and refers to any service that bypasses mobile carrier networks (ATT, Sprint, Verizon, etc.) in favor of powering peer-to-peer interactions via an Internet connection. A prime example of an OTT service is Skype (@Skype). Instead of paying your mobile carrier to make a phone call, you can make a free video call via the Skype mobile app.

Today's fastest growing OTT services, however, revolve around text and multimedia messaging services. Snapchat (@Snapchat), WhatsApp (@WhatsApp), and other OTT apps enable free, peer-to-peer messaging (save for their Internet subscription charges). As a result, OTT messaging services now carry more messaging volume than the mobile carriers SMS infrastructure.[6]

In light of this messaging shift, marketers who rely heavily on SMS would be wise to familiarize themselves with OTT apps to see how brand-to-consumer messaging evolves in the coming years.

SNAPSHOT:	*SMS*
FIRST TEXT MESSAGE:	The first text message was sent December 3, 1992 from a PC to a mobile device over Vodaphone UK's network. It said "Merry Christmas."[7]
PROPRIETARY AUDIENCES:	SUBSCRIBERS. Can also be used to gain email SUBSCRIBERS through text opt-in.
EFFORT REQUIRED:	Low.
WHO OWNS THE DATA:	Mobile carriers own all data. You own the SUBSCRIBER database.
USERS/MESSAGES (WORLD):	Est. 3.5 billion users (2012) sending 19.5 billion messages every day (over 7 trillion messages per year).[8]
SKILLS REQUIRED:	Copywriting, message setup, and execution.
GATEKEEPERS:	Mobile carriers, SMS messaging providers.
STRENGTHS:	Near universal availability of SMS on all cell phones worldwide.
	Low relative cost due to simplicity of messaging requirements (text and link only, no design).
	High open rates (95 percent or greater) due to nature of the channel (immediate, uncluttered, alerts upon message receipt, etc.).
	Easy to set up via SMS providers as well as test messages and offers. Also easy to schedule messaging for future delivery.
	Links can be used to drive SEEKERS to Owned Media.
	Email address capture can be used to gain permission-based email SUBSCRIBERS.
	Geofencing allows you to send location-triggered messaging to SUBSCRIBERS whose mobile device enters a predetermined area.
CHALLENGES:	Consumers more cautious about connecting with companies via SMS (vs. email, Facebook, Twitter, etc.).
	SMS spam complaints handled at mobile-carrier level, with onerous penalties for failure to get explicit permission to send or honor requests to stop messaging.
	SMS inbox is text only for marketers—no design elements to differentiate messaging. Must make sure to identify your brand as the sender or risk inadvertent spam complaints.

Chapter 19

Instagram: Moving Pictures

*We are forever on a quest to take a moment and record it for-
ever in time. Instagram is a tool to remember. Our mission is to
capture and share the world's moments.*[1]
—Kevin Systrom

Once a "neat, little photo app with some cool image filters," Instagram
(@Instagram) has grown into something far, far greater. CEO Kevin Systrom
(@Kevin) now reports to Mark Zuckerberg as part of Facebook's growing
social and mobile media empire. And as of June 2013, Instagram doesn't
just take pictures; it lets users create 15-second videos—9 seconds more than
videos on Twitter's Vine app (@VineApp).

Yes—in Facebook and Twitter's battle for photo and video supremacy,
mere seconds matter. But whether those seconds matter to consumers will be
determined as Instagram and Vine battle it out for king of the mobile-image
app hill. As of this writing, Instagram still reigns supreme, having built the
mobile world's most utilized app for image creation and social sharing—and
the one that more brands use today.

To assess whether this channel has something to offer your company,
you must first download and use the Instagram mobile app. As one of *mobile
first's* pioneers, Instagram is built around the mobile app experience rather
than its website. If you've never used Instagram, think of it as Twitter for

images. You can post your own images and follow other people so their images appear in your image feed. Within Instagram, you can also:

- Take a photo/video and apply artistic filters to it.
- Tag people in your photo/video.
- Geotag your photo/video.
- Add a description.
- Add a hashtag.
- *Share* your image/video with your Instagram and other FOLLOWERS.
- *Share* your image/video with your Facebook FANS.
- Search and browse other people's photos/videos.
- *Like, comment,* or *share* other people's images and videos.

All these capabilities allow Instagram to feed your *Proprietary Audience Development* efforts by delivering:

- SEEKERS who search and browse photos/videos
- AMPLIFIERS who *like, comment,* and *share* photos both inside and outside Instagram (thanks to one-click sharing to Facebook, Flickr, Foursquare, Twitter, and Tumblr)
- FOLLOWERS who receive updates of your images in their feeds

The hands-down dominant brand on Instagram as of this writing is Nike. While its FOLLOWER count (1.7 million) is third behind Victoria's Secret (@VictoriasSecret) and National Geographic (@NatGeo), it has nearly double the mentions (#Nike) over 30 days (13.3 million) of any other brand.[2] The keys to Nike's success include:

- *Access.* Nike uses Instagram to provide FOLLOWERS with a behind-the-scenes glimpse of international sporting events.
- *Brand.* Nike benefits from the habit of AMPLIFIERS to tag their pictures and videos with brand hashtags (like #Nike) to increase their visibility in Instagram search. The same thing happens on Vine videos.
- *Celebrities.* Nike regularly posts photos and videos of its celebrity endorsers to Instagram, and includes celebrity Twitter handles in the captions. This creates Earned Media opportunities as CELEBRITIES and AMPFLIERS share those photos with their FANS and FOLLOWERS.
- *Diversity.* Nike uses Instagram to represent the diversity of products, sports, and CUSTOMERS.

- *Inspiration*. Nike's photos often seek to inspire FOLLOWERS to #justdoit, #makeithappen, or one of their other famous slogans.
- *Language*. As an international brand, Nike tailors its captions to the language of the most relevant segment of their FOLLOWERS.
- *Products*. Nike teases new products, giving FOLLOWERS a first look and AMPLIFIERS an opportunity to be the source of fresh Nike news.

You may not be Nike, but ask yourself if your company has:

- Behind-the-scenes images it can share
- A clearly articulated brand that can be distilled to a hashtag
- Celebrity (national or local) relationships it can leverage
- Inspirational elements to your brand, culture, or EMPLOYEES
- Products that lends themselves to interesting photos
- Passionate CUSTOMERS who share photos with your products or logo

If so, you have a reason to be on Instagram. And if you're facing some skepticism internally, share how these vastly different brands are using the channel to build FOLLOWERS and create visual content for AMPLIFIERS.

- *Oreo* (@Oreo): One of the kings of social media surprised everyone with an ad during Super Bowl XLVII that ended with a CTA to follow Oreo on Instagram. Their FOLLOWERS shot from around 2,000 to over 80,000, and have become key AMPLIFIERS of Oreo's humorous visuals, new recipes (www.snackworks.com), and contests.
- *Maersk* (@MaerskLine on Instagram, @Maersk on Twitter): The worldwide energy-shipping giant may seem like the last company you'd find on Instagram, but they use the channel to connect FOLLOWERS with the scope of what they do and the value of people who do it.[3]
- *TacoBell* (@TacoBell) supported its Doritos Locos Taco launch with a "snap and win" contest for Instagram FOLLOWERS. Interestingly, it was CUSTOMERS posting Instagram photos on their own that spawned the contest and Instagram-inspired TV commercial.[4]
- *TaylorMade Golf* (@TaylorMadeGolf): The club maker gives FOLLOWERS a truly behind-the-scenes look at tournaments around the world, which generates Earned Media on the backs of AMPLIFIERS.

In short, if your brand is highly visual or the nature of your business causes your CUSTOMERS to take a lot of photos, then you should be looking to attract Instagram SEEKERS, AMPLIFIERS, and FOLLOWERS. They're an army of photojournalists (and now, videographers), capable of telling your story from an exponentially greater number of angles than your own internal marketing team ever could.

The Vine That Instagram (and Facebook) Hope to Cut Down

With the move beyond pictures into 15-second video clips, Instagram fired a clear shot over the bow of Twitter's Vine app. If you're not familiar with Vine, don't feel bad—it's not that old. The original, short-form video app launched on January 24, 2013, and led many to question how a six-second video (the time limitation on Vine) could be of any value.[5]

Just weeks after launch, however, Vine found its niche as creators took the six-second limitation as a challenge rather than a limitation. Instant distribution to Twitter allowed AMPLIFIERS to share *vines* (what the videos are called) far beyond the walls of the app itself.

One of the early adopters, comedian Will Sasso (@WillSasso), took to Vine like no other. He's built a Vine audience of over 1 million FOLLOWERS on the back of hilarious impersonations of Hulk Hogan, Arnold Schwarzenegger, and Al Pacino—as well as an ongoing battle with lemons (watch his Vines and you'll see). But his major contribution to the Vine was to demonstrate that funny, episodic content is a great way to grow your FOLLOWERS. Brands like Lowe's (@Lowes) have similarly shown that stop-motion animation, behind-the-scenes footage, and how-to videos can also make Vine extremely useful not only to FOLLOWERS but also proprietary audiences of every type.

Vine has an audience. Instagram has an audience. Instead of looking for one to beat the other, perhaps we're looking at the mobile app version of *Coke versus Pepsi* where there's no winner, just a matter of personal preference.

SNAPSHOT:	*INSTAGRAM*
LAUNCHED:	October 6, 2010 as an iPhone app (purchased in April 2012 by Facebook for a purported $1 billion in cash and stock).[6]
PROPRIETARY AUDIENCES:	FOLLOWERS as well as SEEKERS and AMPLIFIERS.
EFFORT REQUIRED:	Low to moderate depending on composition of photos shared.
WHO OWNS THE DATA:	Intellectual property belongs to copyright holders, but you grant Instagram (Facebook) a nonexclusive, royalty-free license relative to content you create. Your FOLLOWERS are yours, but not portable to other channels.
TOTAL USERS/ UPLOADS:	As of July 2013, 130 million Monthly Active Users (MAUs) worldwide and 45 million photo uploads per day that generate 1 billion *likes* daily and 1,000 comments per second.[7]
SKILLS REQUIRED:	Ability to take a photo and add a caption. Social engagement management.
GATEKEEPERS:	Instagram (Facebook) and users.
STRENGTHS:	Easy-to-use native mobile photo and creation with easy-to-use photo filters, seamless social sharing features, and the ability to embed content in websites.
	Largest photo/video app user base among peer set.
	Ownership, support, and integration with Facebook, the world's largest social network.
	Support for hashtags and "@" names (just like Twitter handles)
CHALLENGES:	Requires a photographer's or videographer's mindset to generate maximum engagement and value.
	May have limited value to companies that aren't visual in nature.

Chapter

20

Podcasts: Listen Carefully

A few years ago I was planning on killing myself in my garage, and now I'm doing the best thing I've ever done in my life in that same garage. It's a podcast. You know what a podcast is?[1]

—Marc Maron

As a former radio D.J. (shout-out to the dearly departed @WOXY), I've always had a soft spot in my heart for podcasts. Birthed by the forces of audio digitization (MP3s), RSS distribution, and Apple's launch of the iPod, podcasting democratized audio content like never before. Instead of needing to get a job at a radio station to reach the masses, you could literally record a show in your garage and distribute it for free to millions of LISTENERS on iTunes.

Of course, the issue is the same you face with any proprietary audience: It takes time to build podcast LISTENERS and SUBSCRIBERS. If you don't invest time (and sometimes money) in the effort, you've created a podcast that nobody hears—and that's of zero value to your company.

Some may think of the podcast a quaint, obsolete relic of Web 1.0, but the channel has undergone quite a renaissance of late as illustrated by the success of comedian-turned-podcaster Marc Maron (@MarcMaron). A veteran of the stand-up comedy scene, Marc was between gigs when he launched his *WTF* podcast (@WTFpod) out of his garage in September 2009. He didn't have a plan, just a desire to do something.[2]

Over 400 episodes later, that "something" turned into Marc's career-defining moment. At a time when others were rushing to social media, Marc picked the medium—podcasting—where his humor, interview skills, and Rolodex of famous friends could shine. As his loyal audience grew, so too did his professional opportunities, culminating in the debut of *Maron*, his TV show on IFC (@IFC) and publication of his autobiography, *Attempting Normal*, in the spring of 2013.

What fascinates me about Marc's success is that he's spent his entire professional career in pursuit of audiences in comedy clubs, at festivals, and on radio and TV. But none of those audiences were his—not until he started building podcast LISTENERS and SUBSCRIBERS. Like all stand-up comedians, Marc was and truly is an entrepreneur; and now, thanks to the Internet, he's building proprietary audiences that don't disappear when he steps offstage.

So, yes—podcasting is still a very viable channel through which you can develop proprietary audiences. Whether it is right for you depends on:

- Your ability to produce high-quality, valuable audio content
- That you publish on a consistent schedule
- That serves the needs of a LISTENERS
- Who have the time and desire to download and listen

These requirements are a bit more demanding than many of the other channels we've discussed. That's because podcasts aren't created with the push of a button. They take time, talent, and marketing savvy to produce and distribute. However, they can help you:

- Educate PROSPECTS and CUSTOMERS with on-demand content
- Mobilize in-the-field training for EMPLOYEES
- Leverage industry INFLUENCERS through interviews
- Push your company's thought leadership out to SEEKERS

Podcasting has particular appeal in B2B industries because of its mobile, on-demand nature. I've seen this firsthand thanks to my co-hosting duties on the *Social Pros Podcast* with Jay Baer (@JayBaer).[3] Jay started the weekly podcast in 2012 as a way to provide *real insights from real social media professionals*. And he discovered was that if you're going to podcast, you should:

- Seek multiple distribution channels to LISTENERS and SUBSCRIBERS, as iTunes does not have a monopoly on the podcast market.

- Increase the long-tail reach of your podcasts with SEEKERS by transcribing each podcast and turning it into a blog post.
- Use interviews to build relationships with INFLUENCERS as they amplify your podcast's value to their proprietary audiences (Earned Media).
- Promote your podcasts to all of your proprietary audiences.
- Ask your podcast participants to do the same (e.g. become AMPLIFIERS).

So, whether you have a "golden voice" or a "face for radio," podcasting might be worth a look. Just be sure you have a target audience with time on the one hand (drivers, travelers, or any folks who have to sit around and wait) and a mobile listening device (iPod, smartphone, etc.) in the other.

All Podcasts Considered

According to the Pew Research Center, about 46 percent of the U.S. adult population knows what a podcast is, and 18 percent listen to news podcasts at least *sometimes*.[4] In December 2012, there were 91,700 podcasts—some 31 percent more than at the end of 2009.[5] So basically, podcasting awareness is flat, listenership is sub-20 percent, and more podcasts are being produced every day.

Sounds like a tough channel, right? Well it is, but it still may be a great one for your company. Just look at what National Public Radio (@NPR) is doing. Through promotion and the continued production of quality content, NPR grew its total monthly podcast downloads in 2012 to 29.3 million—up from 28 million per month in 2012 and 23.3 million in 2010.

Yes, NPR is a radio network, but the growth of its LISTENERS points to the fact that podcasting audiences are still out there if you produce and promote valuable content. The question you must answer is whether your company has the time, talent, and discipline to create a podcast people will want and consume.

SNAPSHOT:	PODCASTS
FIRST APPEARANCE:	2003 saw the first feed-based syndication of MP3 files, but the term *podcasting* was not coined until 2004.[6]
PROPRIETARY AUDIENCES:	LISTENERS and SUBSCRIBERS. Podcasts themselves can drive SEEKER, AMPLIFIER, and JOINER audience growth in any number of ways.
EFFORT REQUIRED:	Moderate to high depending on volume of content production.
WHO OWNS THE DATA:	Listener information and listening data are owned by the podcast delivery services (e.g., iTunes). Podcast creators may have varying levels of access to that information depending on the provider; however, embedding a podcast player does allow you to track listening activity via your analytics provider.
USERS WORLDWIDE:	Difficult, if not impossible, to quantify number of podcasters and listeners worldwide. Suffice it to say that podcasts have the same potential reach of any website—any and all Internet users.
SKILLS REQUIRED:	On-air talent, content production, audio recording, audio editing, skill to upload or coding to post online.
GATEKEEPERS:	None for podcasts hosted on blogs or websites. If syndicated, distribution networks serve as gatekeepers (e.g., Apple iTunes or Stitcher.com)
STRENGTHS:	Instant, worldwide distribution of audio content.
	Serialized audio content allows you to connect with LISTENERS in a more personal, human fashion that print content alone.
	Can be downloaded and then consumed offline by the LISTENER.
	Accessible to SEEKER audiences via dedicated search engines like Google as well as distribution networks like iTunes.
	Provides a more intimate connection with the content producer than the written word.
CHALLENGES:	Takes a greater commitment to listen to audio content than to read the same content.
	As with blogs, the best podcasts require a commitment to produce content on a regular basis. Those without such focus will suffer both in terms of SUBSCRIBER growth and search visibility.

Other Audience Channels: More? You Want More?!?

Believe it or not, I have only scratched the surface of all the channels where your company can build and engage proprietary audiences today. As the Internet matures globally, an increasing number of language- or region-specific channels may factor into your *Proprietary Audience Development* efforts if you hope to communicate with local consumers.

The good news is that *The Audience Imperative* is a global mandate built upon the universal nature of SEEKERS, AMPLIFIERS, and JOINERS. The names of the channels and players may differ from country to country, but the principles and goals remain the same: *Seek to build bigger, more engaged, and more valuable proprietary audiences than your competition.*

With that, here are some very quick snapshots of 20 proprietary audience channels you may not have ever considered.

1. **Baidu.** Baidu.com is China's top search engine with around 70 percent of the market. Other major Chinese search players include Soso.com, Sogou.com, Qihoo.com, and Google China.[1] All are places to capture SEEKERS and drive them to your website through organic and paid means. Many also have social features that may entice AMPLIFIERS.

2. **Bebo.** Bebo.com is a social network that AOL acquired in 2008 for $850 million, only to sell it back to its founders for $1 million in 2013.[2] The site combines email inbox and social

network functionality, so it can be a place to engage SEEKERS, AMPLIFIERS, and JOINERS. However, its small size and uncertain future makes predicting its usefulness difficult.

3. **Bing**. Bing.com is the Microsoft-owned search engine that holds second place in the U.S. market. Its strong integration with Microsoft products makes it an important place to source SEARCHERS outside of Google.

4. **Foursquare**. Foursquare is the leading location-based mobile app in the United States with an estimated 33 million users worldwide.[3] Users *check in* to locations; leave comments, tips, and reviews; and see friends who are nearby. The service has begun testing different paid advertising models and has long offered the ability for stores to offer check-in discounts. Foursquare is therefore a good place to convert SEEKERS to immediate CUSTOMERS.

5. **Kakao Talk** (South Korea), **Line** (Japan), **WeChat** (China), **WhatsApp** (United States). These four OTT messaging apps enable peer-to-peer chatting—and in some cases, video calls—without cellular fees. As of July 2013, Kakao Talk had over 100 million registered users, Line had over 150 million, WeChat had over 300 million, and WhatsApp had over 250 million. As such, each is a way to potentially build SUBSCRIBERS. With their plans to develop more social experiences, each also may become a place to build FANS and FOLLOWERS as well.[4]

6. **Medium**. Medium.com (@Medium) is a publishing platform launched by Blogger and Twitter co-founder Ev Williams (@ev). Touted as the next evolution of blogging, it is effectively a new collaborative publishing platform with the potential to attract SEEKERS to your writing.[5]

7. **Myspace**. Myspace.com (@Myspace) relaunched in 2013 thanks to an investment from Justin Timberlake. The completely rebuilt site now focuses on connecting people with the musicians and other creative people they love.[6] As such, it is a place to attract SEEKERS and FANS for those in a creative industry. How and whether it will expand remains to be seen.

8. **Path**. Path (@Path) is a private OTT messaging and photo sharing service for mobile devices. The service had over 10 million users in April 2013, and its unique selling point is that users can maintain no more than 150 friend connections. So, Path is really more for consumers to foster relationships; however, it is a place where companies may find AMPLIFIERS.[7]

9. **Print Magazines.** With the rise of Content Marketing, brand magazines are experiencing a resurgence. Red Bull has its *Red Bulletin* (www.RedBulletin.com), Ford has its *MyFord Magazine* (www.MyFordMag.com), and consumer review website Angie's List (@AngiesList) publishes a monthly magazine for members with helpful household tips, advice, and coupons. Each demonstrates that print can be a great way to cut through the clutter and build more tactile relationships with print SUBSCRIBERS and CUSTOMERS.

10. **Proprietary Communities.** Lady Gaga made headlines in 2012 when she parlayed her celebrity into a proprietary community of her own: www.LittleMonsters.com. Powered by Backplane (@backplane), the site offers FANS an even more intimate and direct way to connect with the singer than Facebook—and lets Lady Gaga monetize her FAN relationships more directly.

    Starbucks took a different route with its proprietary community, *My Starbucks Idea*. Launched on the Force.com platform (@ForceDotCom), the site allows FANS and CUSTOMERS of Starbucks to contribute product, experience, and involvement ideas for the brand. It is a prime example of how the passion of FANS can be harnessed to benefit everyone.

11. **Qzone.** Qzone (qzone.qq.com) is a social networking service launched in China in 2005. At the end of 2012, the service had approximately 603 million MAU (Monthly Active Users), and it benefits from being a part of parent company Tencent's suite of Internet services.[8] In light of its size, it is a place to engage SEEKERS, AMPLIFIERS, and JOINERS of all types.

12. **Reddit.** Reddit is the self-proclaimed "front page of the Internet," a place where users post stories and vote them up to greater visibility or down to obscurity. According to the Pew Research Center, about 6 percent of U.S. Internet users use the service—but those 6 percent help Reddit drive stories to far greater visibility across the entire Web.[9] As such, Reddit is a place to capture SEEKERS and inspire AMPLIFIERS. But beware: The amplification is not always positive in nature.

13. **Renren.** Renren (renren.com) is "the Facebook of China." Accordingly, it is a place to attract SEEKERS, inspire AMPLIFIERS, and build FANS. As of May 2013, it had approximately 200 million users.[10]

14. **Sina Weibo**. Sina Weibo is a Chinese hybrid of Facebook and Twitter. As of early 2013, it is the fifth most popular social network

worldwide with over 503 million users.[11] Due to its hybrid nature, it is a place to engage SEEKERS, AMPLIFIERS, and JOINERS of all types.

15. **Spotify, Turntable.fm, and Last.fm.** Spotify (@Spotify), Turntable.fm (@turntablefm), and Last.fm (@lastfm) are all streaming music services that allow you to reach LISTENERS and, in some cases, build SUBSCRIBERS for the music you curate. Some offer advertising opportunities, and they can also be used in interesting ways to express the style of brands willing to curate their own channels.

16. **StumbleUpon.** StumbleUpon (@StumbleUpon) is a content discovery service that introduces SEEKERS to images, videos, and other material that may be of interest based on their profile or just random luck. The site allows users to like or dislike content as well as comment and share. As such, it can be a place to attract SEEKERS and AMPLIFIERS.

17. **VKontakte** (RUSSIA). VKontakte.ru is Russia's leading social network with approximately 47 million daily users as of May 2013. It is largely a Facebook clone, so it creates opportunities to engage SEEKERS, build FANS, and inspire AMPLIFIERS.[12]

18. **Vimeo.** Vimeo (@Vimeo) is a video-sharing website akin to YouTube, except with more professional content and less advertising. As of May 2013, about 70 million unique people visited the site each month.[13] It is a potentially useful channel for brands looking for broader distribution of video content to SEEKERS, AMPLIFIERS, and SUBSCRIBERS.

19. **Vine.** Vine is Twitter's six-second video creation and sharing app. Launched in January 2013, the service surpassed Instagram as the most shared visual app on Twitter in June 2013 . . . only to be overtaken by Instagram again when that service added 15-second video creation capabilities.[14] Vine lets you build SUBSCRIBERS and AMPLIFIERS as well as capture SEEKERS who see your videos anywhere they are shared or embedded. As with Instagram, Vine is a great way to provide behind-the-scenes or other unique, short-form content to your proprietary audiences.

20. **Yelp.** Yelp (@Yelp) is the de facto top site for consumer reviews and recommendations of restaurants, stores, nightlife, and entertainment. It attracts SEEKERS looking for things to do; however, your only way to attract them is by providing great products and services that prompt CUSTOMERS to review your offerings on

Yelp's website or mobile app. Thus, if you're confident in your products and services, you should encourage CUSTOMERS to use Yelp. But beware: Negative reviews are a fact of life on Yelp and are not edited or moderated except in extreme circumstances.

For even more proprietary audience channels that may be useful to your company, visit www.AudiencePro.com. For now, however, it's time that we turn our attention to getting your proprietary audience house in order.

Part

The Audience Roadmap

You now know *The Audience Imperative* by heart, as well as the channels you can use to build and engage proprietary audiences. Accordingly, it's time to develop your own *Proprietary Audience Development Strategy*. To do so, how-ever, will take effort, dedication, and teamwork amongst colleagues who may have few organizational incentives to work together save for one:

Proprietary Audience Development is now a core marketing responsibility.

So roll up those sleeves and dig in; the path to more personal, cost-effective marketing and measurable competitive advantage lies straight ahead.

Chapter

Map & Align: Strategy and Team

To map out a course of action and follow it to an end requires courage.

—Ralph Waldo Emerson

As we discussed in Part I, *Proprietary Audience Development* requires a long-term commitment from your company. Here are the four steps you need to take to get off on the right foot:

1. Assemble a team.
2. Map your current landscape.
3. Set your goals.
4. Articulate your strategy.

The time it takes to complete each step will largely depend on the complexity of your organization. But once you're done, you'll emerge with the ability to make much smarter choices about where to invest business resources in order to deliver the greatest bottom-line results.

1. Assemble a Team

You're ready to embrace *The Audience Imperative* and put it to work for your company. But you can't go it alone. You're going to need some allies, encouragement, and support to truly move your company from haphazard development of proprietary audiences to a detailed *Proprietary Audience Development* strategy that fully embraces our *Hybrid Marketing Era*. You need a *Proprietary Audience Development Team* (PAD Team)—a cross-functional group of people who understand that audiences are corporate assets your entire company must build, nurture, and value.

In a perfect world, you'd find these folks by seeing who has a copy of *AUDIENCE* on their desks (an author *can* dream). The more likely scenario, however, is that you'll need to win the support of those who already touch proprietary audiences within your company. These are people with responsibilities like:

- Advertising
- Content Marketing
- CRM
- Digital Marketing
- Direct Marketing
- Email Marketing
- Events
- Mobile Marketing
- Partner Marketing
- Social Media
- Website Development

The great thing about colleagues from each of these disciplines is that they should already have a keen sense of the value of an audience—albeit within the channels they currently serve. Your challenge is to open their eyes to the value of all of your company's proprietary audiences. I recommend selecting only four or five other people for your PAD Team to keep your efforts both manageable and focused. As a first order of business, introduce your team members to *The Audience Imperative* by sharing this book with them or visiting www.AudiencePro.com.

A Team of Many from One

If you are a one-person or small marketing team, you may wonder how you can possibly hope to build a PAD Team to assist your efforts. The answer lies in:

- ***Tapping an existing agency partner***. Agencies and creative partners know your business and bring a wealth of different perspectives to the table. Challenge them to think beyond a short-term, campaign mindset.

- *Networking in your industry.* Your PAD Team doesn't have to reside within your company's four walls. Noncompetitive industry peers can be of great help to one another and serve as a great sounding board for new ideas to grow your proprietary audiences.

- *Networking in your community.* Local marketing organizations are chock full of people just as overwhelmed about where to begin with *Proprietary Audience Development* as you. Seek them out at local AMA (@AMA_Marketing), BMA (@BMANational), DMA (@DMA_USA), Social Media Club (@socialmediaclub), and other professional events. Building a local, noncompetitive, mutually beneficial PAD Team may not only yield ideas, but also meaningful professional relationships.

While it may take a bit more initiative and creativity for smaller companies to assemble a PAD Team, the long-term benefits are well worth the effort.

Audience Exercise #7: Get Out of the Office

To build a sense of camaraderie and shared purpose within your PAD Team, get everyone out of the office and into an environment where real consumers interact—a mall, a restaurant, or even a ball game.

Encourage the team to engage with the environment through their mobile devices. Ask them to document any proprietary audiences or attempts at *Proprietary Audience Development* that they see. Finally, wrap up the trip with lunch or dinner to share observations and ideas that would help build your proprietary audiences. Sharing, after all, isn't just for AMPLIFIERS.

You've probably noticed I'm not suggesting the creation of a team that lives on an org chart in your company—at least not initially. Instead, the best PAD Team will be a loose affiliation of individuals who may report to different leaders within your organization. Their passion to collaborate is driven by their passion to achieve not only the company's goals but also their individual goals—many of which are tied to the performance of proprietary audiences. Thus, if the PAD Team succeeds, they succeed.

Take a Page from Traditional Publishers and Broadcasters

Whether your company is big or small, your PAD Team will likely begin as an informal, collaborative unit. I believe we'll see more formal roles, responsibilities, and titles emerge as marketers begin to embrace the value of *Proprietary Audience Development* —not unlike what happened with Content Marketing. Both Content Marketing and *Proprietary Audience Development* are modeled after the two sides of the traditional publishing/broadcasting business—editorial and circulation. Just as Content Marketing emulates the editorial side with writers, illustrators, researchers, talent, and videographers, so too will *Proprietary Audience Development* emulate the circulation side with future job titles incorporating concepts like:

- Audience Acquisition
- Audience Development
- Audience Management

Your informal PAD Team will not have anyone with any of these titles initially. Over time, however, companies will have to create roles with similar responsibilities in order to create accountability for all PAD efforts.

If you aspire to be a long-term PAD Team member in your company, you would be wise to learn as much as you can from the people who hold circulation and audience development roles in traditional publishing and broadcasting companies. Those folks have been through the Internet's wringer—and have emerged leaner, meaner, and more appreciative of the temporal nature of audiences. Their experiences can help your team better understand that:

- ***Building an audience is hard***. We heard it from Bruce in Chapter 1—but if you really want to feel what this means, talk to your local newspaper's circulation manager. They'll regale you with tales of how brand loyalty, consumer habits, and new technologies will erode proprietary audiences if you don't pay attention to their changing needs.

- ***Audience building takes coordination***. There's a reason radio stations don't play Adele's "Someone Like You" straight into Slayer's "Raining Blood"—those songs appeal to two very different audiences. Audience professionals know this and help develop audiences appropriate for different types of content.

- *Competition is everywhere.* TV shows are incorporating more hashtags, promos, and information on screen than ever because they don't want to lose your attention. Once the social center of the home, the television is now just another device competing for time and eyeballs. As a result, "build it and they will come" is not a Content Marketing strategy; it's a recipe for disaster—a very lonely, unwatched disaster.

- *Measurement matters.* It took years, but mass media finally got the ratings bureaus—the Alliance for Audited Media (print), Arbitron (radio), and Nielsen (television)—to account for online readers, streaming listeners, and on-demand viewers in their ratings.[1] If you can't communicate how you have performed, you're dead in the water.

The only real question is how fully you embrace the opportunity this presents. You need a PAD Team not only to navigate the challenges that all media face today, but also to cure the ailments inflicted on your company by a generation of siloed audience management efforts within Marketing. Ailments like:

1. *Inflammed Data.* Symptoms: Hoarding data in siloed repositories such that consumers in one channel are treated differently (and probably worse) than those in channels where that data is used to personalize messaging.

2. *Rash of Selfishness.* Symptoms: Seeking to boost the performance of channels you manage without any regard for their impact on the rest of marketing's objectives.

3. *Cross-Channel Blindness.* Symptoms: Failing to use cross-channel promotions to build bigger, better audiences, and engagement.

4. *Device Paralysis.* Symptoms: Failing to take mobility into consideration and treating consumers like stationary desktop users instead of the on-the-go, smartphone addicts they are.

5. *Irritable Revenue Syndrome.* Symptoms: Boosting short-term results only to drive proprietary audiences—and LCV—down over the long term.

Thanks to the Internet, every company today is a media company.

With your PAD Team assembled, you can cure what ails you. But you may have to get over your own allergic reaction to a certain word: *audit*.

Red Bull Media House: Building Extreme Proprietary Audiences

If you want to see how Content Marketing and *Proprietary Audience Development* can work together to transform brands into media companies, look no further than Red Bull Media House (@RedBull). Launched in 2007, the content arm of the Red Bull beverage company began producing sports events, documentaries, and even a magazine (*The Red Bulletin*) as a way to increase brand awareness.

Today, however, the unit does that and far, far more. Once a cost center, RBMH now turns a profit all its own thanks to documentary sales on iTunes, licensing deals with NBC, and advertising sales within *The Red Bulletin*. Red Bull hasn't just built a media juggernaut; it's built a kingdom of proprietary SEEKERS, AMPLIFIERS, and JOINERS who are all thirsty for the next great bit of content—as well as the beverage that "gives you wings."

---

2. Audit Your Existing Efforts

It is said that those who don't know their history are doomed to repeat it. You can avoid this fate by rallying your PAD Team to document how your company is building, engaging, and managing proprietary audiences today. No one can map those things for you—not even Google. Instead, your PAD Team will need to venture into the heart of your organization to conduct a PAD Audit.

I know the word *audit* strikes terror in the hearts of many. However, you can't hope to optimize your future PAD efforts unless you know where they stand right now. A PAD Audit requires you to document your existing:

- Paid Media
- Owned Media
- Proprietary Audiences
- Employee- and Partner-Owned Media and Proprietary Audiences

Over the next few pages, we'll explore each of these items; and if you visit www.AudiencePro.com, you'll find a variety of free resources to assist with your PAD Audit. One word of caution as you proceed: Don't let PAD Team members audit the channels that they currently manage. Fresh eyes yield far better observations than those who have a vested interest in the status quo.

Paid Media Discovery

The first step in your PAD Audit is to get your arms around all of your company's Paid Media. This requires that you interview colleagues and analyze your advertising creative and placements to document:

- Channels and ad units used (e.g., print, radio, TV, OOH, online, etc.)
- CTAs, both primary and secondary
- Owned Media used to support your CTAs
- Proprietary audience engagement (e.g., social icons, hashtags, etc.)

So, for instance, if you're in the insurance industry, you might document one of your website banner ads as follows:

- **Channel and ad unit:** Banner ad
- **CTA:** "Get a Free Quote" (no secondary CTA)
- **Owned Media used:** Landing page
- **Proprietary audience engagement:** None until after the click; then, a landing page with email SUBSCRIBER opt-in

As your spreadsheet comes together, you'll quickly see opportunities to hybridize your paid media CTAs to both sell and help build or engage your proprietary audiences. Begin collecting these ideas on a separate spreadsheet while they're fresh in your mind—but don't take action on them yet. We have a lot more auditing to do first.

Owned Media Discovery

Your Owned Media resources provide the foundation for the vast majority of your PAD efforts. To optimize your audience-building potential, therefore, you need to document:

- Each Owned Media asset
- What team/individual(s) in your organization manage each asset (capture names and titles for later relationship-building efforts)
- Current PAD efforts within each asset
- How often each Owned Media asset is updated

Your findings might appear as follows:

ASSET	MANAGED BY	CURRENT PAD EFFORTS	UPDATES
Website	Digital Team (Daniel, Joshua, Lindsay, and Brent)	SEO of website (SEEKERS) Email Opt-In on home page and check-out (SUBSCRIBERS) Social media icons on pages (AMPLIFIERS, FANS, FOLLOWERS)	As needed, priority order determined by Sr. Dir. Website Development
Facebook Page	Social Media Manager (Dawn)	Page attracts SEEKERS and AMPLIFIERS Email tab (SUBSCRIBERS) Occasional CTAs to subscribe/follow (SUBSCRIBERS, FOLLOWERS)	As needed, determined by Social Media Manager
In-Store Signage	Brand Manager, In-Store Experience (Katie M.)	None	Updated monthly

In addition to documenting the Owned Media assets you already have, be sure to also capture what's missing. Your PAD Audit is as much about what you are doing today as it is what you should be doing in the future.

Proprietary Audience Discovery

Once you have documented your Owned Media assets, you're ready to analyze your existing proprietary audience assets—the SEEKERS, AMPLIFIERS, and JOINERS currently at your disposal. To aid in your analysis, let's revisit our list of proprietary audiences:

SEEKERS	AMPLIFIERS	JOINERS
BROWSERS	ADVOCATES	CUSTOMERS
LISTENERS	ANALYSTS	DINERS
PROSPECTS	COMMENTERS	DONORS
READERS	CREATORS	EMPLOYEES
SEARCHERS	INFLUENCERS	FANS
SHOPPERS	REPORTERS	FOLLOWERS
VIEWERS	REVIEWERS	PARTNERS
VISITORS	SHARERS	SUBSCRIBERS

With this list close by, my recommendation is to:

1. Determine which proprietary audiences your company currently attracts, develops and/or engages.

2. Document the following for each of your proprietary audiences:

    a. The channels in which they exist

    b. Who manages acquisition efforts (include names/titles)

    c. Who manages messaging (include names/titles)

    d. Who manages engagement (include names/titles)

    e. Types of current acquisition and engagement efforts

    f. Types of messaging (informational, promotional, etc.)

    g. Types of audience segmentation and personalization used

    h. Frequency of messages

    i. Owned Media leveraged

    j. Technology used to message (name of ESP, social network)

    k. Cross-channel PAD efforts (e.g., promotion of email to FANS)

    l. Consumer data generated (e.g., email, address, purchases, etc.)

    m. Value of proprietary audience (as defined by managing team)

For example, a retailer's audit of a few SEEKER audiences might look like this:

AUDIENCE:	LISTENERS	SEARCHERS	SHOPPERS
Channels:	Radio (paid ads)	Search Engines (Google, Bing) 3rd party mobile apps (Around Me, Google Maps, Yelp)	Physical and online stores.
Management of acquisition, messaging, and engagement:	Brand Ad Team	Digital Marketing Team w/agency assistance	Customer Experience and Stores Teams (Amanda and Scott) CRM Team (Chip).
Types of Acquisition and Engagement:	N/A	SEO (Google focus). PPC (Paid search ads on Google AdWords). Curation of mobile profiles on apps mentioned above	All marketing efforts.

(continued)

(continued)

AUDIENCE:	LISTENERS	SEARCHERS	SHOPPERS
Types of messaging:	30 second spots (promotional)	SEO = Page titles/ snippets PPC = Titles/copy (no Ad Extensions being used)	In-store circulars and signage. Online banners and guided shopping.
Messaging segmentation or targeting:	Yes, by station and daypart (targeting men 18–34)	SEO by keyword. PPC by keyword, audience, device, interest, location (see AdWords options). Foursquare by store location	In-store by product section. Online by product section and personalized product recommendations.
Frequency of messaging:	3 spots per weekday	As searched by SEARCHER.	Messaging only appears to SEARCHER during store visits.
Owned Media leveraged:	Website mentioned	Website/Blog for SEO. Landing Pages for PPC. Profile Pages for Google Maps, Foursquare).	Stores and website.
Technology used to deliver messaging:	Stations handle.	Search engines and individual map, review, and social networks.	Print, no digital in-store signage. Online personalization engine.
Cross-channel PAD efforts:	None	Only on website and PPC landing pages.	No in-store PAD. Online email and social CTAs.
Consumer data generated:	None	None unless conversion on website or landing page.	Upon purchase, full profile and history.
Value of audience:	No ROI tracking currently in place	Varies, but SEO at 200% ROI. PPC at 150% ROI. Mobile not tracked.	In-store LCV = $500/ yr Online LCV = $700/ yr Multichannel LCV = $1000/year

As you can see, your proprietary audience audit can get pretty detailed, even for SEARCHER audiences. Let's take a look now at three AMPLIFIERS audiences for our fictitious retailer:

AUDIENCE:	ANALYSTS	INFLUENCERS	SHARERS
Channels:	Website, Blog, other Owned Media	Websites, Blogs, Email, Facebook, Twitter, Pinterest, and Yelp.	Website, Blog, Email, Facebook, Twitter, Pinterest, Yelp.
Management of acquisition, messaging, and engagement:	Corporate Communications (Mitch)	Proactive, none. Reactive by Social Team (Dawn) and Corp Comm (Mitch)	Website = Digital Team (Daniel). Social Team (Dawn).
Types of acquisition and engagement:	None.	None. All organic engagement initiated by INFLUENCERS.	Website/Blog: social icons on pages and products. Overt efforts to encourage sharing across all social channels.
Types of messaging:	Press releases, analyst briefings	None specific— only receive if also SEEKER or JOINER.	None specific to SHARERS. They share whatever they decide as SEEKERS or JOINERS.
Messaging segmentation or targeting:	Yes, via email and personal outreach.	None.	None at present.
Frequency of messaging:	Quarterly analyst briefings. PR a few times monthly.	None specific to them.	None specific to them.
Owned Media leveraged:	Website, Email	Website, Blogs, Facebook, Twitter, and Pinterest.	Website, Blog, Email, Facebook, Twitter, Pinterest.
Technology used to deliver messaging:	Website, PR Newswire, and scheduled calls	Varies based on point of interaction.	Varies based on point of interaction.

(continued)

(continued)

AUDIENCE:	ANALYSTS	INFLUENCERS	SHARERS
Cross-channel PAD efforts:	None.	None.	Website social sharing. All social channels used to encourage product sharing.
Consumer data generated:	None.	None.	Share counts on social media.
Value of audience:	Not quantified.	Not quantified.	Not quantified.

Finally, let's take a look at how some JOINERS might look to our retailer:

AUDIENCE:	SUBSCRIBERS	FANS	FOLLOWERS
Channels:	Email YouTube	Facebook	Twitter Pinterest
Management of acquisition, messaging, and engagement:	Email Team (Allison) Video Team (Tom)	Social Team (Dawn)	Social Team (Dawn)
Types of acquisition and engagement:	Online opt-in forms; YouTube overlays	Online icons, sharing, and "Like" buttons at website and product level.	Online icons, "Tweet," and "Pin It" buttons at website and product level.
Types of messaging:	YouTube is mainly promotional. Email is information, promotional, triggered, and transactional.	70/30 split promotional to FAN engagement. Photos or video in 50% of posts.	Both Twitter and Pinterest appear to be 80% promotional. Remainder is a mix of engagement and customer service.
Messaging segmentation or targeting:	None for YouTube. Segmentation of email varies greatly by message.	Not in organic posts.	Not in organic tweets or pins.
Messaging frequency:	YouTube monthly. Email varies greatly.	2 posts per day. Avg. of 6 FAN interactions.	On Twitter, 6 tweets per day.

(continued)

(continued)

AUDIENCE:	SUBSCRIBERS	FANS	FOLLOWERS
Current management of messaging and engagement?	Same plus Brand Marketing (Amanda)	Same plus Brand Marketing (Amanda) and Corp Comm (Mitch) assistance	Same plus Brand Marketing (Amanda) and Corp Comm (Mitch) assistance
Owned Media leveraged:	Email, Website, Landing Pages, Social, YouTube channel	Facebook, Website, Blog, YouTube.	Twitter, Pinterest, Website, Blog, YouTube.
Technology used to deliver messaging:	ESP for email. YouTube for video.	Facebook plus third-party page management system.	On Twitter, third-party engagement system. Just using Pinterest for Pinterest.
Cross-channel PAD efforts:	Email promotes social channels.	Tabs to website, email. Occasional posts promoting Pinterest.	Occasional tweets promoting Pinterest, Blog.
Consumer data generated:	Significant via email. Some on YouTube, accessed via advertising.	Tons that can be leveraged through advertising with Facebook.	Some that can be leveraged through advertising relationships with Twitter and Pinterest.
Value of audience:	Email SUBSCRIBER LCV = $1,300. Unknown for YT.	Not currently calculated down to FAN level.	Not currently calculated down to FOLLOWER level.

While you might be tempted to cut corners with your proprietary audience discovery efforts, don't. The more detail you can provide, the better you will be able to identify and prioritize new PAD efforts and phase out the ones costing you time and money.

EMPLOYEE and PARTNER Discovery

The next step in your proprietary audience discovery process is to assess the proprietary audiences your EMPLOYEES and PARTNERS have at their disposal. Many companies overlook these two JOINER audiences—which is a shame since they contain many of your best AMPLIFIERS, FANS, and FOLLOWERS. Assessing PARTNERS is pretty easy. You simply ask them to identify the proprietary audiences to whom they promote partner content, which may include:

- Website
- Blog
- Email
- Podcasts
- Social Media (Facebook, Google+, Instagram, LinkedIn, Twitter, etc.)
- Webinars

You don't need the same level of details as with your own proprietary audiences—just enough to understand:

- Who in their organization manages each channel
- Whether they promote PARTNER content through each channel
- What content they prefer to promote
- Their publishing schedule and rules (if any)
- Whether there is a cost or quid pro quo required to promote content

Your tack needs to be very different with EMPLOYEES. First off, you probably don't have the time to talk to all of your EMPLOYEES to discover who blogs and who's on what social network. Second, any discovery of that nature could come off as creepy and counter to the brand and culture you're seeking to foster.

Accordingly, I recommend a far more laissez-faire approach to your discovery of EMPLOYEE proprietary audiences. Begin by documenting:

- Which company Facebook pages, Twitter handles, and other official social media accounts you currently promote to EMPLOYEES and how
- What forms current EMPLOYEE communications take (channels, messaging, and frequency)
- What monitoring tools like Google Alerts and Radian6 (@MarketingCloud) you currently use to identify and track EMPLOYEE/AMPLIFIERS across blogs, websites, and social media
- Whether your organization asks new hires to provide Twitter and other social media handles as part of their onboarding process

With this PARTNER and EMPLOYEE information in hand, your PAD Team should have a treasure trove of information regarding your company's current PAD efforts across all of your Paid, Owned, and Earned Media. It's therefore time to take your team out for a well-earned adult beverage of their choosing. Just make sure everyone's back in the morning bright and early; you're going to have some very important goals to set.

The Employee Connundrum: Audience Asset or Liability?

While your PAD Audit should assess the viability of leveraging your EMPLOYEES as AMPLIFIERS, you should not feel obligated to do so. Many businesses have very legitimate reasons for restricting the use of social media by EMPLOYEES. Case in point: restaurants.

Restaurants exist to serve CUSTOMERS with their full attention; consequently, many have policies restricting EMPLOYEE use of cell phones during work. I spoke with one restaurateur recently who also bans EMPLOYEES from discussing the restaurant on social media. While this may sound dictatorial, his reason is simple: He wants to make sure the restaurant is presented online in a manner consistent with his vision. It may be funny when an employee tweets out, "Five tables open—come get fat and spend money"; but it doesn't project the image he wants for his restaurant.

So when assessing whether to leverage EMPLOYEES or any proprietary audience for that matter, don't be afraid to go against the grain if it serves your brand without negatively impacting sales.

Document the Holes

With your PAD Audit findings hot off the presses, be sure to document the holes in your existing efforts. What channels are missing, underdeveloped, or understaffed? Where is your Paid Media not working hard enough? Where is there confusion or conflict as to channel ownership or control?

This list of holes in your current *Proprietary Audience Development* efforts will be an indispensable asset as you look to articulate your goals, map your strategy, and prioritize future tactics.

3. Set Your PAD Goals

For your PAD Team to evolve from an off-the-org chart collaborative into the cross-functional, asset-building juggernaut we know it can be, you're going to need to set some goals. Your number one goal, of course, is contained in the PAD acronym itself—*Proprietary Audience Development*. You and your team are seeking to develop proprietary audiences in assets for your company.

But why exactly is that again?

It may seem like a silly question to ask at this point, but it's the question your company's leaders will ask when you inform them of your PAD Team efforts. Why exactly are you investing your time in *Proprietary Audience Development*? Why should your team? And why should your company? Answer these questions in a fashion that satisfies your CEO, CMO, and CFO, and you have found your PAD Goals.

So without further ado, here are some PAD Goals worth consideration as well as some inspiration from brands working toward each:

1. ***Increase marketing-generated sales.*** For many executives, this is the only marketing question of any kind that matters—did your PAD efforts generate sales? If you want to prove that your proprietary audiences are assets to the company, then this should be goal number one of your PAD efforts.

   Inspiration: Restaurant.com (@Restaurant_com) realizes 900 percent more revenue per email thanks to automated messages to SUBSCRIBERS.[2]

2. ***Increase paid media ROI.*** This goal requires collaboration with your Paid Media brethren to add *Proprietary Audience Development* CTAs to their campaigns. Instead of just measuring sales lift, they can also generate value via the SUBSCRIBERS, FANS, and FOLLOWERS driven into your permission marketing loop.

   Inspiration: Papa John's (@PapaJohns) Super Bowl coin toss campaign, which sold pizzas and built SUBSCRIBERS, FANS, and FOLLOWERS.

3. ***Decrease dependency on paid media.*** This may rankle your paid advertising friends, but it's a worthy goal. Larger, more responsive proprietary audiences should give you both the will and the way to phase out your least productive paid media placements.

   Inspiration: Procter & Gamble (@ProcterGamble) shifting paid media budget to more efficient digital media.[3]

4. *Increase marketing efficiency.* With this goal, you seek to realize increases in marketing performance while decreasing the amount and time you spend on marketing. I realize this may scare marketers who are consistently asked "to do more with less." However, it is far better to control the terms of your efficiency through *Proprietary Audience Development* than to have them foisted upon you in an unrealistic time frame.

   Inspiration: Nike (@Nike), which scaled back its advertising costs by 40 percent while increasing investments in Owned Media.[4]

5. *Increase Owned Media ROI.* Proprietary audiences and content are opposite sides of the same coin. Accordingly, if your organization is keen on seeing its Owned Media (content) pay rich dividends, it may be wise to align your PAD Goals with those of the Owned Media/Content Marketing team. This partnership should prove mutually beneficial.

   Inspiration: PetFlow (@PetFlow) generating over $10 million of its $30 million in 2012 revenues from social media.[5]

6. *Increased Earned Media.* PR professionals have long understood that media mentions provide measurable value to companies. If your company isn't dominating the blog, press, and social headlines in your industry, it may be time to focus on developing AMPLFIERS capable of producing more Earned Media mentions for you.

   Inspiration: The Oreo (@Oreo) Super Bowl XLVII blackout tweet that garnered more Earned Media buzz than Oreo's paid advertisement.[6]

7. *Increase CUSTOMER satisfaction.* According to J.D. Power (@JDPower), 87 percent of highly satisfied consumers believe that social media interaction with brands "positively impacted" their likelihood to purchase. If your customer satisfaction scores are suffering, it may be worthwhile to set your sites on *Proprietary Audience Development* as a means to get them moving in the right direction.

   Inspiration: United (@United) investing more in social media to improve customer communications and service.[7]

8. *Decrease CUSTOMER service costs.* As discussed in Chapters 3 and 4, FANS are sometimes your first line of customer service—rushing in on Facebook and other social channels to answer CUSTOMER questions and address complaints before you can get to them. If social media is proving to be a costly channel for your company to manage directly, *Proprietary Audience Development* may be able

to assist by delivering larger, more engaged AMPLIFIERS, FANS, and FOLLOWERS to cap or even reduce those costs.

Inspiration: Dreamfields Pasta (@HealthyPasta) has built a base of loyal Facebook FANS who answer questions regarding product availability, pricing, and use quickly and at no additional cost to the company.

9. *Increase EMPLOYEE satisfaction.* This may seem like an odd goal, but communication lies at the heart of *Proprietary Audience Development.* Therefore, if you're experiencing a drop in EMPLOYEE satisfaction, it may be worth examining how focusing more intently on their needs could positively impact morale. Sometimes, it's as simple as implementing a daily communication to EMPLOYEES or sending automated birthday, anniversary, and special occasion wishes.

   Inspiration: Bonobos (@Bonobos) trains EMPLOYEES outside of customer service to manage social media inquiries. It speeds response times and boosts EMPLOYEE job satisfaction.[8]

10. *Increase PARTNER satisfaction.* As with EMPLOYEES, much of your PARTNERS' satisfaction boils down to communication. Accordingly, helping to improve communications with and promotion of PARTNERS could be a goal that yields not only greater satisfaction but also greater PARTNER sales opportunities.

   Inspiration: Cisco (@Cisco) pushing channel partners to become more active on social media to their mutual benefit.[9]

Whatever PAD Goals you choose, be sure to think like your boss. Results are what matter most in the boardroom; hence, you want to have a *SMART strategy* to support your goals.

4. Articulate Your PAD Strategy

A SMART strategy is:

   Specific—Measurable—Achievable—Relevant—Timely

This classic planning acronym is most often associated with goal setting, but I prefer it to shape strategies, because they require more specific "above the shoulders" thinking than goals. Here's a handy way of thinking about how your PAD Goals, Strategy, and Tactics fit together:

   PAD Goals = Key objectives (your destination on the horizon)
   PAD Strategy = Plan to get there (above-the-shoulders thinking)

PAD Tactics = Means to execute plan
(below-the-shoulders action)

Here's how one PAD Strategy may support one of the PAD Goals we discussed in the prior chapter:

PAD Goal = Increase Paid Media ROI

PAD Strategy = Use Paid Media not just to sell but also to build our proprietary audience of email SUBSCRIBERS

PAD Tactics = Creation and placement of advertisements containing unique CTAs that drive email opt-in

We'll discuss tactics to build and engage your proprietary audiences in Chapter 23, but for now, let's take a look at whether the PAD Strategy we just created is SMART.

1. **Is it *specific*?** Yes. It articulates the use of Paid Media and the desire to build an email SUBSCRIBER database.

2. **Is it *measurable*?** Yes, as long as your tactical execution uses a unique URL to track new email SUBSCRIBERS acquired via Paid Media CTAs.

3. **Is it *achievable*?** Yes, with the help of advertising colleagues.

4. **Is it *relevant*?** Yes. The strategy achieves the goal by adding a new metric to Paid Media measurements: total email SUBSCRIBERS gained.

5. **Is it *timely*?** Yes. Email produces higher customer acquisition rates than any other digital channel save for SEO and PPC advertising.[10]

As you develop your PAD Strategies, run them through this SMART analysis to ensure they are aligned with your PAD Goals—and that you can execute them in a measurable fashion through specific PAD Tactics. To generate and prioritize your PAD Strategies, you must dig into your PAD Audit findings and determine:

1. **Where are your biggest opportunities?** Where is your company currently underinvesting, understaffing, or just not focusing on *Proprietary Audience Development* efforts that could yield quick wins in terms of revenue or cost savings? Those are obviously places in need of PAD Strategies that will generate new value for your company.

Not too long ago, I presented our *SFF* research series to a *huge* CPG company that had been investing heavily in building Facebook FANS and Twitter FOLLOWERS. At the end of the presentation, it hit them—in their rush to embrace social media, they had neglected their email SUBSCRIBERS. With a new product launch on the horizon, reengaging their existing email SUBSCRIBERS—and reinvesting in SUBSCRIBER growth— was a huge, SMART opportunity.

2. **Where is your low-hanging fruit?** Quick wins build both confidence and loyalty within your PAD Team. They also attract favorable attention from marketing leadership.

   For instance, nearly every company I know could stand to acquire more email SUBSCRIBERS from its Facebook FANS and vice versa. To do so takes very little additional effort—just complementary, regularly promoted CTAs sent via email and posted to Facebook. The results speak for themselves—SUBSCRIBER and FAN growth for zero cost.

3. **What critical proprietary audiences are missing from your mix?** Your PAD Audit should highlight holes in your existing Proprietary Audience Develpment efforts. For instance, you may be tweeting, but not building FOLLOWERS. You may be creating content, but not enabling AMPLIFIERS with one-click sharing buttons. Identifying and prioritizing development of missing proprietary audiences could be the key to developing a strategy that will yield immediate, tangible results.

4. **What strategic initiatives can your existing staff support?** The quickest way for a PAD Strategy to fail is to pin all your hopes on getting more budget or dedicated staff. Your PAD Audit should yield a clear idea of the players already on the field with whom you can collaborate and achieve some immediate results. And don't wait for everything to be "perfect" to get started. Nothing ever is.

5. **What existing marketing initiatives are underperforming?** Your PAD Audit should also reveal some marketing efforts that aren't producing results commensurate with their costs. As part of your strategic planning, consider whether you can shift some (or all) of the budget for these initiatives to support your PAD Team's efforts. Granted, this is tricky political business in many large organizations; the goal is to find the win-win for all involved. No one wants to be on the losing team.

6. **What data are you underutilizing or gathering inefficiently?** A major retailer recently confided to me that they had consumer data strewn across 120 different databases. *One hundred and twenty!* If you can highlight these inefficiencies and be a part of the team that eliminates them, that's a big accomplishment. If you can also integrate those data sources to power more relevant, personal, and timely messages to your proprietary audiences, you've delivered on one of the key opportunities of *Proprietary Audience Development*: true one-to-one marketing.

7. **What existing marketing staff is underutilized?** I can't stand the sight of underworked people. While a few people are inherently lazy, most will rise to a challenge. Underutilized staff is therefore a management issue. Assess underutilized staff members' skills and challenge them to contribute to your *Proprietary Audience Development* efforts. It's a way to build your PAD Team—and consensus about the value of proprietary audiences—without adding to your payroll.

8. **Where is additional investment (budget or staff) warranted?** If you've done all of these things, you may be ready to ask leadership for more budget or staff to take your PAD efforts to the next level. You'll have a much more convincing case when you've got a proven track record of success. You may be a ways off from this ask—but still, keep your wish list handy. You never know when some "use it or lose it" budget may fall in your lap.

With these key questions answered, you're in a perfect position to articulate your initial PAD Strategy. Remember: A PAD Strategy should be a SMART, above-the-shoulders statement of how you will achieve your PAD Goals. Let your PAD Team share and debate different ideas; then prioritize your PAD Goals and Strategies based on the value they will deliver to your company and your ability to support them with your existing budget and staff. Finally, review your prioritized PAD Goals and Strategies with each Marketing practice leader so they can begin to take ownership of the PAD Tactics that will help each goal become a reality.

Chapter 23

Build & Engage: Audiences on Demand

Hysteria is impossible without an audience.[1]
—Chuck Palahniuk

PAD Tactics are the "below the shoulders" efforts of how you'll execute your PAD Strategies. These initiatives may include:

- Audience acquisition initiatives
- Audience engagement efforts
- Budget reallocations
- Cross-channel marketing
- Data integration initiatives
- Events
- Marketing automation
- Marketing team alignment and staffing
- Optimization of message content, design, or frequency
- Paid, Owned, and Earned Media development
- Software implementations

While I'd love to cover how all these different tactics serve PAD Strategies, the vagaries of book publishing only permit me to cover two within these pages. However, they're the most important PAD Tactics of all: how you can *build and engage* proprietary audiences of your very own.

The all-important tasks of building and engaging proprietary audiences are inextricably linked—a clear reflection of our *Hybrid Marketing Era*. This is to say that while the best audience-building tactics boost engagement, many of the best engagement tactics will also help you acquire new SEEKERS, AMPLIFIERS, and JOINERS.

What follows are 27 PAD Tactics to build and engage proprietary audiences. For the majority, I have included references to resources that will help you better understand each tactic's use and value. Consider this just the beginning of your journey into *tactical Proprietary Audience Development*. For additional PAD Tactics, in-depth analysis, and inspiration, I encourage you to explore our resources at www.AudiencePro.com.

Tactic #1: Talk to People

Don't be fooled: Word of mouth scales. Indeed, in my youth, if you wanted anything spread through the family, you made one call: to Aunt Bonnie.* From there, distribution of your message to the rest of the family was assured.

One of the best ways to build SEEKERS, AMPLIFIERS, and JOINERS is simply to talk to people. If you have a store, train your staff to tell CUSTOMERS about your website, social channels, and email program. If you're a restaurateur, encourage DINERS to Instagram and comment on their experience online. If you're in B2B sales, explain to PROSPECTS where your company engages online and why. In our electronic message–heavy world, we sometimes forget that personal, face-to-face interactions are often the most effective.

Resource Recommendations:

Word of Mouth Marketing: How Smart Companies Get People Talking by Andy Sernovitz (@Sernovitz)
At Your Service by Frank Eliason (@FrankEliason)

---

*Names have been changed to protect the innocent—namely—at family reunions.

Tactic #2: Websites & BLOGS

Your website and blog are the epicenter of all your *Proprietary Audience Development* efforts. They should link and promote all of the means to *subscribe, like, and follow* your brand. In so doing, they drive significant growth of your email SUBSCRIBERS, Facebook FANS, and Twitter FOLLOWERS, as well as other JOINER audience growth. Audit your website annually to ensure you are promoting all points of engagement with your company.

One important point of emphasis today: *Make sure your website and blog render properly on mobile devices.* Nothing kills website-powered proprietary audience acquisition efforts faster than a bad mobile experience.

Resource Recommendations:

MarketingProfs (@MarketingProfs)—www.marketingprofs.com
Website Magazine (@WebsiteMagazine)—www.websitemagazine.com

Tactic #3: Content Marketing

As we discussed back in Chapter 5, Content Marketing and *Proprietary Audience Development* are sides of the same coin. For your content to make an impact, it needs an audience; and to attract, engage, and retain proprietary audiences, you need meaningful content. Your website is the hub of your Content Marketing efforts. However, thanks to the ever-shrinking costs of production and the instantaneous, worldwide distribution afforded by the Internet, you can publish a wide range of content including:

- Articles
- Games
- Music
- Infographics
- Interviews
- Podcasts
- Presentations
- Streaming events
- Videos
- Webinars
- White papers

Every piece of content you create should contribute to the growth of your proprietary audiences. This benefits both the Content Marketing Team and the company as a whole, as *all of your future content* will reach a larger audience the next time out. So with every type of content you produce, be certain to:

- Optimize it for search engines to attract SEEKERS.
- Make social sharing easy for AMPLIFIERS.
- Sell the benefits of becoming a SUBSCRIBER (email, YouTube, etc.).
- Encourage *likes* and *follows* to create FANS and FOLLOWERS.

In short, Content Marketing and *Proprietary Audience Development* should be hand-in-glove activities where the success of one drives the other.

Resource Recommendations:

Content Marketing Institute (@CMIContent)—
    www.contentmarketinginstitute.com
Content Rules by Ann Handley (@AnnHandley) and C. C. Chapman
    (@cc_chapman)

Tactic #4: Search Engine Optimization

A search for "SEO" books on Amazon (@Amazon) produces around 12,000 results. Go read and learn from a recent one like *Search Engine Optimization* from my friend Kristopher Jones (@KrisJonesCom). At a time when Owned Media is critical to attract SEEKERS and create AMPLIFIERS who deliver Earned Media, you have to do everything in your power to ensure your content (from your website to blogs, videos, images, etc.) is optimized to garner the highest, most visible placements on Google, Bing, and other search engines. If you don't, you're leaving money—and audiences—on the table.

> **Resource Recommendation:**
>
> *Search Engine Land* (@SEngineLand)—www.searchengineland.com
> *Search Engine Watch* (@SEWatch)—www.searchenginewatch.com

Tactic #5: Organic Growth

Organic growth isn't so much a tactic as a natural outcome of your company having a presence on Facebook, Twitter, LinkedIn, and other social networks that consumers can use to reference or engage you. For instance, by simply having a Twitter handle (@jkrohrs), I pick up a few new FOLLOWERS each week—either because of recommendations Twitter makes or due to SEEKERS finding me via search.

Facebook FANS can grow this way too. In fact, Tony Clark (@TonyClarkCP), the digital communications manager for "Roller Coaster Capital of the World" Cedar Point (@CedarPoint), says that's exactly their situation. With over 3 million park visitors each year, Cedar Point's Facebook FANS have grown from 30,000 a few years ago to over 1.2 million as of this writing—much of it on the back of VISITORS sharing their stories and pictures with family and friends.

While not every business has millions of consumers walking through their gates each week, organic growth can be a powerful source of proprietary audience growth. But, as the lottery always says, "You have to play to win." So even if you can't tend to Facebook and Twitter constantly, it's still wise to have official accounts for your business to facilitate these types of organic social interactions.

> **Resource Recommendations:**
>
> *Contagious: Why Things Catch On* by Jonah Berger (@j1berger)
> *Fascinate: Your 7 Triggers to Persuasion and Captivation* by Sally
>   Hogshead (@SallyHogshead)

Tactic #6: Product Packaging

There isn't a man, woman, or child alive today that hasn't spent some mindless time staring at a book cover, cereal box, or package containing the product of their latest desire. Product packaging often flies under marketers' radar, but this key Owned Media asset is a veritable blank canvas of *Proprietary Audience Development* opportunity.

Your company's humble product boxes and packages can be used to:

- *Send SEEKERS to your website or app:* Turn *showrooming** SHOPPERS to your advantage by providing a bar code or QR code that takes SHOPPERS (and CUSTOMERS) to instructions, demonstrations, and helpful videos.

- *Encourage AMPLIFIERS to share:* With CUSTOMERS creating *unboxing and haul videos,*** packaging should clearly state how they can reference your company on Facebook, Twitter, and other social channels. Don't make consumers hunt for your Twitter handle; print it on the box.

- *Convert CUSTOMERS to email SUBSCRIBERS:* Packaging and printed instructions offer the opportunity to capture email SUBSCRIBERS by touting the benefits of subscription. There's not a product warranty process today that shouldn't leverage email opt-in, just as there isn't a fast food company that shouldn't use its bags, cups, and boxes to turn every meal into a long-term communication opportunity.

One last thought: Don't forget your products themselves. Larger, longer-lasting products like automobiles and appliances afford the space to print a URL, bar code, or QR code right on them—resources that CUSTOMERS can use should they have issues in the future.

Audience Exercise #8: Read Your Breakfast

Go spend a half-hour in the cereal aisle of your local grocery store. General Mills (@GeneralMills), Kellogg's (@Kelloggs_US), and Post Brand Cereals (@PostCereals) long ago mastered the box as marketing art form. But I want you to document how 10 cereals are engaging their captive, breakfast morning audience of READERS. In your opinion, which brands walk away from the breakfast table with more SUBSCRIBERS, FANS, and FOLLOWERS? Which create more AMPLIFIERS? What could they be doing better—and why?

---

*Showrooming is when a consumer enters a brick and mortar store, scans a product to find the best price, and then buys that product elsewhere (usually online).

**Unboxing videos are videos that document CUSTOMERS opening and unpacking new purchases. Haul videos document CUSTOMERS showing everything they bought during a shopping trip.

Tactic #7: Email Opt-In Form

Tried and true, a simple form requesting VISITORS to subscribe to your email communications remains one of the best ways to grow your email SUBSCRIBERS. The key—as with any opt-in form—is to:

- *Make it simple*: The more fields you have, the fewer SUBSCRIBERS you'll gain. Ask for only the data you need (and see Tactic #8, Social Login).

- *Set expectations*: Uncertainty as to "what you're getting yourself into" is one of the prime reasons VISITORS abandon opt-in processes. Clearly articulate the frequency of messaging and the content SUBSCRIBERS can expect to receive.

- *Send a Welcome Email*. New SUBSCRIBERS *want to hear from you*; and yet, only 74 percent of the retailers we recently surveyed send welcome emails.[2] Engagement begins with the first email. Communicate clearly with new SUBSCRIBERS early and they'll engage more in the future.

There are a variety of places where you can place your email opt-in forms:

- Your website or blog home page
- Your most frequented pages
- The bottom of blog posts
- Your *About Us* page
- On a Facebook tab
- Within a Twitter card
- Within a Google AdWords ad

The bottom line: Place email opt-in CTAs in places where SEEKERS/VISITORS are most likely to see the value in an ongoing relationship with your company.

> **Resource Recommendations:**
>
> *The New Inbox* by Simms Jenkins (@SimmsJenkins)
> *Marketing Sherpa* (@MarketingSherpa)—www.marketingsherpa.com

Tactic #8: Social Login

One of the worst things you can have in any registration process is *friction*—annoyances that cause people to abandon your form. Many VISITORS do not want to create *yet another* username/password combination for a website, contest, or email registration. *Social Login* eliminates this point of friction by letting consumers register with an existing social media profile. Facebook and Google are the most used social login options today.[3]

Social Login also provides you with more data than a traditional opt-in form. (See Figure 23.1.) For instance, when a user opts to register for an email program using Facebook Social Login, you can acquire the following information in as little as two clicks:

- Name
- Gender
- Email address
- Marital status
- Birthday
- Location

You can request more information, but be advised that more onerous requests will result in fewer VISITORS converting into SUBSCRIBERS.

A Social Login option not only makes your company appear more "up to date" to VISITORS; it also delivers a more engaged SUBSCRIBER base. Samsung (@Samsung) found those who subscribed via its Social Login option were 34 percent more likely to open emails, 63 percent more likely

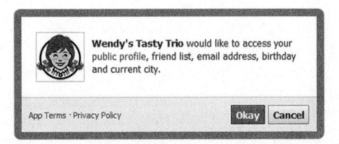

FIGURE 23.1 Wendy's Facebook Social Login Confirmation. Note how it clearly explains what personal data will be shared with Wendy's

to click, and a whopping 506 percent more likely to leave product reviews.[4] With 92 percent of consumers indicating they will abandon a website when they forget their login credentials, Social Login has moved from a *nice to have* to a *must have* feature in very short order.[5]

Resource Recommendations:

Convince & Convert (@JayBaer)—www.convinceandconvert.com
Social Media Examiner (@SMExaminer)—
    www.socialmediaexaminer.com

Tactic #9: Social Icons

If you recall my rant from Chapter 5, you already know that I'm not a fan of plastering social icons everywhere. You should limit the use of Facebook, Twitter, and other social network icons to those places where they will inspire the SEEKER to engage—preferably by becoming an AMPLIFIER and extending the reach of your content. These are some places social icons do work:

- At the end and beginning of blog posts or articles
- In association with images and product photography
- In association with podcasts and online videos

These are places social icons don't work (absent additional context promoting specific reasons to engage):

- At the end of TV commercial without any further context
- As static-cling stickers on your mall or store windows
- In the header of your website, far removed from content

In fact, I recently had a conversation with a high-volume retailer that had decided to remove social icons from their emails altogether because they weren't being used and took up valuable real estate. If you determine that your AMPLIFIERS, FANS, or FOLLOWERS aren't using your social icons, ditch them.

Tactic #10: Overlays & POP-UPS

FIGURE 23.2   Overlay on Motley Fool (@MotleyFool) Homepage

Overlays are one of the most polarizing SUBSCRIBER acquisition methods in use today. These opt-in CTAs are deployed on your website or blog and encourage VISITORS to subscribe to email, download your app, or engage with you. (See Figure 23.2.) To many SEEKERS, they are annoyances that interrupt the browsing experience.

To conversion-minded marketers, however, overlays are often worth the risk in order to convert SEEKERS (who can appear and disappear at will) into SUBSCRIBERS you can reengage. Overlays are not for everyone, but they are worth testing to see if your immediate engagement losses are more than covered by your SUBSCRIBER gains and returning traffic.[6]

Tactic #11: Signage & DOOH Advertising

Take stock of your company's Owned Media signage and then put on your PAD Team hat. Signage in stores, restaurants, and offices can promote the SUBSCRIBER relationship via calls to opt-in for email/SMS or to download your Mobile App. Waiting rooms may be the perfect place to showcase the benefits of becoming a Facebook FAN or AMPLIFIER. Fleet vehicles make for the perfect, mobile CTAs that attract FOLLOWERS seeking company information.

The options to build proprietary audiences through signage only increase when you examine Digital Out-of-Home (DOOH) advertising solutions. Billboards, bus stops, concerts, elevators, escalators, malls, sporting events, and taxis are just a few of the places where you can use Paid Media to inspire social engagement from mobile-enabled consumers. Need inspiration? Just head to Times Square in New York City, where social media campaigns leveraging DOOH happen every week.

> ### Resource Recommendations:
>
> *Digital Outsider* (@MediaPost)—
>   www.mediapost.com/publications/digital-outsider
> *The Web Outside* (@TheWebOutside)—www.theweboutside.com

Tactic #12: Cross-Channel Promotion

As you grow your SUBSCRIBER, FAN, and FOLLOWER audiences, you gain the ability to use each audience to build the other. Emails become opportunities to encourage social engagement on Facebook and Twitter. Facebook posts and pages give you the ability to integrate email opt-in forms. And tweets let you promote both email opt-in and Facebook engagement.

If you're resistant to this idea because you're afraid you'll inundate your proprietary audiences with messaging, keep in mind:

- JOINERS are always in control and can *unsubscribe, dislike,* or *unfollow* whenever they see fit.
- Each channel should be doing very different things: email providing convenience to SUBSCRIBERS, Facebook providing camaraderie for passionate FANS, and TWITTER providing timely information to SEEKERS, AMPLIFIERS, and FOLLOWERS.

Cross-channel promotion through all of your Owned Media not only makes sense; it works without costing you a dime.

Tactic #13: E-Commerce Checkout

For almost any type of online purchase, the seller must obtain the CUSTOMER'S email address. This is the perfect time to ask CUSTOMERS to also become an email SUBSCRIBER, Facebook FAN, Twitter FOLLOWER, or other type of JOINER. However, in an attempt to avoid overwhelming the buyer and losing the sale, most sellers opt only to ask for email opt-in. Whatever you choose, the checkout process is one worth optimizing to build proprietary audiences.

To Pre-Check or Not Pre-Check, That is the Question

As a shortcut to building email SUBSCRIBERS, many companies include pre-checked opt-in boxes in their online forms. While legal in some countries, this practice adds SUBSCRIBERS to your database who *haven't provided explicit permission to message them*. Such people aren't SUBSCRIBERS; they're CAPTIVES. Regardless of the law, it's time to ditch the pre-checked box. Your email performance, engagement, and deliverability rates will thank you for the change.

Tactic #14: Post-Purchase Confirmation & Communications

After a purchase is completed, you have one final moment of consumer attention that you can leverage for *Proprietary Audience Development. Word of Mouth* author Andy Sernovitz (@Sernovitz) calls it "The Love Moment" because the CUSTOMER may never have as much affinity for your brand again (we certainly hope that's not the case, but it is possible).

To take full advantage of this moment, use the data you know about the CUSTOMER to integrate relevant AMPLIFIER and JOINER opportunities into your *post-purchase communications*. These may include CTAs to:

- Become an email or SMS SUBSCRIBER (if they aren't already).
- *Like* your company on Facebook (thereby becoming a FAN).
- *Follow* your company on Twitter, Google+, LinkedIn, or other appropriate social networks (thereby becoming a FOLLOWER).
- *Like*, *comment*, *share*, *pin*, or *review* products on social networks (thereby becoming an AMPLIFIER).
- *Download* your mobile app (thereby becoming a SUBSCRIBER).

You don't want to overwhelm a CUSTOMER with all these options, so test which ones generate the most value for your business and stick with those. Other post-purchase opportunities to acquire new JOINERS include:

- *Printed receipts* with opt-in and engagement CTAs
- *Emailed receipts* from online and physical stores
- *Shipping confirmations* with calls to engage and review
- *Review solicitations:* Amazon (@Amazon) has mastered these—turn CUSTOMERS into AMPLIFIERS (through sharing product reviews)

Resource Recommendations:

Internet Retailer (@IR_Magazine)—www.internetretailer.com
Marketing Experiments (@MktgExperiments)—
   www.marketingexperiments.com

Tactic #15: Search Advertising

PPC search advertising is the advertising format that built Google. For as little as a penny per click (depending on the keyword), companies can bid for traffic. For Google, AdWords is a veritable golden goose that won't stop laying very valuable eggs.

However, if you're going to pay for clicks, you must ensure—as with all your other online advertising—that your SEEKERS land on a page where their interest can be captured (by becoming a PROSPECT or CUSTOMER). Promoting email subscription is a perfect way to do this, and in B2B marketing, it often serves as the point of initiation for *marketing automation*. When SEEKERS provide email addresses to download a white paper, they become SUBSCRIBERS around whom a company can build automated marketing campaigns.

Unbeknownst to many advertisers, clicks are not the only actions available within PPC search ads. Take the paid search result shown in Figure 23.3 that appears when I search for the company Brooks Brothers (@Brooks Brothers) on Google.[7]

FIGURE 23.3 A Brooks Brothers PPC Ad Leveraging Google's Email Opt-In Ad Extension

This ad leverages Google's *Ad Extensions* offering, which lets advertisers include more than one CTA in their paid search ads.[8] The main and sale links drive SEEKERS, while the subscription form builds email SUBSCRIBERS without ever leaving Google.

Only testing will determine whether this tactic works for you. Regardless, it serves to demonstrate that even Google recognizes the importance of helping its advertisers develop SUBSCRIBERS.

Resource Recommendations:

SEO Book (@SEOBook)—www.seobook.com

WordTracker (@WordTracker)—www.wordtracker.com/academy

Tactic #16: Facebook, Twitter, & Other Social Advertising

As social media usage expands rapidly, so too do your opportunities to advertise to social media users. If you want to build FANS and FOLLOWERS on a specific social network, first look to see if it offers a Paid Media option to do just that:

- Facebook lets you promote pages to gain new FANS.
- Twitter lets you promote profiles to gain new FOLLOWERS.
- LinkedIn ads can be used to gain new FOLLOWERS.

You can also use these same channels to build email, SMS, or mobile app SUBSCRIBERS through sponsored stories, posts, and—in some cases—more traditional banner or sidebar ads.

Social advertising really shines through when the creative leverages organic posts. Facebook Sponsored Stories and Twitter Sponsored Posts are two such examples. Each permits advertisers to amplify preexisting post or tweet content to paid audiences based on demographics, interests, location, profession, and more. The depth of data that you can leverage for ad targeting on Facebook, in particular, boggles the mind—and creates tremendous opportunities to capture SEEKERS, create AMPLIFIERS, and build JOINERS.

LinkedIn also deserves mention here because of its depth of professional data. No other site maps business connections like LinkedIn, and this affords marketers the ability to build their proprietary audiences through ads targeted by company, profession, education, and more. As other social networks carve out their niche audiences, rest assured that you'll find more ways to build and engage yours.

Resource Recommendations:

All Facebook (@AllFacebook)—www.allfacebook.com
We Are Social (@WeAreSocial)—www.wearesocial.com

Tactic #17: In-App Mobile Advertising

At a recent conference, the CMO of a major online retailer shared the following bit of insight with me, provided it would be unattributed:

> Over two years, we spent hundreds of thousands of dollars trying to boost downloads of our mobile app. Two months into running a Facebook Mobile Ads for Apps campaign, we generated 10 times the downloads at a fraction of the cost.

Wow, right? As one of Facebook's newest ad units, Mobile Ads for Apps appear in your Facebook app news feed and put you just two clicks away from download—one for the ad, and one in your phone's App Store. It's a near-frictionless example of perfect advertising placement: smack dab in front of mobile consumers while they're using their mobile devices.

But that's just one of the many mobile advertising options available today. Google, Facebook, and other advertising networks offer search, banner, overlay, video, and other ad units increasingly tailored to the mobile experience. Your challenge? To find ad units that work seamlessly to help build and engage your SEEKERS, AMPLIFIERS, and JOINERS. Great examples include:

- *Google AdWords within Google Mobile Maps*: Ads that take SEEKERS straight to your site and enable one-click to call.
- *YouTube TrueView ads*: Ads that promote your video next to other video content. You only pay when SEEKERS click and become VIEWERS.
- *Twitter Cards*: Allow you to supercharge your tweets with email opt-in forms, mobile app downloads, deep links into previously installed apps, video, and more. They entice SEEKERS, inspire AMPLIFIERS, and enable the development of SUBSCRIBERS, FANS, and FOLLOWERS.

With mobile usage only set to grow, the efficacy of mobile advertising as a PAD Tactic will only increase. As with any Paid Media in *The Hybrid Marketing Era*, you should design it to both sell and build audiences or engagement. Where smaller, mobile ad formats don't allow for dual CTAs, make sure your landing page or post-click process accommodates your *Proprietary Audience Development* needs.

Resource Recommendations:

Interactive Advertising Association (@IAB)—www.iab.net
Mobile Marketing Association (@MMAGlobal)—
    www.mmaglobal.com

Tactic #18: Television, Video, & Radio Advertising

You hear a lot of marketers disparage television advertising these days. Certainly channel-skipping DVR users, commercial-free streaming services, and the fragmentation of VIEWER attention create legitimate cause for concern. According to eMarketer (@eMarketer), however, the average American spends 278 minutes a day watching TV—up 11 minutes since 2009.[9] This finding (combined with YouTube's growing viewership) certainly suggests television isn't dying—the way we consume it is just evolving.

Accordingly, if you're going to spend precious dollars to produce and run a TV, YouTube, or any other video advertisement, you need to make sure it advances your *Proprietary Audience Development* efforts by doing any number of these things:

- Directing SEEKERS to visit your website
- Asking VIEWERS to become a SUBSCRIBER, FAN, or FOLLOWER with a clear CTA with stated benefits
- Turning VIEWERS into AMPLIFIERS (and hopefully, FOLLOWERS) with inclusion of a provocative hashtag (#Sharknado, anyone?)[10]
- Encouraging CUSTOMERS to become AMPLIFIERS by sharing product experiences on Facebook, Twitter, and elsewhere
- Turning VIEWERS into DONORS with an SMS call to action*

It's not enough to slap up your URL, flash a hashtag, or show social media icons within your commercials. To truly drive proprietary audience growth, you must make your CTAs clear and persistent enough for consumers to engage with them. And if that's not a challenge your creative director is willing to tackle, go get another one who understands both advertising and *Proprietary Audience Development*.

---

*A PSA during Super Bowl XLVII for The Wounded Warrior Project (@WWPinc) did just this by asking VIEWERS to text WWP to 50555 to donate $10. As of July 2013, the short code still worked for those wanting to go from READER to DONOR. I donated, and if the short code still works as you read this, so can you.

> ### From Viewer to Engaged
> ### SEEKER—Shazam!
>
> You may know Shazam (@Shazam) as the mobile app that took first-generation iPhone users by storm with its ability to "listen" to a song and provide the title, artist, album, and purchase options. Today, Shazam can listen to just about anything including television commercials. Advertisers like Old Navy (@OldNavy), Toyota (@Toyota), and Pepsi (@Pepsi) pay Shazam to "tag" their commercials so VIEWERS can use the app to listen to them and then be connected to the brand's website, offer, or promotion. From there, those VISITORS may become CUSTOMERS, AMPLIFIERS, or JOINERS of any type. So don't just listen to TV next time, try Shazam-ing it.

Tactic #19: SMS

There's one thing that every single cell phone in the world can do in addition to make calls, and that's send text messages. Along with email, SMS is an original permission-based SUBSCRIBER channel. And as discussed in Chapter 18, SMS also remains an extremely cost-effective way to communicate with mobile consumers at scale. Considering that around 95 percent of text messages are read within 15 minutes of receipt, SMS is a great way to cut through the clutter and trigger real-world consumer engagement.[11]

You can build and engage SMS SUBSCRIBERS in a number of ways, including:

- *Alerts*: Service alerts can encourage SMS SUBSCRIBERS to become SEEKERS of more information or AMPLIFIERS of timely public safety (e.g., Amber Alerts) or weather (e.g., tornado warnings) issues.

- *Automated keyword response*: With SMS, you can set up specified *keywords* that, if texted to your specific short code (number), will generate an automated response. This is a great way to manage and respond to FAQs in a mobile setting.

- *Coupon codes*: Text offers can turn SMS SUBSCRIBERS into not only CUSTOMERS but also AMPLIFIERS if codes are allowed to be shared.

- *Email acquisition*: SMS users text the word SUBSCRIBE and their email address to your short code. In an instant, you convert mobile consumers to valuable email SUBSCRIBERS.

- *Geofencing*: This service allows you to push SMS messages to SUBSCRIBERS within a specified city, proximity, or radius—a great way to push SHOPPERS into nearby stores.

- *Linked content*: For those SMS users with Internet access, the provision of linked content within SMS messages provides far more detail than a short message ever could. Such links help turn your SMS SUBSCRIBERS into READERS, LISTENERS, and VIEWERS in a single click.

Text messages may be short, but they can be long on value with a bit of creative thinking about how to engage your mobile CUSTOMERS and PROSPECTS.

> ### Resource Recommendations:
>
> *Mobile Marketer* (@MobileMktrDaily)—www.mobilemarketer.com
> *Mobile Marketing Magazine* (@MMMagTweets)—
>   www.mobilemarketingmagazine.com

Tactic #20: Mobile Apps

If you have successfully built a mobile app, congrats—you have yet another proprietary channel through which to build and engage audiences. It is critical to your app's long-term success (engagement) that you seek permission from each SUBSCRIBER upon initial download to send them *push messaging*. Push messages are *in-device messages* that pop up on the iPhone screen and within the messaging center on Android devices. They enable you to:

- Encourage reengagement.
- Notify users of app updates and new features.
- Notify users of activities within their games or accounts.

At initial launch of the app, you should also seek to encourage your mobile app SUBSCRIBERS to opt-in to email communications. Obtaining an external means of communication with your mobile app SUBSCRIBERS is one of the most important things you can do to ensure the continued use of your app. Without the ability to email mobile app SUBSCRIBERS, you lack an *external, non–app-based communication channel* through which you can reengage dormant users. And in a growing universe of 1.5 billion apps, those who can't communicate with mobile app SUBSCRIBERS both inside and outside their apps risk watching their app usage wither away to nothing.

A few other quick notes about in-app PAD efforts:

- *Make sharing easy.* If your app allows users to create content—be it a picture or even just their high score in a game—provide social sharing links so your SUBSCRIBERS can easily become AMPLIFIERS.
- *Encourage other channel engagement.* Promote the benefits of being your FAN or FOLLOWER across your active social networks.
- *Use push messaging to serve, not just sell.* When storms approached Austin during SXSW 2013, conference organizers used push messaging to alert the thousands of SXSW app-carrying attendees. The Weather Channel (@WeatherChannel) similarly leverages GPS data (e.g., geofencing) to offer location-specific weather alerts to its app users wherever they may be.

Resource Recommendations:

Youtility: Why Smart Marketing Is About Help Not Hype by Jay Baer (@JayBaer)

Urban Airship (@UrbanAirship)—http://urbanairship.com/blog

Tactic #21: Direct Mail, Print Advertising, & Circulars

Printed materials possess a unique ability to capture and direct our attention. They're tactile, visual, and don't require a plug, battery, or electricity of any kind. You may find any number of the following types of print materials useful in your own PAD efforts:

- Business cards
- Coupons
- Direct mail
- Flyers

- Free-standing inserts
- Magazines
- Newspapers
- Pamphlets
- Postcards
- Store circulars

Print's issue is one of cost and distribution. If you have both, then you can use print materials to:

- *Gain SUBSCRIBERS*. Much like a TV commercial, your direct mail and print ads should do more than just sell. Use personalized URLs and QR codes to direct READERS to social login pages to gain direct, lower-cost audiences for future marketing.
- *Stir AMPLIFIERS*. Instead of asking DONORS to mail letters on your behalf, ask them to post, tweet, and share. Include an SMS call to action (like The Wounded Warriors Project did), and your print piece becomes an immediate DONOR acquisition tool.
- *Showcase FANS and FOLLOWERS*. When print READERS see comments from real people like them, it increases affinity for your brand. So why not showcase real Facebook posts, tweets, Instagram pictures, and more? They only humanize your brand.

Direct mail and print stand out in our hyper-digital age. However, their production costs demand that you leverage them more like TV advertising—not only to sell but also to build your proprietary audiences.

To QR Code or Not QR Code? That Is the Question

QR codes and their ilk are quick ways to deliver mobile SEEKERS to a website, landing page, or mobile app. QRs should be deployed where they provide some convenience; however, they should rarely appear without a corresponding short URL that enables SEEKERS who don't have a QR code reader to reach the same destination. Absent a URL option, you're limiting your potential audience, since less than 40 percent of consumers aged 18–34 scan QR codes with any regularity.[12]

Tactic #22: Co-Marketing

With Co-marketing, two companies leverage their brands, products, or proprietary audiences for mutual benefit. Taco Bell (@TacoBell) and Doritos (@Doritos) did this when they partnered to develop the Doritos Locos Taco.[13] After only 70 days on the market, Taco Bell had sold 100 million units—unprecedented success for a new product, let alone one launched without a written contract between the two companies.*

Co-marketing can be just as exciting for *Proprietary Audience Development* as it is for product development. The key is to look for a partner that:

- Offers different but complementary products or services
- Commands the attention of CUSTOMERS whom you'd like to attract
- Has Owned Media assets that their CUSTOMERS utilize regularly
- Generates Earned Media regularly through AMPLIFIERS

Once you've identified a partner, you need to map out how you can each leverage your Owned/Earned Media assets and your proprietary audiences to mutual benefit. For Minnesota's Cub Foods (@CubFoods) and Holiday Stationstores, this means promoting food and gas discounts via website, email, and store signage.[14] For your company, it could be as simple as an email, a blog post, a webinar, or a series of tweets. Whatever the case, the keys to making Co-marketing work are:

- Clear communication between the partners
- Mutually beneficial growth of proprietary audiences
- Relevance of all promotions to your proprietary audiences

Fail at that last point—relevance—and you'll lose, not gain, audience members. And neither you nor your partner wants that.

Resource Recommendations:

Entrepreneur Magazine (@EntMagazine)—www.entrepreneur.com
Getting to Yes: Negotiating Agreement without Giving In by Roger
    Fisher and William L. Ury

---

*Yes, the Doritos Locos Taco was launched with a handshake between the CEOs of Taco Bell and Frito-Lay (@FritoLay), Doritos' owner. Sometimes, you have to go with your gut and not wait on the lawyers.

Tactic #23: Contests & Giveaways

Contests and giveaways can be a great way to build a proprietary audience fast. In fact, recent research found that including a $500 giveaway incentive on email opt-in landing pages increased the volume of new SUBSCRIBERS by 700 percent.[15] There's no question; people like free stuff.

However, as you look to implement contests or giveaways, always seek to:

- *Segment your new contest- or giveaway-acquired SUBSCRIB-ERS, FANS, or FOLLOWERS wherever possible.* This allows you to gauge performance and response versus similar audiences not provided with incentives.

- *Balance your cost to acquire a new SUBSCRIBER, FAN, or FOLLOWER versus their LCV.* You never want to find yourself upside down, paying more to acquire an audience member than the potential value they'll deliver to you as a CUSTOMER.

- *Align prizes, giveaways, and incentives with your brand.* Cash awards and iPads will undoubtedly attract a lot of new audience members; however, what you want are quality JOINERS who will convert. Prizes aligned with your brand or products do this better than generic ones.

- *Test different prizes, giveaways, and incentives.* Sometimes the promise of something bigger (one prize of $1,000) is more motivating than everyone receiving $5.

As your contests and giveaways generate SUBSCRIBERS, FANS, and FOLLOWERS, be sure to communicate with them immediately and regularly after registration. There's nothing more wasteful than watching a brand spend the time and money building a proprietary audience only to let it atrophy from lack of engagement. You should encourage entrants to become AMPLIFIERS of the contest while it's ongoing and become CUSTOMERS during and after the promotion.

Resource Recommendations:

About.com (@AboutDotCom)—http://contests.about.com
ePrize (@ePrize)—www.eprize.com/engage/blog/

Tactic #24: Hashtags

Back in August 2007, while Twitter was in its infancy, open source advocate Chris Messina (@ChrisMessina) suggested that people use the number/hash symbol (#) as shorthand for associating topics on Twitter.[16] In the years, since, the lowly hashtag has joined "@" as one of the can't-live-without symbols of the social media era. It has jumped from Twitter to Instagram to Facebook, and now exists as cultural shorthand around the globe.

Hashtags can benefit your *Proprietary Audience Development* efforts by:

- *Exposing you to bigger audience.* Hashtags for events enable attendees and sponsors alike to join the conversation and gain some FOLLOWERS from those who follow the hashtag and like what you say (e.g., #SXSW).

- *Connecting conversations.* FANS and FOLLOWERS can propel their favorite TV shows to far greater notoriety through the use of hashtags. The *Game of Thrones* (@GameOfThrones) episode featuring the infamous "Red Wedding" on HBO (@HBO) generated the network's highest recorded number of social interactions—largely thanks to tracking the #GoT hashtag.[17]

- *Fueling creative campaigns.* JELLO (@JELLO) did this with its provocative #JELLOfml hashtag. The campaign surprised consumers who tweeted #fml ("fuck my life"—a commonly used hashtag among people having a *really* bad day) with a reply that encouraged them to "fun my life" (hence the #JELLOfml hashtag). A website in support (www.jellofml.com) showcased all of the AMPLIFIERS and garnered a lot of media attention.[18]

Hashtags can also backfire. Just Google "hashtag PR disasters" and you'll see what I mean. What you need to know is this: *Hashtags alone do not create proprietary audiences.* However, as part of a well-constructed creative campaign, they can drive SEEKERS, AMPLIFIERS, and JOINERS into your arms.

Resource Recommendations:

AllTwitter (@AllTWTR)—www.alltwitter.com
Social Fresh (@SocialFresh)—www.socialfresh.com

Tactic #25: Events

What better place to build and engage proprietary audiences than events that draw audiences all their own? Chances are that your company participates in one or more of the following types of events:

- Community events
- Concerts
- Conferences
- Networking events
- Parades
- Sponsored events
- Sporting events
- Tradeshows
- Tweet-ups
- Webinars

You can build proprietary audiences at events by:

- *Providing entertainment*. Nearly every professional sports team now engages ATTENDEES with opportunities to see their texts and tweets up on the Jumbotron. These aren't just time-fillers; they're a great way to create SMS SUBSCRIBERS and Twitter FOLLOWERS.

- *Offering clear CTAs*. Events are a form of Paid or Owned Media. As such, you want to leverage them in all the ways you would your commercials or website—with appropriate CTA encouraging ATTENDEES to become website VISITORS as well as SUBSCRIBERS, FANS, and FOLLOWERS.

- *Participating in the social conversation*. Use official event hashtags in your Facebook posts, Instagram photos, and tweets to attract AMPLIFIERS as well as potential new FANS and FOLLOWERS.

- *Providing a service*. There's no better way to disseminate information at large events than SMS. Consider providing a *time-limited* SMS program where ATTENDEES can opt-in for agenda, safety, and weather updates via SMS. While short term, these SMS SUBSCRIBERS can quickly become AMPLIFIERS due to the value of the service you provide.

At events, you should seize every opportunity to convert ATTENDEES into SEEKERS, AMPLIFIERS, or JOINERS—something you can do only if your PAD Goals are front of mind.

Audience Exercise #9: Be in the Audience Moment

The next time you're an ATTENDEE at an outdoor event, take a good look around. Are SMS, website URLs, or mobile apps promoted as a way to engage with sponsors? Does any signage encourage you to become a SUBSCRIBER, FAN, or FOLLOWER? If you were in charge of the event, what would you do differently and why? What would your changes cost versus what they would deliver? Ask these questions, and trust me—you'll never look at an event the same way again.

Tactic #26: Social Widgets & Mosaics

Social widgets enable you to showcase a curated stream of content from Facebook, Twitter, Instagram or any other social network you leverage. They can be placed on giant screens at your events or integrated straight into your website or other Owned Media. The net effect is to entice SEEKERS to engage with social content such that they become AMPLIFIERS and/or FANS and FOLLOWERS.

To get a feel for how far you can push social widget integration on your website, go check out www.Interscope.com (@Interscope). The website for the record label of Lady Gaga (@LadyGaga), Eminem (@Eminem), and Imagine Dragons (@ImagineDragons) abandoned static page design in favor of a mosaic of constantly updated posts, tweets, images, and videos from all of its artists. The impact is stunning, and you'd be hard-pressed as a VISITOR not to explore some of Interscope's other artists (something the artists must love, since it helps them build their proprietary audiences too).

Resource Recommendations:

Mass Relevance (@MassRelevance)—www.massrelevance.com/blog
SocialMedia.org (@SocialMediaOrg)—www.socialmedia.org

Tactic #27: Appending

I've chosen to wrap up our discussion of the best ways to build and engage your proprietary audiences with a tactic that causes a lot of confusion and concern among marketers and consumers today: *appending*. The first thing you need to grasp is that there are three different types of appending efforts for marketers:

1. *Data appending*. The process of adding behavioral, demographic, or psychographic information to a PROSPECT or CUSTOMER record.

2. *Email appending*. The process of adding an email address to an existing PROSPECT or CUSTOMER record.

3. *Reverse appending*. The process of adding personal information like a name or postal address to a SUBSCRIBER's record where you already have obtained permission to communicate (via email, SMS, etc.).

Consumers benefit from *appending* because it allows companies to better tailor their marketing and customer service communications to each customer's needs. This helps deliver on the promise of one-to-one marketing long ago envisioned by Peppers and Rogers (@PeppersRogers)—when communications become more relevant, timely, and meaningful to each individual.

The downside of *appending* concerns permission, privacy, and security.

- *Permission*. In permission marketing channels like email, it is of questionable efficacy and legality to assume that just because someone is a PROSPECT or CUSTOMER, they also want to be a SUBSCRIBER. This is why *email appending* is against the policies of major ESPs.

- *Privacy*. While social media and the NSA have both helped erode our expectations of personal privacy today, it is still a hot-button issue for consumers. Marketers must therefore always seek to comply with prevailing local and international laws regarding the acquisition and use of personal data.

- *Security*. The last thing any company wants to do is expose consumers to personal risk. And yet every year we hear of thefts of credit card numbers and personal account information. As Spider-Man's late, great Uncle Ben said, "With great power comes great responsibility." If your company is going to leverage Big Data, it must also have *Big Security*.

In short, appending opens both a world of personalization and a Pandora's box of legal issues. This is one tactic where you're best advised to consult your attorney before doing anything. Both laws and social mores are evolving too fast to suggest otherwise.

Looking for More?

No single book could hold all of the PAD Tactics available today. For that reason, if you're looking for more ideas and inspiration, I invite you to visit www.AudiencePro.com, where my colleagues and I:

- Maintain an ever-growing list of ways you can build and engage your proprietary audiences.
- Debate the merits of PAD Tactics with experts from across the entire spectrum of marketing today.
- Provide how-to instructions, images, and videos to help you put each PAD Tactic into practice.

While I hope to see you on the site, our *Proprietary Audience Development* roadmap's next point of interest calls for a bit of color—red, to be exact.

Serve, Honor, Deliver, Surprise & Delight: The Red Velvet Touch

Get someone else to blow your horn and the sound will carry twice as far.

—Will Rogers

A funny thing happened on the way to writing this chapter. My employer, ExactTarget (@ExactTarget), was acquired by Salesforce.com (@salesforce)—two companies built upon a "customer first" mentality. This caused me to reflect on an initiative we launched back in 2008 called *SUBSCRIBERS RULE!* The result of a brainstorm with our CMO Tim Kopp (@TBKopp) and two of my whip-smart colleagues, Morgan Stewart (@mostew) and Chip House (@CEHouse), *SUBSCRIBERS RULE!* expressed our shared belief that permission marketing could be distilled into three tenets: *Serve* the individual, *honor* their unique preferences, and *deliver* them timely, relevant content that makes their lives better.

We had the idea to represent the entire initiative with a single image: the sign language symbol for *love*, which musical FANS also display proudly while shouting "Rock on!" at concerts. This *love/rock* duality hammered home the point that is our job as marketers to both *serve* and *celebrate* consumers—for it is their *permission* that fuels much of the most effective marketing today. The *SUBSCRIBERS RULE!* initiative culminated in the distribution of thousands of orange, foam hands shaped like the *SR!* logo. (See Figure 24.1.) In fact, if you walk the halls of ExactTarget today or check out our Instagram page, you'll see more than a few of our EMPLOYEES, CLIENTS, and PARNTERS proudly displaying their *SR!* foam hands.

FIGURE 24.1   The Logo for *SUBSCRIBERS RULE!*

In the years since we launched *SUBSCRIBERS RULE!*, its tenets have become engrained in our company's culture. And upon our acquisition by Salesforce.com, we found ourselves aligned with a kindred spirit focused on helping every company become *a customer company*. It was all pretty cool kismet indeed, but with the rise of mobile and social media, it struck me that we needed to add two more tenets to our *SUBSCRIBERS RULE!* philosophy in order to reflect the need for customer-centricity today: *surprise* them with access, and *delight* them with your company's humanity.

Surprise and delight has long been a rallying cry of customer service and social media advocates, as surprising and delighting CUSTOMERS increases loyalty and creates AMPLIFIERS. But it struck me that adding these two tenets means that *SUBSCRIBERS RULE!* has evolved into something more vivid for our email, mobile, and social age: *The Red Velvet Touch*.

I know it sounds strange, but indulge me. *Red velvet is the fabric of audience*. Consider the rationale behind each tenet:

1. ***Serve the individual.*** Marketing is now in the customer service business. Amidst the cacophony of social media activity, there are CUSTOMERS reaching out for help—even at this very moment. It is not enough to serve the masses; we must use technology to anticipate individual needs. We must seek to provide high-touch, *velvet glove service* around everything we do.

2. ***Honor their unique preferences.*** Consumers now control the on/off switch of nearly every digital channel. We must request their permission, honor their decisions, and use our *Big Data* to their advantage. The consumer is king, sitting on a *red velvet throne*.

3. ***Deliver them timely, relevant content that makes their lives better.*** Our proprietary audiences have expectations and finite attention; they want us to inform and entertain them. They have filled our *red velvet theater* waiting for the show they were promised.

4. ***Surprise them with unexpected access.*** Today's passionate FANS can be vocal AMPLIFIERS of your brand one minute and extensions of your CUSTOMER service staff the next. Remove the *red velvet rope* that creates *us versus them thinking* and celebrate the value of passionate people both inside and outside your organization.

5. ***Delight them with your company's humanity.*** Brands can no longer afford to be stoic monoliths. Social media demands that they let their humanity shine through in real time with real people. This means baking the proverbial *red velvet cupcake* or two regardless of whether or not it produces immediate ROI (#JustBecause).

Is *The Red Velvet Touch* concept a bit kitschy? Maybe—but that's what also makes it memorable and perhaps a device that can help your PAD Team's proprietary audience engagement efforts reach new heights. Let's take a look at each tenet and some companies delivering *The Red Velvet Touch* today.

1. Serve (The Red Velvet Glove)

The Red Velvet Touch immediately casts *marketing as a service*. We're not just selling widgets; we're helping customers to meet real needs. We do this because in a social world where Earned Media is on the rise, each CUSTOMER touch lays the foundation for them to become an AMPLIFIER.

Our *Proprietary Audience Development* efforts support this *serve-first* tenet by giving your company direct, one-to-one means to interact with CUSTOMERS and PROSPECTS at scale. They also lay the groundwork for *Youtility*, a term Jay Baer coined in 2012—and the subject of his 2013 book of the same name.[1]

Youtility is the notion that the best marketing provides a service to customers:

> *The difference between helping and selling is just two letters.* But those letters make all the difference. Your company needs to become a Youtility. Sell something, and you make a customer. Help someone, and you make a customer for life.[2]

When everything around our brands is always-on, hyper-competitive, and socially amplified, we must *serve individuals* or run the risk of creating some very vocal detractors. Here are a few recent examples of how brands can *serve individuals* within their proprietary audiences:

- *GE's "Talking" GeoSpring Hybrid Water Heater.* GE (@GE) is giving its products a voice by enabling them to "talk" to owners via its *Nucleus* energy management system. In the case of its GeoSpring Water Heater, this means the unit can send maintenance alerts via text or smartphone app. The result is high-touch service for the CUSTOMER and increased sales and loyalty for the brand.[3]

- *Nivea's Solar Charger Print Ad.* In Brazil, Nivea (@Nivea) ran a print ad on the back of magazines that doubled as a solar-powered cell phone charger. Talk about serving today's mobile consumers! The ad gave consumers an electricity fix for their mobile devices, while also converting READERS into AMPLIFIERS the world around.[4]

- *CustomMade.com Maker Emails.* CustomMade (@CustomMade) helps connect skilled artisans ("Makers") with CUSTOMERS to enable one-of-a-kind creations. In addition to using video to share amazing Maker stories, CustomMade keeps CUSTOMERS informed of their Maker's progress via photos and email updates.* The transparent process transforms SEEKERS into PROSPECTS, SUBSCRIBERS into CUSTOMERS, and everyone into FANS and AMPLIFIERS of this company dedicated to handcrafted quality.

---

*For a stellar (if not interstellar) CustomMade Maker story, search "R2D2 Engagement Ring" on YouTube.

The notion of marketing as a service resonates across the full spectrum of proprietary audiences as well as Paid, Owned, and Earned Media. And it also puts you in a great position to tackle the second tenet of *The Red Velvet Touch*: *Honor their unique preferences.*

2. Honor (The Red Velvet Throne)

Picture a king or queen on their throne, scepter in hand, bejeweled crown in place while all of their subjects hang on their every word. *That* is the world your company operates in today—only you're not the one in charge.

Thanks to Internet-powered mobile and social channels, consumers stormed the castle and assumed the throne long ago. With a smartphone in hand, consumers now walk into your office, restaurant, or store with access to more information about your business than even your sharpest salesperson.

We keep our consumer lords and ladies happy by *honoring their individual preferences*. This eliminates the feeling that they're merely a faceless number to your company and increases the potential for positive word of mouth. And we do this by leveraging both *technology* and *data* to deliver personalized experiences in all of our Owned Media channels. Examples today include:

- *Beyond the Rack's Mass Mobile Personalization*: The fast-growing flash sale retailer leverages SUBSCRIBER interests, purchase behaviors, and real-time inventory to serve up content to its mobile shopping app and emails that's not only tailored to each individual but also assured to be in stock. This boosts the SHOPPER's sense of urgency as well as sales.

- *Scholastic's Product Recommendations*: Proving an old dog can teach you new tricks, the nearly century-old bookseller leverages a recommendation engine to help personalize SHOPPERS' website and email product recommendations based on whether they're a teacher or a parent.[5]

- *The Weather Channel Mobile App*: The latest iteration of the Weather Channel's (@WeatherChannel) award-winning app lets SUBSCRIBERS map driving routes and pushes National Weather Service (@usNWSgov) alerts to your home screen based on your exact location.

The *Honor* tenet is really the realization of the vision set forth by Don Peppers (@DonPeppers) and Martha Rogers (@Martha_Rogers) over

20 years ago in their seminal book, *The One-to-One Future*. However, if the past two decades have taught marketers anything, it is that technology alone cannot transform mass media mentalities into customer-centric thinking. It takes people with:

1. *Vision* to chart a course toward one-to-one marketing programs.
2. *Accurate consumer data* that's put to timely use.
3. *Technological acumen* to select and integrate the right marketing software solutions to provide truly personal brand experiences.

As I said earlier, Big Data isn't big if it's wrong or unused. The coming years will only increase the ease with which you can truly deliver on the promise of *The One-to-One Future*. The only question is whether your company has the discipline and respect for each consumer's express permission and preferences to make that future a reality.

3. Deliver (The Red Velvet Theater)

The third tenet of *The Red Velvet Touch* calls to mind a classic theater filled with gold trim, ornate furnishings, and red velvet seats. I'm fortunate here in my hometown of Cleveland, that I can visit Playhouse Square (@PlayhouseSquare) to see no fewer than five such theaters, each with its own personality. No matter the theater, however, the audience always expects to see the show they were promised. All audiences come to have their expectations met—or better yet, exceeded.

> *All audiences come to have their expectations met—or, better yet, exceeded.*

To achieve your PAD Goals, your company must meet or exceed the expectations you've set with each proprietary audience. This is no small feat. We live in an age where local customer service outrage—regardless of its legitimacy—can generate international headlines.[6] Accordingly, you would be wise to regularly reassess whether you are delivering *timely, relevant content that improves people's lives.*

That "improvement" could be a coupon, your latest promotional flyer, or an entertaining video. The key is that it meets or exceeds expectations; if it doesn't, you stand to lose SUBSCRIBERS, FANS, and FOLLOWERS over time. Some great examples of brands over-delivering to their audiences today include:

- *Amazon Prime*: This Amazon (@Amazon) service began simply as a delivery service promising unlimited, free, two-day shipping to members. Over time, and without any obligation to do so, Amazon added the additional benefits of Amazon Instant Video (free streaming movies and TV shows) and the free Kindle Lending Library (free digital books). When you look up "exceeding expectations" in the dictionary, the Amazon Prime logo should appear.[7]

- *Cedar Point In-Park Messaging*: When you're the Roller Coaster Capital of the World, you can be sure of two things: big crowds and even bigger expectations. Cedar Point (@CedarPoint) manages these expectations by using in-park digital signage, push messaging within its mobile app, and Twitter to keep VISITORS informed of incoming weather, ride maintenance, and other issues that may impact their visit. This multipoint communication strategy helps minimize frustration so that the park's AMPLIFIERS are positive about their experience—rain or shine.

- *LinkedIn Year-End Email*: LinkedIn (@LinkedIn) launched this stealthy bit of email marketing genius in 2011. A prime example of how email can help social media, the message shows SUBSCRIBERS a mosaic of their CONNECTIONS who changed jobs in the prior year. It not only sends an avalanche of VISITORS to LinkedIn, but also delivers on its promise to keep you connected to the people who may aid your career in the future.[8]

As you wrestle with how to *deliver timely, relevant content that improves lives*, understand that the vast majority of a company's problems come from a lack of communication. Companies that over-deliver usually also over-communicate—but all within the bounds of consumer expectations. If you want to keep your red velvet theater filled to capacity, make sure that when you take the stage, you deliver on each and every promise made to your proprietary audiences.

4. Surprise (The Red Velvet Rope)

Most people have a love/hate relationship with the red velvet rope. On *this* side of it, you're an outsider, hoping and praying that fortune smiles on you so they let you *in there* where all sorts of amazing things must be happening.

Of course, the view once you're inside may not be as *fantastic* as those kept outside imagine—but perception is reality when it comes to access.

In the past, companies hung the red velvet rope in front of their brands, guarded by lawyers and rules and incredibly didactic brand standards that dictated exactly who could tweak, touch, and shape the brand. Today, however, brands are a living, breathing expression of consumer experiences. The trademark may belong to the company, but the brand is shaped just as much—if not more—by its passionate FANS as by the marketing team.

You can eliminate *us vs. them* thinking by inviting your most passionate FANS to help shape your message, products, and services. In the process, you'll gain AMPLIFIERS who can't believe that their ideas are being heard, while you also capture the interest of attentive FANS who want similar access. Initiatives granting this kind access behind the red velvet rope today include:

- *Beck's Song Reader*: Beck Hansen (@Beck) turned heads in December 2012 by releasing *Song Reader*, an "album" that consisted of sheet music for 20 songs he had written but not recorded. His wish? That FANS the world around would record their own interpretations—which they did, by the thousands. At www.SongReader.net, Beck shares all of the FAN creations and, in so doing, turns into a FAN and AMPLIFIER himself.

- *Melt Bar & Grilled Tattoo Club*: As I shared in Chapter 4, the Tattoo Family at Melt Bar & Grilled (@MeltBarGrilled) has over 500 members. In addition to their discount, the Family also receives updates on Melt events and sandwiches before regular email SUBSCRIBERS. If you watch the *Man vs. Food* episode recorded at Melt in 2010, you'll see a lot of Tattoo Family members in the crowd because they were the first to know that Adam Richman (@AdamRichman) was coming to town to tackle *The Melt Challenge*—a monster, 5-lb. grilled cheese sandwich. The winner in the end? Both Adam and Melt's most loyal FANS.[9]

- *Samsung's Jay Z App*: Sometimes, the red velvet rope you remove doesn't have to be yours. Samsung (@SamsungMobileUS) surprised Jay Z (@S_C_) FANS by announcing during the 2013 NBA Finals that the hip-hop legend's new album, *Magna Carta . . . Holy Grail*, would be provided free and exclusively to Samsung Galaxy owners on July 4, 2013, at 12:01AM—72 hours before its release to the rest of the world. The catch? You had to download a mobile app that also provided exclusive content and behind-the-scenes footage. Surprise? Check. Access? Check. Unbelievable generation of SUBSCRIBERS, FANS, and FOLLOWERS? Triple-check.

When FANS get closer to the brands they love, good things can happen. Accordingly, tear down—or at least occasionally remove—your company's red velvet rope and mingle face to face with your FANS.

5. Delight (The Red Velvet Cupcake)

Who doesn't love cupcakes? Their recent renaissance from back-of-the-pantry snack into decadent, upscale treat is a testament that sometimes the smallest things make the greatest rewards. I know you have a lot of work. I know hitting the numbers and making payroll is serious business; however, every once in a while, you need to stop and thank the people who got you there—your CUSTOMERS. You need to delight them with the occasional red velvet cupcake. Here are a few brands that have done just that:

- *Meat Pack Hijack Mobile App*: Meat Pack (@TheMeatPack) is an edgy shoe chain in Guatemala. To promote new discounts, it developed *HiJack*, a mobile app feature that uses GPS to determine when a SUBSCRIBER is in a competitive store. It then offers a *Countdown Discount*—a timed discount that shrinks from 100 percent to nothing depending on how fast you get to the store. The recovering attorney in me is a bit worried about the liability issues posed when sneakerheads run full speed through Guatemalan malls; but Meat Pack successfully "hijacked" over 600 customers during the initial test run. That's CUSTOMER delight at full speed.[10]

- *Pepperidge Farm's Care Package*: When blogger Rob Gunther (@Strictly_Rob_G) published his post "The Milano: An Ode to Pepperidge Farm," he thought it would get a few laughs from friends, but little else. The post caught the eye of Pepperidge Farm (@PepperidgeFarm), which liked it so much they sent him an entire case of Milano cookies free of charge. In so doing, they not only created a FAN for life; they turned Rob into an AMPLIFIER extraordinaire who shared his story with Reddit (@Reddit) and AGBeat (@AGBeat), thereby creating Earned Media impressions worth far, far more than a case of Milanos.[11]

- *The White Castle Hall of Fame*: In the early 1990s, White Castle (@WhiteCastle) hired a psychologist to interview FANS and discover what drove their passion for the chain's beloved sliders. The answer? An insatiable craving. And with that, *The Craver Nation* was born. Part FAN club, part email SUBSCRIBER program, the pinnacle of *Craver Nation* achievement is induction into the *White Castle Hall of Fame.* While nominations are open, MEMBERS are selected by a panel of judges and inducted in a ceremony every October. And yes, the writers, directors, and stars of *Harold & Kumar Go to White Castle* are honored—and *delighted*—to be MEMBERS of the White Castle Hall of Fame.[12]

Delight is the icing on your *Proprietary Audience Development* cake (or cupcake). Done well, it serves to engage SUBSCRIBERS, FANS, and FOLLOWERS in ways that create AMPLIFIERS and increase positive sentiment about your brand. But as we all know, marketers cannot live on icing alone, and that's why we conclude our journey down your proprietary audience roadmap with a stop in the future—one in which you constantly test and evolve your efforts.

Test & Evolve: What Marketers Can Learn from 5,000 Years of Football

It was the best of times, it was the worst of times, it was the age of wisdom, it was the age of foolishness, it was the epoch of belief, it was the epoch of incredulity, it was the season of Light, it was the season of Darkness, it was the spring of hope, it was the winter of despair, we had everything before us, we had nothing before us, we were all going direct to Heaven, we were all going direct the other way ...[1]

—Charles Dickens

This quote from *A Tale of Two Cities* is one of the most famous openings of any novel ever written. In a single sentence, Dickens conveys the head-snapping duality of his era; a time when optimism and pessimism existed simultaneously to inspire—and torture—the hearts of men.

And I can't help but feel it summarizes today's marketing environment perfectly.

Right now is the "best of times" for your business in that you've never had more ways to reach consumers. It's also the "worst of times," because *you've never had more ways to reach consumers.* Frankly, if you aren't feeling overwhelmed, you aren't human.

Seriously, what businesses—what marketing departments other than the largest in the world—can fully leverage the variety of channels, advertising formats, and technologies out there today? The answer: none. Being great at marketing today is as much about knowing where to place your bets as where *not* to place them.

Being great at marketing today is as much about knowing where not to place bets as where to place them.

And that's why the last stop in your *Proprietary Audience Development* roadmap requires you to test and evolve your efforts on an ongoing basis. You're not going to get things perfect out of the gate. You're going to make mistakes and probably bite off more than you can chew. Since you can't do it all, you need to *test, measure, and assess* which of today's *Proprietary Audience Development* channels work best for your business and then realign your efforts accordingly.

Test, Measure, and Assess

"Test, measure, and assess" is really the mantra of any marketer pulling their weight today. Unlike Don Draper's era, nearly all of our digital marketing channels deliver real-time performance metrics straight to our desktop. As a result, we can use A/B, multivariate, and other testing methodologies to improve campaign performance *during our campaigns*. This permits us to:

- Boost conversions by defaulting to higher-performing CTAs.
- Cease efforts in channels that underperform.
- Convert high-performing organic posts and tweets with high engagement to Sponsored Posts or Tweets with greater reach.
- Initiate reengagement campaigns to those who initially don't respond.
- Replace out-of-stock items with CTAs for in-stock items.
- Shift ad spend toward audience segments with higher response.
- Shift messaging to dayparts with higher response rates.

Ultimately, all of these efforts allow you to prioritize of your investment of time and money in those *Proprietary Audience Development* channels of greatest value to your organization. Remember: You're seeking the tactical mix that works best for you—and this may be vastly different than your competition because of differences in your:

- Abilities
- Brand
- Budget
- Corporate policies
- Market position
- PAD goals
- Physical properties
- Proprietary audiences
- Staffing
- Status (public or private)

What works for other brands can serve to guide your testing efforts; but ultimately, it is what works for you company—your brand—that must guide your tactical investments. As channels evolve and laws change, you must also be prepared to accept that what worked last year may not work next. Slowly but surely, through your testing, measuring, and analysis, it will become apparent which PAD channels benefit your business the most. Over time, you will also *evolve* your mix of channels, messaging, and staffing to best increase the size, engagement, and value of your proprietary audiences.

How does that make you feel? Exhilarated? Terrified? Well, rest easy—because I have one final handy-dandy analogy to ease your mind about the workload ahead. Anybody got a ball?

Marketing Lessons from 5,000 Years of Football

One of the perks of my position is that I get to speak to audiences around the world, ranging from C-level executives to front-line marketing folks who make the magic happen. During one such speaking trip to the United Kingdom a few years back, I had the pleasure of riding to the airport with a cabbie who had an encyclopedic knowledge of football—what we Yanks refer to as *soccer*.

While I had played the game as a youth, I had lost touch with it over the years—something that's easy to do in the NFL/NBA/MLB-obsessed U.S. of A. This cabbie piqued my interest, however, with one statement:

Mate, there are over 7,000 football clubs in the U.K. alone.

Wait . . . what?!? My mind couldn't comprehend the number. Granted he was including professional, semi-professional, and amateur clubs; but still, 7,000 seemed well beyond the realm of possibility to someone living in the bubble of North American sports.

Nevertheless, I pressed on, peppering him with question after question. He told me about the birth of football in 1863 and that *soccer* was actually the original British term for the game—a contraction of *Association Football.* * I was also introduced to the concept of *relegation*, a process by which the bottom three or so teams from an upper division are demoted each year in favor of the promotion of an equal number of teams from a lower division. **

Upon returning home, I promptly fired up our television and discovered I now had access to the Fox Soccer channel (@FoxSoccer). I called this "a sign from God." My wife calls it "the beginning of my lost years." In an instant, I became an absolute English Premier League (@PremierLeague) junkie, developed my affinity for the Tottenham Hotspur Football Club (@TottenhamHotspur), and sought out anything and everything I could read about *The Beautiful Game.* ***

As my madness fully took hold, I discovered some fascinating parallels between the spread of soccer around the world and the Internet-powered channels that dominate our marketing conversations today:

1. ***The game was nothing new.*** FIFA (@FIFA) recognizes the third century BC game of Cuju (pronounced *Tsu-Chu)* to be the precursor to the modern game of soccer.[2]

   Similarly, when you examine all of our marketing channels today, you realize they are really just technologically supercharged word of mouth—which has been around since humans developed language.

---

*For this reason—and for clarity—I will refer to the international game of football as soccer from here on out.

**It was not lost on me that, had relegation been in place in the NFL, my beloved Cleveland Browns would have been demoted nearly every year since their return to the league. Thank heavens for the monopolistic socialism of the NFL. Without it, I might never have been able to see 20 different quarterbacks under center since 1999.

***I owe my love of Tottenham Hotspur to my uniquely American fascination with their name, the play of former Spur Gareth Bale (@GarethBale11), and the lobbying of Joseph Jaffe (@JaffeJuice). For this, I owe an apology to lifelong Arsenal FAN and colleague Mark Charalambous (@Mark_Chara), who took me to my first EPL game—Arsenal's 3–0 victory over West Bromwich Albion (@WBAFCofficial). You tried your best Mark, but I'm a Spur not a Gooner.

2. *Chaos ruled the early days*. Early versions of soccer and rugby were played in England from the eleventh century on. Those games, however, more closely resembled mob rule than an actual sport. Indeed, a French observer of one such a game in 1829 commented, "If this is what the English call playing, it would be impossible to say what they would call fighting."[3]

   The early days of Internet marketing were a similar Wild West of chaos; brands were unsure how to play the game and fought over URLs, and a great many start-up deaths ensued when the dot-com bubble burst in 2000.

3. *Rules take time, experience, and consensus to create*. Until they were codified in 1863 and 1871, respectively, soccer and rugby weren't distinct sports. Prior to 1863, you could show up to play a game of "soccer" only to discover that the home team's rules required 18 men on a side and allowed the use of hands and violent shin kicking. Even now, the rules of soccer continue to evolve. Tackles are more tame, penalties more severe, and in 2013, FIFA finally introduced goal line technology to ensure that goals are called accurately.

   Do you know—I mean *really know*—the rules of Facebook, Pinterest, or Twitter marketing? You might have a sense of them, but it's not like there's a rulebook to guide your efforts. As Internet marketers, we're a lot like England in the 1800s when lots of different games dotted the countryside. They called them *soccer* or *rugby*; we call ours *social media*. Right now, the home teams (Facebook, Twitter, etc.) are writing the rules. But increasingly, the participants—brands and consumers—are leveraging their personal experience to dictate what's right or wrong in terms of taste, timing, and privacy. This isn't a process that we can rush; the distinct rules for each social channel will become clear. But we have to accept that rulemaking takes time, experience, and unfortunately, some bruised shins.

4. *The game travels with the forces that move people*. The reason soccer emerged as the world's game is because of two forces: British colonialism and the emergence of steam locomotion. The first took the game to distant shores, and the second allowed professional teams from Manchester to travel to London to develop regional—not just local—rivalries.

   The twin forces impacting marketing are the Internet and mobility. The Internet enabled email, Google, Facebook, Twitter, and other U.S. innovations to connect and inspire the globe.

Mobile devices then took that one step further, untethering consumers from desktop computers while transforming them into rivals for attention with brands themselves.

5. ***Simplicity drives adoption, but not necessarily ROI.*** Author Julian Norridge sums up the global spread of soccer thusly:

> The appeal was the same as it was to the English working class. The rules were simple. It was flexible—you could play almost anywhere. It was cheap—all you needed was a ball and something to mark out goals. You weren't as likely to get injured as you might be at rugby. And, above all, it was skillful and exciting.[4]

And yet, for all its global adoption, the vast number of soccer clubs around the world struggle to make ends meet. The "whales" of Manchester United (@ManUtd) and Real Madrid (@RealMadrid) may not worry about finances, but the ROI for the "minnows" is often too little to survive.

The rapid adoption of social media in marketing is a testament to its ease of use; it is far easier to post to Facebook or tweet than to develop a data-driven email program. However, your brand's ROI from the "easy" channels may not be as great as that of the whales in your industry. To survive, therefore, you must play more than one game.

Fortunately, there are a lot of games called football. Soccer may be the world's game, but there's also rugby football, Gaelic football, Australian rules football, Canadian football, and American football. They play with different balls, rules, and uniforms, but the objective is the same: Score more points than the opposition. The lesson for marketers is that the game you're best at—the marketing channel that delivers the greatest ROI—may not be the most popular game in the world. Popularity, however, doesn't matter. Profitability does.

The Many Ways to Accommodate Your Audience

And one final lesson from 5,000 years of football: You don't have to do it all at once. As an American, I'm brainwashed by our professional sports franchises to believe that they all need huge, new stadiums every few decades or so to stay competitive. And yet, when you travel to the Mecca of world soccer—Manchester, England—you see something very different at Old Trafford, the home of Manchester United.

Old Trafford isn't a bright, shiny new stadium. It opened in 1910, was bombed in World War II, reopened in 1949, and has been renovated incrementally ever since.[5] Today, Old Trafford is sold out every game, and serves as the foundation of the global marketing juggernaut that is the Manchester United Football Club.

Manchester United could have built a new stadium years ago, but they opted to stick not only with what worked but also what kept their FANS passionate—a connection to over 100 years of history. Meanwhile, the team found other means of revenue—kit sponsors, television, in-game advertising, and its website—to grow its global presence and revenues. It did all of these things incrementally, on the back of its success on the pitch.

This isn't the only path to success. Just across town, United's bitter rivals, Manchester City (@MCFC), opened a new stadium in 2002. In 2012, City won the Premier League title. And in 2013, United swiped it right back. There are many paths to building a winning club—and that's the faith that keeps many of the 6,998 or so smaller clubs all around England literally building upon success—adding to their stands as their budgets and FAN growth permit.

As you contemplate how to evolve your PAD efforts moving forward, know that there's no one right way. If you're a brand with deep pockets, then perhaps you can have it all in the form of a fully-staffed PAD Team and individuals to manage each channel—emerging or otherwise. However, if you're like the majority of companies and have to make tough budgetary decisions, then rest assured that your "PAD stadium" can evolve more slowly, growing section by section, success upon success, and enlisting the help of your SUBSCRIBERS, FANS, and FOLLOWERS as needed. After all, they are just a push button away.

The Next Big Thing

The *game* of marketing today is so complex because it is not one game, it is many—each with a set of rules evolving in real time that serve to confuse the uninitiated and drive up sales of Excedrin (@Excedrin). We are literally marketing today in wet cement—new channels so fresh that there are no *mentors* to show us the way only early adopters who plow ahead without knowing if they're on to *the next big thing* or *a huge waste of time*.

At such moments, I cling to things that I know will matter now and always—and I encourage you to do the same. Personally, those things are the moments I share with friends and family. Professionally, as a marketer, those things are brand, content, product, sales, service—and now, *Proprietary Audience Development*. Channels may rise and fall, but SEEKERS, AMPLIFIERS, and JOINERS will always be assets that the smartest companies build, nurture, and value in order to beat the competition.

So perhaps the next big thing in marketing isn't a thing at all. It's the hard work necessary to embrace all that *Proprietary Audience Development* has to offer your company.

It's the game that never ends.*

---

*Sort of like cricket. But that's a longer conversation for another book.

Conclusion

A live concert to me is exciting because of all the electricity that is generated in the crowd and on stage. It's my favorite part of the business.

—Elvis Presley

Since I began *AUDIENCE* with thoughts from The Boss, I figured I'd best send you off with some words from The King. Elvis Presley didn't inherit a single audience; in fact, he was born in Tupelo, Mississippi, about as far away from a stage as you can get. He succeeded and became The King of Rock and Roll because of his talent, determination, and loyal audiences—audiences that generated unbelievable amounts of electricity every time he took the stage.

Audiences are still electric today, and they're willing to generate all of the energy your company needs to thrive. Your challenge—and that of every marketer in this *Hybrid Marketing Era*—is to step off stage each night with more SEEKERS, AMPLIFIERS, and JOINERS than you started with. You do this by delivering on each mandate contained in *The Audience Imperative*:

Use your Paid, Owned, and Earned Media not only to sell in the short term but also to increase the size, engagement, and value of your Proprietary Audiences over the long term.

Some brands will be able to do this organically with very little effort because of the nature of their products and services. For instance, it is far easier for Coke (@Coke) to gain FANS than RC Cola (@RoyalCrownCola) because of Coke's deep marketing pockets and far larger global distribution network. Do not, however, let the riches of other brands cast you into marketing poverty.

There are proprietary audiences looking right now to connect with your brand. They want the convenience of email, the passionate camaraderie of Facebook, and the inside scoop from Twitter. They reward brands that serve, honor, deliver, surprise, and delight them with loyalty that makes the cash register ring (and sometimes transcends all logic). This is not Don Draper's marketing era; it is ours. And it's high time we restructured our goals, our strategies, and our marketing to serve our new King: the hyper-connected, ever-mobile, always social consumer.

Introduction: Why AUDIENCE?

1. Alfred North Whitehead, *Science and the Modern World* (New York: Macmillan, 1925).

Chapter 1 Audiences as Assets: Think Like The Boss

1. Ken Tucker, "Springsteen Speaks," *Entertainment Weekly*, February 28, 2003, www.ew.com/ew/article/0,,261357,00.html.
2. "Fold the Front Page," *Graphic Detail* (blog), June 4, 2013, www.economist.com/blogs/graphicdetail/2013/06/daily-chart-1?fsrc=scn/tw_ec/fold_the_front_page.
3. Motorola, "2013 Media Engagement Barometer—Unveiling Our Global Media Habits, One Question at a Time," *Arris Solutions Blog*, March 19, 2013, www.arriseverywhere.com/2013/03/motorolas-2013-media-engagement-barometer-unveiling-our-global-media-habits-one-question-at-a-time/.
4. Reuters, "The Internet of Things: By 2020, You'll Own 50 Internet-Connected Devices," *HuffPost Tech*, April 22, 2013, www.huffingtonpost.com/2013/04/22/internet-of-things_n_3130340.html.
5. KeithWagstaff, "Netflix Loses 800,000 Subscribers after Price Hike, Qwikster Debacle," *Time*, October 24, 2011, http://techland.time.com/2011/10/24/netflix-loses-800000-subscribers-after-price-hike-qwikster-debacle/.

Chapter 2 The Audience Imperative: Our Hybrid Source of Business Energy

1. Andy Goldsworthy, *Midsummer Snowballs* (New York: Harry N. Abrams, 2001), 34.
2. Roger Deakin, "Review: Vegetal; Theatre de la Ville, Paris," *The Independent*, March 12, 1996, www.independent.co.uk/arts-

entertainment/art/review-vegetal-theatre-de-la-ville-paris-1341614 .html.

3. Cecil Adams, "Did Oil Really Come from Dinosaurs?," *The Straight Dope*, May 12, 2006, www.straightdope.com/columns/read/2652/ did-oil-really-come-from-dinosaurs.

4. *Wikipedia*, s.v. "Super Bowl Advertising," accessed June 9, 2013, http:// en.wikipedia.org/wiki/Super_Bowl_advertising; Nielsen, "Super Bowl XLVII: How We Watch and Connect across Screens," *Newswire*, February 5, 2013, http://www.nielsen.com/us/en/newswire/2013/ super-bowl-xlvii-draws-108–7-million-viewers-26–1-tweets.html.

5. This is, of course, a turn of John Wanamaker's famous quote, "Half of my advertising is wasted, I just don't know which half"; *Advertising Age*, "John Wanamaker," March 29, 1999, http://adage.com/article/ special-report-the-advertising-century/john-wanamaker/140185/.

6. Caitlin A. Johnson, "Cutting Through Advertising Clutter," *CBS News Sunday Morning*, February 11, 2009, www.cbsnews.com/8301-3445_162-2015684.html.

7. Angus MacKenzie, "2013 Motor Trend Car of the Year: Tesla Model S," *Motor Trend*, January 2013, www.motortrend.com/oftheyear/ car/1301_2013_motor_trend_car_of_the_year_tesla_model_s/viewall .html.

Chapter 3   Your Proprietary Audiences: Seekers, Amplifiers & Joiners

1. Julius "Dr. J." Irving, as quoted by Vincent Malozzi, *Doc: The Rise and Rise of Julius Irving* (Hoboken, NJ: John Wiley & Sons, 2009), 46.

2. ABI Research, "More Than 30 Billion Devices Will Wireless Connect to the Internet of Everything in 2020," May 9, 2013, http://www.abiresearch .com/press/more-than-30-billion-devices-will-wirelessly-conne.

3. Aaron Smith, "Smartphone Ownership—2013 Update" (Washington, DC: Pew Research Center, June 5, 2013), http://www.pewinternet .org/~/media//Files/Reports/2013/PIP_Smartphone_adoption_2013 .pdf

4. Kristina Wong, "iViu Technologies Partners with Hi-Time Wine Cellars on Mobile App," OC Metro, April 10, 2012, http://www.ocmetro .com/t-iViu-Technologies-HiTime-Wine-Cellars-partner-on-mobile-app-04-10-2012.aspx

5. Jay Rosen, "The People Formerly Known as the Audience," *Press Think* (blog), June 27, 2006, http://archive.pressthink.org/2006/06/27/ppl_ frmr.html.

6. "Faberge Shampoo," YouTube video, 0:29, posted by "mybeautyads," December 29, 2007, http://www.youtube.com/watch?v=TgDxWNV4wWY.

7. Gary M. Stern, "Social Network Feedback Sparks Tempur-Pedic's Sales," *Investor's Business Daily*, February 4, 2011, http://news.investors .com/management-managing-for-success/020411–562136-social-network-feedback-sparks-tempur-pedics-sales.htm?p=full.

8. Ernest Dichter, "How Word-of-Mouth Marketing Works," *Harvard Business Review*, November–December 1966, 147–66.

9. *The New York Times* Customer Insight Group, "The Psychology of Sharing: Why Do People Share Online?," 2012, http://nytmarketing. whsites.net/mediakit/pos/.

10. Nandita Verma, "Consumers Choose Email over Social for Referrals," *SocialTwist* (blog), July 8, 2013, http://blog.socialtwist.com/marketing/ referral-marketing-email-or-social; Jose Antonio Sanchez, "The State of Digital Content," *Uberflip* (blog), March 27, 2013, www .uberflip.com/blog/the-state-of-digital-content;"SUBSCRIBERS,FANS& FOLLOWERS REPORT #14: The 2012 Channel Preference Survey," ExactTarget, April 2012, http://pages.exacttarget.com/SFF14-US?ls= Website&lss=Micro.SubscribersFansFollowers.ChannelPreference&lss m=Corporate&camp=701A0000000cOGNIA2.

11. Andy Sernovitz, *Word of Mouth Marketing: How Smart Companies Get People Talking* (Austin, TX: Greenleaf Book Group Press, 2012), 6.

12. Rich Thomaselli, "Carnival Doesn't Shy Away From Triumph Crisis— But Is Damage Done?," *Advertising Age*, February 14, 2013, http://adage .com/article/news/carnival-cruises-pr-response-triumph-crisis/239819/.

13. Seth Godin, *Permission Marketing* (New York: Simon & Schuster, 1999), 43.

14. Jeffrey K. Rohrs, "The Bill of Four Rights," *ExactTarget Blog*, October 12, 2007, www.exacttarget.com/blog/the-bill-of-four-rights/.

Chapter 4 The VIP Joiners: Subscribers, Fans & Followers

1. Amanda Palmer, "The Art of Asking," TED2013 video, 13:48, February 2013, www.ted.com/talks/amanda_palmer_the_art_of_asking .html.

2. Cord Jefferson, "Amanda Palmer's Million-Dollar Music Project and Kickstarter's Accountability Problem," *Gawker*, September 19, 2012, http://gawker.com/5944050/amanda-palmers-million+dollar-music-project-and-kickstarters-accountability-problem.

3. Ibid.

4. Marcus Wohlsen, "Email Is Crushing Twitter, Facebook for Selling Stuff Online," *Wired*, July 1, 2013, www.wired.com/business/2013/07/email-crushing-twitter-facebook/.

5. Derek Halpern, "Why You MUST Build Your Email List—And How to Get Started," *Social Triggers* (blog), http://socialtriggers.com/build-an-email-list/.

6. *Online Etymology Dictionary*, s.v. "fan," accessed August 5, 2013, www.etymonline.com/index.php?term=fan.

7. Charles Mackay, *Extraordinary Popular Delusions and the Madness of Crowds*, with an introduction by Professor Norman Stone (Hertfordshire, England: Wordsworth Editions, 1995).

8. General Mills, "General Mills History of Innovation: The Pillsbury Bake-Off Contest," http://generalmills.com/~/media/Files/history/hist_bakeoff.ashx.

9. "Springtime in Atlanta. March 27th–March 30th, 2013," Atlanta Chapter of the Coca-Cola Collectors Club, accessed August 5, 2013, http://theatlantachapter.webs.com/springtimeinatlanta.htm.

10. "What Is IMM?," *IMM 2013* (FAQ), accessed August 5, 2013, www.imm2013.eu/index.php?lang=en&Itemid=506.

11. Jessica Lee, "78% of Brand's Facebook Fans Are Already Customers," *ClickZ*, July 1, 2013, www.clickz.com/clickz/news/2278389/78-of-a-brands-facebook-fans-are-already-customers-study.

12. "Facebook 'Like' Button Replaces 'Become a Fan,'" *HuffingtonPost*, June 19, 2010, www.huffingtonpost.com/2010/04/19/facebook-like-button-repl_n_543439.html.

13. "Jayne's Hat," ThinkGeek.com product page, www.thinkgeek.com/product/f108/.

14. Ellie Hall, "'Firefly' Hat Triggers Corporate Crackdown," *BuzzFeed*, April 9, 2013, www.buzzfeed.com/ellievhall/firefly-hat-triggers-corporate-crackdown.

15. "SUBSCRIBERS, FANS & FOLLOWERS REPORT #16: Retail Touchpoints Exposed!," ExactTarget, 2012, http://pages.exacttarget.com/SFF16E-US?ls=Website&lss=Micro.SubscribersFansFollowers.RetailTouchpoints&lssm=Corporate&camp=701A0000000czJzIAI, 28.

16. Darren Rovell, "Steelers' Antonio Brown Spends Super Bowl Week with Twitter Fan Turned BFF," *CNBC*, February 9, 2012, www.cnbc.com/id/46326110/Steelers_Antonio_Brown_Spends_Super_Bowl_Week_with_Twitter_Fan_Turned_BFF.

17. "SUBSCRIBERS, FANS & FOLLOWERS REPORT #20: Marketers from Mars," ExactTarget, 2013, http://pages.exacttarget.com/SFF20-US?ls=Website&lss=Micro.SubscribersFansFollowers.MktrsFromMars&lssm=Corporate&camp=701A0000000eR4AIAU.

Chapter 5   Beyond Don Draper: Paid, Owned & Earned Media

1. Cathryn Humprhies and Matthew Weiner, "Season 3, Episode 2: Love Among the Ruins," *Mad Men*, November 2009, www.slantmagazine .com/house/2009/08/mad-men-mondays-on-tuesday-season-3-episode-2-love-among-the-ruins/.

2. "The New Multi-screen World: Understanding Cross-Platform Consumer Behavior," Google Think Insights, August 2012, www.google. com/think/research-studies/the-new-multi-screen-world-study.html.

3. Jeffrey K. Rohrs, "Punt, Pass, & Kick: Email, Mobile, & Social Misses at Super Bowl XLVII," *ExactTarget Blog*, February 4, 2013, www.exacttarget.com/ blog/punt-pass-kick-email-mobile-social-misses-at-super-bowl-xlvii/.

4. Jackie Kass, "Super Bowl Sponsor Papa John's Forgoes Commercial for Free Pizza Coin Toss," *Examiner.com*, January 30, 2013, www .examiner.com/article/super-bowl-sponsor-papa-john-s-forgoes-commercial-for-free-pizza-coin-toss.

5. Search for "Brooks Brothers" conducted on Sunday, May 27, 2013, via Google. Screen capture is of the first sponsored result from that search.

6. "Search Ads: Ad Extensions," Google Ads, accessed August 5, 2013, www.google.com/ads/innovations/search.html#tab=extensions.

7. ExactTarget, "SUBSCRIBERS, FANS & FOLLOWERS REPORT #16," 6.

8. Joe Pulizzi, as quoted in Content Market Institute, "Getting Started," accessed August 5, 2013, http://contentmarketinginstitute.com/getting started/.

9. Ryan Boyko, "Referee Bias Contributes to Home Field Advantage in English Premiership Football," *Journal of Sports Sciences* 25, no. 11 (2007), www.tandfonline.com/doi/full/10.1080/02640410601038576#. UbkGGZwmwdo.

10. C. E. Shannon, "A Mathematical Theory of Communication," *The Bell System Technical Journal*, 27 (July & October 1948), 379–423, 623–56, http://cm.bell-labs.com/cm/ms/what/shannonday/shannon1948.pdf.

11. Nick Burcher, *Paid, Owned, Earned: Maximizing Marketing Returns in a Socially Connected World* (London: Kogan Page, 2012), 18.

12. Rebecca Lieb and Jeremiah Owyang, *The Converged Media Imperative: How Brands Must Combine Paid, Owned, and Earned Media* (San Mateo, CA: Altimeter Group, July 19, 2012), www.altimetergroup.com/2012/ 07/the-converged-media-imperative.html.

13. Ibid., 20.

14. "Introducing Sponsored Stories," Facebook Marketing video, 2:06, January 25, 2011, www.facebook.com/video/video.php?v=1010032 8087082670.
15. "Audiences," Facebook, accessed August 5, 2013, www.facebook.com/help/459892990722543/.
16. "Twitter Ads Self Service," Twitter Business, accessed August 5, 2013, https://business.twitter.com/products/twitter-ads-self-service.

Chapter 6   Increase What Matters: Size, Engagement & Value

1. Lieb and Owyang, *The Converged Media Imperative: How Brands Must Combine Paid, Owned, and Earned Media," Altimeter Group (July 19, 2012) (*http://www.altimetergroup.com/2012/07/the-converged-media-imperative.html*).
2. "What's the Difference between Impressions and Reach?," Facebook, accessed August 5, 2013, www.facebook.com/help/274400362581037/.
3. "Sponsor Your Page Posts," Facebook, accessed August 5, 2013, https://www.facebook.com/notes/facebook-marketing/sponsor-your-page-posts/10150675727637217.
4. "Inbox Tabs and Category Labels," Google Help, accessed August 24, 2013, https://support.google.com/mail/answer/3055016?hl=en.
5. "Priority Inbox Overview," Google Help, accessed August 5, 2013, https://support.google.com/mail/answer/186531?hl=en.
6. Matt McGee, "Edgerank is Dead: Facebook's News Feed Alorithm Now Has Close to 100K Weight Factors," *MarketingLand*, August 16, 2013, http://marketingland.com/edgerank-is-dead-facebooks-news-feed-algorithm-now-has-close-to-100k-weight-factors-55908
7. "What Is EdgeRank?," accessed August 5, 2013, www.whatisedgerank.com/.
8. Rebecca Corliss, "Photos on Facebook Generate 53% More Likes Than the Average Post," *Hubspot Blog*, November 15, 2012, http://blog.hubspot.com/blog/tabid/6307/bid/33800/Photos-on-Facebook-Generate-53-More-Likes-Than-the-Average-Post-NEW-DATA.aspx.
9. ReturnPath, "EmailMostlyMobile," December 11, 2012, www.returnpath.com/resource/email-mostly-mobile/.
10. Matt McGee, "Your Tax Dollars at Work: State Department Spends $630,000 Buying Facebook Fans," *MarketingLand*, July 3, 2013, http://marketingland.com/your-tax-dollars-at-work-state-department-spends-630000-buying-facebook-fans-50575.

11. Kevin Kelleher, "Mobile Growth Is About to Be Staggering," *CNNMoney*, February 20, 2013, http://tech.fortune.cnn.com/2013/02/20/mobile-will-growth-is-about-to-be-staggering/.

12. Benedict Evans, "Mobile Is Eating the World," Slideshow presented at BEA, May 17, 2013, www.slideshare.net/bge20/2013-05-bea.

13. Leigh Shevchik, "Mobile APPeal: Exploring the Mobile Landscape," *New Relic* (blog), March 13, 2013, http://blog.newrelic.com/2013/03/13/mobile-appeal-why-the-future-is-mobile/.

14. LCV is sometimes also abbreviated as LTV for simply "Lifetime Value," or CLV for "Customer Lifetime Value."

15. Cynthia Clark, "Keeping Tally: Understanding the Significance of Mapping Customers' Lifetime Value," *1to1media*, May 27, 2013, www.1to1media.com/view.aspx?DocID=34294.

16. Gene Marks, "Putting a Dollar Value on a Facebook Fan," *You're the Boss* (blog), *The New York Times*, April 23, 2013, http://boss.blogs.nytimes.com/2013/04/23/putting-a-dollar-value-on-a-facebook-fan/.

17. Jay Baer, "A New Way to Calculate What Facebook Is Worth to Your Business," *Social Media ROI* (blog), *Convince & Convert*, 2012, http://www.convinceandconvert.com/social-media-roi/a-new-way-to-calculate-what-facebook-is-worth-to-your-business/.

Chapter 7 A Larger Font: Our Long-Term Responsibilities

1. Viola Spolin, *Improvisation for the Theater* (Third Edition, Northwestern University Press 1999), p. 13, http://books.google.com/books?id=W24B26mGvQkC.

2. eConsultancy and Adobe Systems, "Quarterly Digital Intelligence Briefing: Digital Trends for 2013," January 2013, http://econsultancy.com/us/reports/quarterly-digital-intelligence-briefing-digital-trends-for-2013.

3. Jonathan Espinosa, "Facebook Reveals Ad Unit Improvements, Will Phase Out Questions and Offers Products," *InsideFacebook*, June 6, 2013, www.insidefacebook.com/2013/06/06/facebook-reveals-ad-unit-improvements-will-phase-out-questions-and-offers-products/.

4. David Emery, "No, Facebookers, Bill Gates Isn't Giving Money to Everyone Who Shares This Photo," About.com, February 14, 2013, http://urbanlegends.about.com/b/2013/02/14/bill-gates-giving-away-money.htm.

5. Hibah Yousuf, "False White House Explosion Tweet Rattles Market," *CNNMoney*, April 23, 2013, http://buzz.money.cnn.com/2013/04/23/ap-tweet-fake-white-house/.

6. "Child-Snatching Eagle Video Created as Student Project," *CBC News*, December 19, 2012, www.cbc.ca/news/canada/montreal/story/2012/12/19/montreal-golden-eagle-viral-video.html.

7. Brad McCarty, "Haven't You Heard? Email Is Dead According to Facebook's COO," *The Next Web*, June 24, 2010, http://thenextweb.com/socialmedia/2010/06/24/havent-you-heard-email-is-dead/.

8. Chris Anderson and Michael Wolff, "The Web Is Dead. Long Live the Internet," *Wired*, August 17, 2010, www.wired.com/magazine/2010/08/ff_webrip/.

9. Mark Schaefer, "Twitter Is Dying—and It's All Your Fault," *Social Media Today*, October 5, 2011, http://socialmediatoday.com/markwschaefer/371341/twitter-dying-and-it-s-all-your-fault.

10. Patrick Evans, "Facebook Is Dead for Gen Y; What's Next?," *Engage: GenY* (blog), *MediaPost*, November 18, 2011, www.mediapost.com/publications/article/162602/facebook-is-dead-for-gen-y-whats-next.html#axzz2Siu7BWvn.

11. Dan Rowinski, "Jason Calacanis: 'Blogging Is Dead' & Why 'Stupid People Shouldn't Write,'" *ReadWriteWeb*, December 29, 2011, http://readwrite.com/2011/12/29/redux_jason_calacanis_blogging_is_dead_why_stupid_people.

12. Ken Krogue, "The Death of SEO: The Rise of Social, PR, and Real Content," *Forbes Entrepreneurs* (blog), *Forbes*, July 20, 2012, www.forbes.com/sites/kenkrogue/2012/07/20/the-death-of-seo-the-rise-of-social-pr-and-real-content/.

13. Bill Lee, "Marketing Is Dead," *HBR Blog Network, Harvard Business Review*, August 9, 2012, http://blogs.hbr.org/cs/2012/08/marketing_is_dead.html.

14. Dominique Turpin, "The CMO Is Dead," *On Marketing* (blog), *Forbes*, October 3, 2012, www.forbes.com/sites/onmarketing/2012/10/03/the-cmo-is-dead/.

15. Amil Husain, "Advertising Is Dead," *Huffington Post Business*, March 22, 2013, www.huffingtonpost.com/amil-husain/advertising-is-dead_1_b_2932332.html.

Chapter 8   Website: Marketing's Magnetic Center

1. "User Experience Quotes," TheoMandel.com, accessed August 5, 2013, http://theomandel.com/resources/user-experience-quotes/.

2. "Wendy's Refresh Continues with New, Interactive Website," *QSR Magazine*, May 24, 2013, www.qsrmagazine.com/news/wendys-refresh-continues-new-interactive-website.

3. Lee Odden, "Landing Page Optimization Deep Dive: Interview with Tim Ash," *TopRank Online Marketing Blog*, April 2010, www.toprankblog.com/2010/04/landing-page-optimization-deep-dive-interview-with-tim-ash/.

4. Stan Schroeder, "The World's First Website Gets Its Original Web Address Back," *Mashable*, April 30, 2013, http://mashable.com/2013/04/30/worlds-first-website/.

5. Allison McCarthy, "Worldwide Internet Users: 2013 Forecast Report and Comparative Estimates," *eMarketer*, May 17, 2013, www.emarketer.com/corporate/reports, available to *eMarketer* SUBSCRIBERS.

Chapter 9   Email: The Bedrock Audience

1. Fred Wilson, "Social Media's Secret Weapon," *AVC*, May 14, 2011, www.avc.com/a_vc/2011/05/social-medias-secret-weapon-email.html.

2. See www.AVC.com.

3. "The Man Who Made You Put Away Your Pen," *NPR*, November 15, 2009, http://www.npr.org/templates/story/story.php?storyId=120364591.

4. Andrew Webster, "Internet Society Inducts Al Gore, Craig Newark [sic], and 31 Others into New Internet Hall of Fame," *The Verge*, April 23, 2013, www.theverge.com/2012/4/23/2969378/internet-society-hall-of-fame; "Internet Hall of Fame Innovator: Raymond Tomlinson," Internet Hall of Fame, www.internethalloffame.org/inductees/raymond-tomlinson.

5. Cecil Adams, "Was Chuck Barris a Hit Man for the CIA?," *The Straight Dope*, February 7, 2003, www.straightdope.com/columns/read/2437/was-chuck-barris-a-hit-man-for-the-cia.

6. Kate Stoodley, "Father of Spam Speaks Out on His Legacy," *eSecurity Planet*, November 19, 2004, http://www.esecurityplanet.com/trends/article.php/3438651/Father-of-Spam-Speaks-Out-on-His-Legacy.htm.

7. David Streitfeld, "Opening Pandora's In-Box," *Los Angeles Times*, May 11, 2003, www.latimes.com/technology/la-fi-spam11may11001420,1,5168218,full.story.

8. Dave Crocker, "Email History," *The Living Internet.com*, accessed August 6, 2013, www.livinginternet.com/e/ei.htm.

9. "Marketing Strategy Outlook Survey," Ascend2, February 2012, http://ascend2.com/home/reports/.

10. Mark Brownlow, *National Client Email Report*, Direct Marketing Association, 2012, http://alchemyworx.cachefly.net/2012/alchemy_worx/aw_p5424_nl_dma/html/National_Client_Email_Report_2012.pdf, 13.

11. Marcus Wohlsen, "Email Is Crushing Twitter, Facebook for Selling Stuff Online," *Wired*, July 1, 2013, www.wired.com/business/2013/07/email-crushing-twitter-facebook/.

12. Eckerle, Courtney, "Email Marketing: Reactivation Campaign for Performing Arts Center Sees 738% ROI," *MarketingSherpa*, July 9, 2013, www.marketingsherpa.com/article/case-study/reacitivation-campaign-email-marketing-roi.

13. "eBags Boosts Fall Sales with New ExactTarget-Powered Cross-Channel Marketing on Facebook, Email and Mobile," *Business Wire*, November 7, 2012, www.businesswire.com/news/home/20121107006069/en/eBags-Boosts-Fall-Sales-ExactTarget-Powered-Cross-Channel-Marketing.

14. "Thomas Cook Client Success," ExactTarget, accessed August 6, 2013, http://pages.exacttarget.com/EN-ThomasCookClientSuccess.

15. Dylan Tweney, "Sept, 1979: First Online Service for Consumers Debuts," *Wired*, September 24, 2009, http://www.wired.com/thisday intech/2009/09/0924compuserve-launches/.

16. Sara Radicati and Thomas Buckley, *Email Market, 2012–2016* (Palo Alto, CA: The Radicati Group, October 2012), www.radicati.com/wp/wp-content/uploads/2012/10/Email-Market-2012-2016-Executive-Summary.pdf.

17. ExactTarget, "SUBSCRIBERS, FANS & FOLLOWERS REPORT #14," 11–12.

18. Matt McGee, "Email Is Top Activity on Smartphones, Ahead of Web Browsing & Facebook," *MarketingLand*, March 28, 2013, http://market ingland.com/smartphone-activities-study-email-web-facebook-37954.

Chapter 10   Facebook: Making It Personal

1. "Letter from Mark Zuckerberg," Facebook, Inc. Form S-1 Registration Statement, February 1, 2012, www.sec.gov/Archives/edgar/data/1326801/000119312512034517/d287954ds1.htm#toc287954_10.

2. "Facebook Find Reunites Mother and Son after 12 Years," *FoxNews.com*, September 12, 2011, www.foxnews.com/tech/2011/09/12/mother-and-son-reunited-after-12-years-on-facebook/; "Facebook Reunites 50-Year-Old Long Lost Love," *KABC*, July 31, 2010, http://abclocal

.go.com/kabc/story?section=news/bizarre&id=7585869;DixieLouviere, "How Facebook Helps Me Reunite People with Their Pets after Natural Disasters," *Huff Post Good News*, May 25, 2013, www.huffingtonpost .com/dixie-louviere/how-facebook-helps-me-reu_b_3333778.html.

3. Ashwini Nadkarni and Stefan Hofmann, "Why Do People Use Facebook?," *Personality and Individual Differences* 52, no. 3 (2012): 243–9, www.ncbi.nlm.nih.gov/pmc/articles/PMC3335399/.

4. Shea Bennett, "The Top 15 Social Networks Worldwide," *AllTwitter*, May 14, 2013, www.mediabistro.com/alltwitter/top-social-networks -worldwide_b42350.

5. ExactTarget, "SUBSCRIBERS, FANS & FOLLOWERS REPORT #16," 6.

6. Chris Crum, "Oscars: *The Social Network* Wins 3 Academy Awards," *WebProNews*, February 28, 2011, www.webpronews.com/oscars-the -social-network-wins-3-academy-awards-2011–02.

7. Donald Melanson, "Facebook Reports $1.81 Billion in Revenue for Q2 2013, 1.15 Billion Monthly Active Users," *Engadget*, July 24, 2013, http://www.engadget.com/2013/07/24/facebook-q2–2013-earnings/.

8. "Facebook's Growth in the Past Year," Facebook, May 17, 2013, www .facebook.com/photo.php?fbid=10151908376831729&set=a.101519 08376636729.1073741825.20531316728&type=1&theater.

9. "SUBSCRIBERS, FANS & FOLLOWERS REPORT #10: The Meaning Of Like," ExactTarget, 2011, http://pages.exacttarget.com/ SFF10-US?ls=Website&lss=Micro.SubscribersFansFollowers.Meaning ofLike&lssm=Corporate&camp=701A0000000Ov4UIAS, 12.

Chapter 11 Twitter: Real-Time Characters

1. Mike Isaac, "Under CEO Dick Costolo, Twitter Is Growing Up," *Wired*, January 30, 2012, www.wired.com/business/2012/01/ twitter-costolo-allthingsd/.

2. Jay Baer, "Are Consumer Expectations for Social Media Customer Service Realistic," *The Social Habit*, October 2012, http://socialhabit .com/uncategorized/customer-service-expectations/.

3. Teisha Seabrook, "The World's Fastest Responding Brands on Twitter," *SocialBakers*, www.socialbakers.com/blog/1748-the-world-s-fastest-responding- brands-on-twitter.

4. "Capture User Interest with the Lead Generation Card," Twitter Advertising, May 22, 2013, https://blog.twitter.com/2013/capture- user-interest-lead-generation-card.

5. "Twitter Came to Life Five Years Ago This Week; Creator Jack Dorsey Remembers," *L.A. Times*, March 13, 2011, http://latimesblogs.latimes .com/technology/2011/03/twitter-came-to-life-five-years-ago-this-week-founder-jack-dorsey-shares-history.html.

6. "Twitter Now the Fastest Growing Social Platform in the World," *GlobalWebIndex*, January 28, 2013, www.globalwebindex.net/twitter-now-the-fastest-growing-social-platform-in-the-world/.

7. Hayley Tsukayama, "Twitter Turns 7: Users Send over 400 Million Tweets per Day," *The Washington Post*, March 21, 2013, http://articles.washingtonpost.com/2013-03-21/business/37889387_1_tweets-jack-dorsey-twitter.

Chapter 12 Blogs: A Website by Another Name

1. Andrew Sullivan, "Why I Blog," *The Atlantic*, November 1, 2008, www .theatlantic.com/magazine/archive/2008/11/why-i-blog/307060/2/.

2. Farhad Manjoo, "Flash: Blogging Goes Corporate," *Wired*, May 9, 2002, www.wired.com/culture/lifestyle/news/2002/05/52380.

3. See Tumblr's "About" page, www.tumblr.com/about. Charlie Rose, "Charlie Rose Talks to Tumblr's David Karp," *Bloomberg Businessweek*, May 30, 2013, www.businessweek.com/articles/2013-05-30/charlie-rose-talks-to-tumblrs-david-karp.

4. Tristan Louis, "Is Tumblr The Next Geocities?," *Forbes*, May 18, 2013, www .forbes.com/sites/tristanlouis/2013/05/18/is-tumblr-the-new-geocities/.

Chapter 13 Mobile Apps: Audiences on the Go

1. Bruce Horovitz, "Starbucks CEO Schultz on Digital Innovation," *USA Today*, April 25, 2013, www.usatoday.com/story/money/business/2013/04/24/starbucks-howard-schultz-innovators/2047655/.

2. Jason Ankeny, "Starbucks: Mobile Payments Now 10% of All U.S. Transactions," *FierceMobileContent*, June 19, 2013, www.fiercemobile content.com/story/starbucks-mobile-payments-now-10-all-us-transactions/2013-06-19.

3. Allison Stadd, "79% of People 18–44 Have Their Smartphones with Them 22 Hours a Day," *AllTwitter*, April 2, 2013, www.mediabistro .com/alltwitter/smartphones_b39001.

4. Luke Wroblewski, "Why Mobile Matters," *LukeW.com*, February 21, 2012, www.lukew.com/ff/entry.asp?1506.

5. Margaret Kane, "Apple Launches New iTunes with App Store," *CNET*, July 10, 2008, http://news.cnet.com/8301–1023_3–9987100–93.html.

6. Ryan Lawler, "Mary Meeker's 2013 Internet Trends: Mobile Makes Up 15% of All Internet Traffic, With 1.5B Users Worldwide," *TechCrunch*, May 29, 2013, http://techcrunch.com/2013/05/29/mary-meeker-2013-internet-trends/.

7. Sam Costello, "What Are iPad Sales All Time?," About.com, last modified April 25, 2012, http://ipod.about.com/od/ipadmodelsandterms/f/ipad-sales-to-date.htm.

8. ABI Research, "Android Will Account for 58% of Smartphone App Downloads in 2013, with iOS Commanding a Market Share of 75% in Tablet Apps," March 4, 2013, www.abiresearch.com/press/android-will-account-for-58-of-smartphone-app-down.

9. Lavey-Heaton, Megan, "App Store Hits 50 Billion Apps Downloaded," TUAW.com, May 15, 2013, www.tuaw.com/2013/05/15/app-store-hits-50-billion-apps-downloaded/.

Chapter 14   LinkedIn: The Professional Audience

1. Jennifer Van Grove, "LinkedIn's Next Target: Yammer, Salesforce Chatter?," *CNET*, February 25, 2013, http://news.cnet.com/8301-1023_3-57571235-93/linkedins-next-target-yammer-salesforce-chatter/.

2. Itamar Orgad, "New Ways to Get Insights from LinkedIn Influencers," *LinkedIn Blog*, January 29, 2013, http://blog.linkedin.com/2013/01/29/new-ways-to-get-insights-from-linkedin-influencers/.

3. Chris Seper, "Why I Cheer When My Employees Leave," LinkedIn, January 25, 2013, www.linkedin.com/today/post/article/2013012510 5449-107961-why-i-cheer-when-my-employees-leave?trk=mp-reader-card.

4. Nick Besbeas, "What HP's 1 Million LinkedIn Followers Means for Marketers," *LinkedIn Blog*, February 28, 2013, http://blog.linkedin.com/2013/02/28/what-hps-1-million-linkedin-followers-means-for-marketers-infographic/.

5. See the Philips Innovations in Health LinkedIn discussion, www.linkedin.com/groups/Innovations-In-Health-2308956?gid=2308956&trk=hb_side_g.

6. See the Connect: Professional Women's Network, www.linkedin. com/groups/Connect-Professional-Womens-Network-Powered-4409416?trk=corpblog_0113.

7. Leena Rao, "LinkedIn Acquires Professional Content Sharing Platform SlideShare for $119M," *TechCrunch*, May 3, 2012, http://techcrunch. com/2012/05/03/linkedin-acquires-professional-content-sharing-platform-slideshare-for-119m/.

8. "Why You Should Use SlideShare?," SlideShare, accessed August 6, 2013, http://www.slideshare.net/about.

9. "Most Popular (All Time)," SlideShare, http://www.slideshare.net/ popular/all-time.

10. Mark Walsh, "LinkedIn Launches SlideShare Ads," *Online Media Daily* (blog), *MediaPost*, March 12, 2013, www.mediapost.com/publications/ article/195571/#axzz2XFK5fv000.

11. "Exporting Your Connections," LinkedIn Help Center, http://help. linkedin.com/app/utils/auth/callback/%2Fapp%2Fanswers%2Fdetail% 2Fa_id%2F3.

12. Sean Ludwig, "LinkedIn Reports Strong Q2 Results, Membership Grows to 238M Users," *VentureBeat*, August 1, 2013, http:// venturebeat.com/2013/08/01/linkedin-reports-strong-q2-results-membership-grows-to-238m-users/.

Chapter 15 YouTube: Internet Built The Video Star

1. Jake Coyle, "YouTube Says the Battle with TV Is Already Over," *The Seattle Times*, May 2, 2013, http://seattletimes.com/html/entertainment/ 2020906479_apusyoutubebrandcast.html.

2. Greg Sterling, "Report: YouTube Generated $350M in Mobile Revenue in Past Six Months," *MarketingLand*, June 6, 2013, http://marketingland .com/report-youtube-now-generating-350m-in-mobile-revenue-for-google-47165.

3. "The Orabrush Story: How a Utah Man Used YouTube to Build a Multi-million Dollar Business," *Google Official Blog*, November 15, 2011, http://googleblog.blogspot.com/2011/11/orabrush-story-how-utah-man-used.html.

4. Grady Smith, "The New Face of YouTube," *Entertainment Weekly*, March 1, 2013, www.ew.com/ew/article/0,,20679715,00.html.

5. "Evolution of Dance," YouTube video, 6:01, posted by Judson Laipply, April 6, 2006, www.youtube.com/watch?feature=player_embedded&v= dMH0bHeiRNg.

6. "About YouTube," YouTube.com, accessed August 6, 2013, www.youtube .com/yt/about/.

7. Associated Press, "Google Buys YouTube for $1.65 billion," *NBC News*, October 10, 2006, www.nbcnews.com/id/15196982/ns/business-us_business/t/google-buys-youtube-billion/#.UbByd5zNnE1.

8. "Statistics," YouTube.com, accessed August 6, 2013, www.youtube. com/yt/press/statistics.html.

9. "Videos about Making Videos," YouTube.com, accessed August 6, 2013, www.youtube.com/user/videotoolbox.

10. Jason Calacanis, "I Ain't Gonna Work on YouTube's Farm No More," *Launch Blog*, June 2, 2013, http://blog.launch.co/blog/i-aint-gonna-work-on-youtubes-farm-no-more.html.

11. Pierce Sharpe, "Cheerios Ad Sparks Racist Comments on YouTube," *WTVR*, June 3, 2013, http://wtvr.com/2013/06/03/cheerios-ad-comments/.

Chapter 16   Google+: The Great Unknown

1. Tom Waits, "What's He Building?," *Mule Variations*, Anti-, 2009.

2. Danny Sullivan, "Google: 'Game Changing' Features Will Boost Google+ Adoption," *MarketingLand*, May 17, 2013, http://marketingland.com/ google-game-changing-features-will-boost-google-adoption-44377.

3. Ibid.

4. Greg Finn, "Google Rewards App Developers Using Google+ Sign-In With Better Visibility on Google Search," *Search Engine Land*, April 30, 2013, http://searchengineland.com/google-sign-in-now-pushing-app-activities-directly-into-search-results-157755.

5. Matt McGee, "Google+ Adds Content Recommendations for Mobile Websites," *MarketingLand*, May 13, 2013, http://marketing land.com/google-adds-content-recommendations-for-mobile-websites-43556.

6. Jay Baer, "Social Media Lessons from the Open Source Movement," *Social Pros Podcast, Convince & Convert*, January 30, 2013, www. convinceandconvert.com/social-pros-podcast/social-media-lessons -from-the-open-source-movement/.

7. Beth Hayden, "12 Ways to Connect, Create, and Collaborate Using Google Hangouts," *Copyblogger*, March 13, 2013, www.copyblogger. com/google-hangout-content/.

8. Rand Fishkin, "Is Google+ Approaching Twitter's Marketing Value?," *Moz. com*, April 6, 2013, http://moz.com/rand/is-google-approaching-twitters-marketing-value/.

9. "Social Platforms GWI.8 Update: Decline of Local Social Media Platforms," *GlobalWebIndex*, January 22, 2013, www.globalwebindex.net/social-platforms-gwi-8-update-decline-of-local-social-media-platforms/.

10. Jemima Kiss, "On Social Media Marketing: Plus Points," *The Guardian*, June 2, 2013, www.guardian.co.uk/technology/2013/jun/03/google-plus-social-media-jemima-kiss.

11. Cyrus Shepard, "Amazing Correlation Between Google +1s and Higher Search Rankings," *The Moz Blog*, August 20, 2013, http://moz.com/blog/google-plus-correlations.

12. "Welcome to Google+ Social Statistics," accessed August 6, 2013, http://socialstatistics.com/.

Chapter 17   Pinterest: A Collection of Beautiful Followers

1. Tom Simonite, "Q+A Ben Silbermann," *MIT Technology Review*, February 19, 2013, www.technologyreview.com/qa/511096/pinterests-founder-algorithms-dont-know-what-you-want/.

2. Chris Crum, "Here Are Some Clear Business Uses for Pinterest," *WebProNews*, December 6, 2012, www.webpronews.com/here-are-some-clear-business-uses-for-pinterest-2012–12.

3. Cameron Scott, "Pinterest Drives More Traffic to Niche Retailers Than to Major Sites," *SocialTimes*, December 21, 2012, http://socialtimes.com/pinterest-drives-more-traffic-to-niche-retailers-than-to-major-sites_b114245.

4. Justin Smith, "Facebook vs. Pinterest: You're Investing, But What Are Your Goals?," *The Bloomreach Blog*, April 25, 2013, http://bloomreach.com/2013/04/facebook-vs-pinterest-youre-investing-but-what-are-your-goals/.

5. Daniel P. Maloney, "Pinterest Followers and Engagement: NOT The Same," *Business2Community*, January 16, 2013, www.business2community.com/pinterest/pinterest-followers-and-engagement-are-not-the-same-0378642.

6. Nicholas Carlson, "Pinterest CEO: Here's How We Became the Web's Next Big Thing," *Business Insider*, April 24, 2012, www.businessinsider.com/pinterest-founding-story-2012-4?op=1.

7. Josh Horwitz, "Semiocast: Pinterest Now Has 70 Million Users and Is Steadily Gaining Momentum Outside the US," *The Next Web*, July 10, 2013, http://thenextweb.com/socialmedia/2013/07/10/

semiocast-pinterest-now-has-70-million-users-and-is-steadily-gaining-momentum-outside-the-us/.

8. Reuters, "Pinterest Is Worth $2 Billion Because Its 25 Million Users Are Rich, Female, and Like to Spend," *Business Insider*, February 28, 2013, www.businessinsider.com/pinterest-is-worth-2-billion-because-its-25-million-users-are-rich-female-and-like-to-spend-2013-2.

Chapter 18 SMS: Cutting through the Clutter

1. McKay Allen, "How IHOP Generates Sales: SMS Marketing Case Study," *Bsuiness2Community*, March 26, 2013, www.business2community.com/marketing/how-ihop-generates-sales-sms-marketing-case-study-0445725.
2. Ibid.
3. Chantal Tode, "P.F. Chang-owned Pei Wei Adds 5,000 Consumers to email database via Mobile," *Mobile Commerce Daily*, November 1, 2011, www.mobilecommercedaily.com/pei-wei-adds-over-6000-names-to-email-subscriber-list-via-mobile.
4. David Kirkpatrick, "Mobile Marketing: How Redbox Drove 1.5 Million Texts and Added 200,000 Mobile Participants in 10 Days," *MarketingSherpa*, October 6, 2011, www.marketingsherpa.com/article/case-study/how-redbox-drove-15-million.
5. Allegra Tepper, "The Power of Text Message Marketing," *Mashable*, July 13, 2012, http://mashable.com/2012/07/13/text-message-marketing-infographic/.
6. David Meyer, "Chat Apps Have Overtaken SMS by Message Volume, but How Big a Disaster Is That for Carriers?," *GigaOM*, April 29, 2013, http://gigaom.com/2013/04/29/chat-apps-have-overtaken-sms-by-message-volume/.
7. Lance Whitney, "Father of SMS Reflects on 20th Anniversary of First Text Message," *CNET*, December 3, 2012, http://news.cnet.com/8301-1035_3-57556747-94/father-of-sms-reflects-on-20th-anniversary-of-first-text-message/.
8. Pamela Clark-Dickson, "OTT Messaging Traffic Will Be Twice the Volume of P2P SMS Traffic by End of 2013," *Informa Telecoms & Media* (blog), April 29, 2013, http://blogs.informatandm.com/12861/news-release-ott-messaging-traffic-will-be-twice-the-volume-of-p2p-sms-traffic-by-end-2013/.

Chapter 19 Instagram: Moving Pictures

1. Anthony Wing Kosner, "Instagram Simplifies Making Video Pictures While Lightt Aims at Ongoing Movie of Life," *Forbes*, June 21, 2013, www.forbes.com/sites/anthonykosner/2013/06/21/instagram-simplifies-making-video-pictures-while-lightt-aims-at-the-ongoing-movie-of-life/.
2. For current brand popularity on Instagram, see Nitrogram 50, "Most Popular Brands on Instagram," http://50.nitrogr.am/sort-photos.
3. Jay Baer, "Social Pros 6—Instagram Lessons from a Giant B2B Company," *Social Pros Podcast, Convince & Convert.com*, 2012, www.convinceandconvert.com/social-pros-podcast/social-pros-6-instagram-lessons-from-a-giant-b2b-company/.
4. Lauren Johnson, "Taco Bell Builds on Doritos Locos Taco Promotion with Instagram," *Mobile Marketer*, October 10, 2012, www.mobilemarketer.com/cms/news/content/13959.html.
5. Michael Sippey, "Vine: A New Way to Share Video," *Twitter Blog*, January 24, 2013, https://blog.twitter.com/2013/vine-new-way-share-video.
6. Dan Primack, "Breaking: Facebook Buying Instagram for $1 billion," *CNNMoney*, April 9, 2012, http://finance.fortune.cnn.com/2012/04/09/breaking-facebook-buying-instagram-for-1-billion/.
7. "Stats," Instagram Press Center, accessed August 6, 2013, http://instagram.com/press/#

Chapter 20 Podcasts: Listen Carefully

1. Don Steinberg, "The King of Podcast Comedy Expands His Rule," *The Wall Street Journal*, April 18, 2013, http://online.wsj.com/article/SB10001424127887324030704578426732432948580.html.
2. Peter Hartlaub, "Marc Maron Talks of TV, 'WTF,' New Book," *San Francisco Chronicle*, June 5, 2013, www.sfchronicle.com/tv/article/Marc-Maron-talks-of-TV-WTF-new-book-4576225.php.
3. See the Social Pros Podcast, www.convinceandconvert.com/social-pros-podcast/.
4. Laura Santhanam, Amy Mitchell, and Kenny Olmstead, "Audio: Digital Drives Listener Experience," *The State of the News Media 2013: An Annual Report on American Journalism*, Pew Research Center, http://stateofthemedia.org/2013/audio-digital-drives-listener-experience/.
5. See Podcast Alley, www.podcastalley.com/index.php.

6. Stephanie Ciccarelli, "History of Podcasting," Voices.com, accessed August 6, 2013, http://www.voices.com/resources/articles/podcasting/history-of-podcasting.

Chapter 21 Other Audience Channels: More? You Want More?!?

1. Steven Millward, "These Two Graphs Show Painful Drops for Google and Baidu in China Search Engine Market," *Tech In Asia*, July 4, 2013, www.techinasia.com/china-baidu-qihoo-google-search-market-share-war/.
2. Ryan Tate, "Bebo's $849M Implosion Teaches a Brutal Lesson in Social Networking," *Wired*, July 2, 2013, www.wired.com/business/2013/07/bebo-lesson/.
3. Ricardo Bilton, "After a $41M Loan, Foursquare Still Needs to Prove It's an Actual Business," *VentureBeat*, April 11, 2013, http://venturebeat.com/2013/04/11/foursquares-quest-for-legitimacy/.
4. Prasant Naidu, "South Korea's Messaging App Kakao Talk Has Passed 100 Million Registered Users," *Yahoo!*, July 3, 2013, http://smallbusiness.yahoo.com/advisor/south-korea-messaging-app-kakao-talk-passed-100–154014274.html.
5. Lauren Indvik, "Medium's Plan to Serve the Next Generation of Bloggers," May 28, 2013, http://mashable.com/2013/05/28/medium-ev-williams/.
6. David Taintor, "Myspace Relaunches with $20 Million Ad Campaign," *AdWeek*, June 12, 2013, www.adweek.com/news/technology/myspace-relaunches-20-million-ad-campaign-150217.
7. Jennifer Van Grove, "Path Said to Be Seeking Valuation of $1 Billion," *CNET*, June 14, 2013, http://news.cnet.com/8301-1023_3-57589380-93/path-said-to-be-seeking-valuation-of-$1-billion/.
8. CIW Team Staff, "Tencent Active IM Users Close to 800 Million, Social Network Qzone over 600 Million in 2012," *China Internet Watch*, March 21, 2013, www.chinainternetwatch.com/2054/tencent-active-im-users-close-to-800-million-social-network-qzone-over-600-million-in-2012/.
9. Stephanie Mlot, "Pew: 6 Percent of American Adults Use Reddit," *PCMag*, July 3, 2013, www.pcmag.com/article2/0,2817,2421391,00.asp.
10. Trefis Team, "Renren Rides China's Social Networking and Gaming to $3.20," *Great Speculations* (blog), *Forbes*, May 3, 2013, www.forbes.com/sites/greatspeculations/2013/05/03/renren-rides-chinas-social-networking-and-gaming-to-3-20/.

11. "Which Social Networks Are Growing Fastest Worldwide?," *eMarketer*, May 13, 2013, www.emarketer.com/Article/Which-Social-Networks-Growing-Fastest-Worldwide/1009884; Josh Ong, "China's Sina Weibo Grew 73% in 2012, Passing 500 Million Registered Accounts," *The Next Web*, February 21, 2013, http://thenextweb.com/asia/2013/02/21/chinas-sina-weibo-grew-73-in-2012-passing-500-million-registered-accounts/.

12. Tom Balmforth, "Russia's Top Social Network under Fire," *Radio Free Europe/Radio Liberty*, May 28, 2013, www.rferl.org/content/russia-vkontakte-under-fire/24999478.html.

13. Eric Larson, "Five Reasons to Choose Vimeo Instead of YouTube," May 30, 2013, http://mashable.com/2013/05/30/vimeo-over-youtube/.

14. Jon Russell, "It's Time to Stop Comparing Instagram and Vine using Twitter," *The Next Web*, June 29, 2013, http://thenextweb.com/insider/2013/06/29/its-time-to-stop-comparing-instagram-and-vine-using-twitter/.

Chapter 22   Map & Align: Strategy and Team

1. See "ABC Introduces New Name—Alliance for Audited Media—to Reflect Leadership in New World of Media," Alliance for Audited Media, November, 15, 2012, www.auditedmedia.com/news/news-releases/2012/abc-introduces-new-name-%E2%80%93-alliance-for-audited-media.aspx; Ben Robins, "Summary of Arbitron's Total Audience Measurement," NPR Digital Services, January 23, 2012, http://digitalservices.npr.org/post/summary-arbitrons-total-audience-measurement; "Nielsen and Twitter Establish Social TV Rating," Nielsen, December 17, 2012, www.nielsen.com/us/en/press-room/2012/nielsen-and-twitter-establish-social-tv-rating.html.

2. Adam Sutton, "Email Marketing: 900% More Revenue-per-Email from Restaurant.com's Automated Strategy," *MarketingSherpa*, November 27, 2012, www.marketingsherpa.com/article/case-study/automated-email-strategy-ecommerce#.

3. Jack Neff, "P&G to Slash $10 Billion in Costs over Five Years," *AdAge*, February 23, 2012, http://adage.com/article/cmo-strategy/p-g-slash-10-billion-costs-years/232914/.

4. Scott Cendrowski, "Nike's New Marketing Mojo," *Fortune*, February 13, 2012, http://management.fortune.cnn.com/2012/02/13/nike-digital-marketing/.

5. Stefany Moore, "How $200,000 in Facebook Ads Becomes $10 million in E-commerce Sales," *InternetRetailer*, March 6, 2013, www.internetretailer .com/2013/03/06/how-200000-facebook-ads-becomes-10-million-sales.
6. Angela Watercutter, "How Oreo Won the Marketing Super Bowl With a Timely Blackout Ad on Twitter, *Underwire* (blog), *Wired*, February 4, 2013, www.wired.com/underwire/2013/02/oreo-twitter-super-bowl/.
7. Gregory Karp, "United's Social Media Efforts Getting off the Ground," *Chicago Tribune*, June 9, 2013, http://articles.chicagotribune.com/2013-06-09/business/ct-biz-0609-united-social-media-20130609_1_social-media-instagram-google-plus/2.
8. Heather Clancy, "Why Bonobos lets its customer service 'ninjas' improvise solutions to complaints," *SmartPlanet*, August 2, 2012, www. smartplanet.com/blog/business-brains/why-bonobos-lets-its-customer-service-8216ninjas-improvise-solutions-to-complaints/25549.
9. Kristin Bent, "Cisco to Partners: Use Social Media—You Can Bet Your Competitors Are," *CRN*, April 17, 2013, www.crn.com/news/networking/240153030/cisco-to-partners-use-social-media-you-can-bet-your-competitors-are.htm.
10. Marcus Wohlsen, "Email Is Crushing Twitter, Facebook for Selling Stuff Online," *Wired*, July 1, 2013, www.wired.com/business/2013/07/email-crushing-twitter-facebook/.

Chapter 23 Build & Engage: Audiences on Demand

1. Chuck Palahniuk, *Invisible Monsters*, (New York: W.W. Norton, 1999), 50.
2. ExactTarget, "SUBSCRIBERS, FANS & FOLLOWERS REPORT #16," p. 16.
3. Michael Olson, "Social Login Trends Across the Web for Q1 2013," *Janrain*, April 8, 2013, http://janrain.com/blog/social-login-trends -across-the-web-for-q1–2013/.
4. Bill Piwonka, "How to Leverage Social Login to Boost User Engagement, *Website Magazine*, June 1, 2013, www.websitemagazine.com/content/blogs/issues-pro/pages/how-to-leverage-social-login-to-boost-engagement.aspx.
5. Ibid.
6. Jon Correll, "Opt-In Email Newsletter Popup Best Practices for 2012," *ConversionVoodoo*, January 2012, www.conversionvoodoo.com/blog/

2012/01/opt-in-email-newsletter-popup-best-practices-landing-page-optimization-shoemoney/.

7. Search for "Brooks Brothers" conducted on Sunday, May 27, 2013, via Google. Screen capture is of the first sponsored result from that search.

8. Google Ads, "Search Ads: Ad Extensions."

9. "eMarketer: Consumers Spending More Time with Mobile as Growth Slows for Time Online," *eMarketer*, October 22, 2012, www.emarketer.com/newsroom/index.php/consumers-spending-time-mobile-growth-time-online-slows/.

10. Brian Stelter, "'Sharknado' Tears Up Twitter, if Not the TV Ratings," *The New York Times*, July 12, 2013, /www.nytimes.com/2013/07/13/arts/television/sharknado-tears-up-twitter-if-not-the-tv-ratings.html?_r=0.

11. Al Urbanski, "Avenue Goes Off in a New Mobile Direction," *Direct Marketing News*, February 12, 2013, www.dmnews.com/avenue-goes-off-in-a-new-mobile-direction/article/280129/.

12. "US Ahead of Western Europe in QR Code Usage," *eMarketer*, January 28, 2013, www.emarketer.com/Article/US-Ahead-of-Western-Europe-QR-Code-Usage/1009631.

13. Austin Carr, "Deep inside Taco Bell's Doritos Locos Taco," *Fast Company*, May 1, 2013, www.fastcompany.com/3008346/deep-inside-taco-bells-doritos-locos-taco.

14. CSD Staff, "Holiday Stationstores and Cub Foods Launch Rewards," *Convenience Store Decisions*, September 28, 2012, www.csdecisions.com/2012/09/28/holiday-stationstores-and-cub-foods-launch-rewards/.

15. Ayaz Nanji, "The Impact of Contests on Email Leads," *Marketing Profs*, citing research from *Incentivibe*, May 29, 2013, www.marketingprofs.com/charts/2013/10844/the-impact-of-contests-on-email-leads-infographic.

16. Ashley Parker, "Twitter's Secret Handshake," *The New York Times*, June 10, 2011, www.nytimes.com/2011/06/12/fashion/hashtags-a-new-way-for-tweets-cultural-studies.html.

17. Michael Krebs, "Violent 'Game of Thrones' episode is most social in HBO history," *Digital Journal*, June 8, 2013, http://digitaljournal.com/article/351818.

18. Tim Nudd, "Jell-O Hijacks Twitter's Profane #FML Hashtag, Changes It to Mean 'Fun My Life,'" *AdWeek*, May 23, 2013, www.adweek.com/adfreak/jell-o-hijacks-twitters-profane-fml-hashtag-changes-it-mean-fun-my-life-149788.

Chapter 24 Serve, Honor, Deliver, Surprise & Delight: The Red Velvet Touch

1. Jay Baer, "Is Youtility the Future of Marketing?," *Integrated Marketing and Media* (blog), *Convince & Convert*, 2012, www.convinceandconvert.com/integrated-marketing-and-media/is-youtility-the-future-of-marketing/.
2. Jay Baer, "The Key to Social Media Success Is Just 2 Letters," *Convince and Convert*, 2012, http://www.convinceandconvert.com/integrated-marketing-and-media/the-key-to-social-media-success-is-just-2-letters/.
3. Steven Castle, "GE Touts the iPhone-Connected Hybrid Water Heater," *GreenTech Advocates*, October 25, 2012, http://greentechadvocates.com/2012/10/25/ge-touts-the-iphone-connected-hybrid-water-heater/.
4. David Gianatasio, "Solar Panel Inside Nivea Print Ad Generates Power to Charge Your Cellphone," *AdWeek*, May 30, 2013, www.adweek.com/adfreak/solar-panel-inside-nivea-print-ad-generates-power-charge-your-cell-phone-149882.
5. See the Scholastic case study at www.igodigital.com/resources/case_studies/scholastic.
6. "Dunkin' Donuts to Recognize Employee Who Calmly Dealt With Customer Freakout," *Huff Post Business*, June 12, 2013, www.huffingtonpost.com/2013/06/12/dunkin-donuts-employee-to-be-honored-_n_3428439.html.
7. Wohlsen, Marcus, "Why Amazon Prime Could Soon Cost You Next to Nothing," *Wired*, March 13, 2013, www.wired.com/business/2013/03/amazon-prime-could-soon-cost-next-to-nothing/.
8. See http://pinterest.com/pin/38210296811402525/; Jodi Glickman, "The Best Networking Email You'll Get All Year," *CNNMoney*, February 1, 2011, http://management.fortune.cnn.com/2011/02/01/best-networking-email-linkedin/.
9. "Grilled-Cheese Victory," Man v. Food Nation video, 2:48, Travel Channel, www.travelchannel.com/video/grilled-cheese-victory-12442.
10. "Meat Pack: Hijack," Ads of the World video, 1:36, December 2012, http://adsoftheworld.com/media/ambient/meat_pack_hijack.
11. Lani Rosales, "Pepperidge Farm Surprises a Blogger, Wins a Fan for Life," *AGBeat*, February 6, 2013, http://agbeat.com/social-media/pepperidge-farm-surprises-a-blogger-wins-a-fan-for-life/.
12. See White Castle Hall of Fame, accessed August 6, 2013, www.whitecastle.com/cravers/hall-of-fame.

Chapter 25 Test & Evolve: What Marketers Can Learn from 5,000 Years of Football

1. Charles Dickens, *A Tale of Two Cities*, 1859. http://www.gutenberg.org/files/98/98-h/98-h.htm.
2. Julian Norridge, *Can We Have Our Balls Back, Please? How the British Invented Sport (and Then Almost Forgot How to Play It)* (London: Penguin, 2008), 157.
3. Ibid., 160.
4. Ibid., 188.
5. "Old Trafford," The Stadium Guide, accessed August 6, 2013, www.stadiumguide.com/oldtrafford/.

Acknowledgments

*A*UDIENCE would not have been possible without the assistance, contributions, and support of a great many wonderful people over the years.

First and foremost, I'd like to thank Tim Kopp, whose unyielding belief in me helped make the *SUBSCRIBERS, FANS & FOLLOWERS Research Series* (*SFF*) and this book possible. Many thanks also to ExactTarget's founders, Scott Dorsey, Peter McCormick, and Chris Baggott, who gave me a key to the building as well as personal and professional opportunities beyond my wildest imagination. This book also would not be in your hands were it not for the legal magic of Todd Richardson and Scott Gotshall, and the publishing magic of John Wiley & Sons, Inc., Richard Narramore, Christine Moore, and Tiffany Colon—many thanks to all of you from this occasionally verbose recovering attorney.

Second, I'd like to thank the man, the myth, the legend: Morgan Stewart. We hatched the idea for *SFF* together back in late 2009, and our back-and-forth over the years helped clarify many of the ideas you'll find in *AUDIENCE*. I'd also like to thank everyone who contributed to any part of the *SFF Series*, from the original *SWAT Team* of Katie Martin, Jen Ribble, Teresa Wilcox, and Elizabeth Kjeldsen, to other key contributors including Kyle Lacy, Dave Eckert, Lauren Esposito, Jenn Milks, and the team at Trendline Interactive. I'd also be remiss if I didn't thank Chip House, Mitch Frazier, Kevin Bobowski, Scott Thomas, Benham Roberts, Shawn Herring, Mallory Lee, Fletch Fletcher, Amy Condle, Beth Leleck, Allison Lightner, Charlie McAtee, Katie Wheeler, Stephanie Sandilla, Daniel Walker, Jonathan Gandolf, and Chris Mascaro for their *SFF*-related support over the years; Amanda Leet, Daniel Incandela, and their team for their amazing interactive efforts; and Scott Roth, Sameer Kazi, Jean-Philippe Baert, Jason deBoer, Teresa Becker, Nick Badgett, Lindsay Niemic, Judd Marcello, Ryan Bonnici, Solange Carvalho, and Johanna Zuber for helping to take *SFF* global.

Third, I'd like to thank my amazing team of thought leaders, team players, and doers of good. Heike Baird, Joel Book, Tom Corey, Bo Dietrick, Dawn DeVirgilio, Kyle Lacy, Tony Mulinaro, Jen Ribble, Andrea Smith, Mathew Sweezey, and Chad White—the X-Men have nothing on your mutant super powers. And yes, that is a compliment of the highest order.

AUDIENCE would also be nothing without insights from real brands, companies, and people. To that end, I'd like to thanks Cam Balzer, Mark Bishop, Dylan Boyd, Mark Charalambous, Tom Chokel, Tony Clark, Jeff Cunning, Sam Decker, John DeFoe, David DeVore, Michael Donnelly, Kip Edwardson, Jesse Engle, Matt and Marcus Fish, Rand Fishkin, Gary Foodim, Margaret Francis, Adam Giuffre, Keith A. Grossman, Alix Hart, Dan Heimbrock, Brent Hieggelke, Gabe Joynt, Sameer Kazi, Pete Krainik, Scott Kveton, Judson Laipply, Dick Lynch, Mac Mahaffee, Susan Marshall, Scott McCorkle, Nick McCullough, Kenny Miller, Howard Mittman, Chris Moody, Len Peralta, Eric Prugh, Evan Rossio, Tom Sather, R. J. Talyor, Jason Therrien, Matt Thomson, Scott Townsend, Bryan Wade, Ryan Warren, and Rick Wion. Thanks also to Jason Redlus and his top-notch crew at the Argyle Executive Forum, whose stage was the perfect forum for me to evolve many of my ideas regarding proprietary audiences.

AUDIENCE also stands on the shoulders of a lengthy list of thought leaders who advanced the cause of responsible, permission-based marketing in the Internet era. To this end, I owe a debt of gratitude to authors (and, in many cases, dear friends) Chris Anderson, Tim Ash, Josh Bernoff, Jay Baer, Matt Bailey, John Battelle, Jonah Berger, Rohit Bhargava, Pete Blackshaw, Matt Blumberg, Nick Burcher, Jennifer Evans Cairo, C. C. Chapman, Matt Cutts, David Daniels, Frank Eliason, Jason Falls, Porter Gale, Paul Gillin, Seth Godin, Ann Handley, Jeffrey Hayzlett, Sally Hogshead, Joseph Jaffe, John Jantsch, Simms Jenkins, Kristopher B. Jones, Aaron Kahlow, Peter Kim, Jim Kukral, Steven Levy, Sage Lewis, Charlene Li, Rebecca Lieb, Dr. Flint McLaughlin, Jeanniey Mullen, Amber Naslund, Lee Odden, Jeremiah Owyang, Don Peppers, Joe Pulizzi, Paul Roetzer, Martha Rogers, Robert Rose, Ted Rubin, Andy Sernovitz, Peter Sheahan, Aaron Strout, Stefan Tornquist, Shar VanBoskirk, Gary Vaynerchuk, D. J. Waldow, Chad White, and Steve Yastrow.

Last, I'd like to thank some folks from past lives without whom I wouldn't have reached this very moment: my parents—Kenn and Karen Rohrs, my Cho-Cam-Ro family, Tim and Janet Barnett, David Blaine, Greg Boser, Tom Bralliar, Ben Bykowski, Leslie Caruthers, Tiffan Clark, the 1462 Comm Ave. Crew (Andrew Strickman and Adam Zoll), Paul Elliott, Peter Fasano, Todd Friesen, Mike Hamlin, Dawn Hanson, Erin Howe, the boys in Hollerado, Andrew Kordek, Professor Pnina Lahav, Marlo Lyons, Christine Marx, Chris Miller, Ellen Moreau, the Optiem Team (Joe Kubic, Clyde Miles, and Mark Nuss), Daniel Oron, Professor Glenn Platt, Tony Rohrs, Laryce Sasaki, David Stone, the Third Door Media Team (Chris Elwell, Sean Moriarty, Chris Sherman, and Danny Sullivan), Thom Ruhe, the old Vantage One Team (Tim Mueller, Brian Powers, and Dan Rose), Professor Robert Vogel, Deb Wilcox, Julie Winterbottom, and the dearly departed WOXY (@woxy—*forever* the Future of Rock 'n' Roll, BAM!).

Index

Advertising, 19–21, 95, 96, 216, 217, 219, 220. *See also* Paid Media
ADVOCATES, 11, 31, 67, 126, 186
Alerts, 110, 111, 113, 217, 219, 232
Altimeter Group, 68, 211
Amazon, 203, 212, 234
AMPLIFIERS. *See also* specific audience channels
  about, 11, 26, 29–40, 50–52, 59, 65, 67, 186, 245, 247
  and Red Velvet Touch, 229–231, 234–237
  and strategy, 184, 186, 189, 191–193, 196, 198
  and tactics for building and engaging proprietary audiences, 201, 203, 205, 208, 210, 212, 214–217, 219–225
  types of, 11, 186. *See also* specific subgroups
ANALYSTS, 11, 31, 67, 186, 189–190
Appending, 226, 227
Ash, Tim, 107
At Your Service (Eliason), 201
Attempting Normal (Maron), 169
Attention, attracting, 18–20. *See also* Business energy creation
Audience Imperative, 10, 70, 247
AudiencePro.com, 1, 176, 180, 184, 201, 227
Audiences
  about, 1–3
  as business assets, 12, 13
  engagement, 70, 77–82, 109
  importance of, 7, 8, 91–93
  proprietary. *See* Proprietary audiences
  reach, 71, 75–77
  size, 70–77
  types of, 11, 186. *See also* specific audiences
  value of, increasing, 70, 82–90
Automated keyword response, 217

B2B, 83, 111, 140, 141, 143, 156, 169, 201, 213
Baer, Jay, 88, 169, 208, 219, 231
Baidu, 172
Bebo, 172, 173
Berger, Jonah, 204
Bieber, Justin, 52
Big Data, 74, 226, 230, 233
Bing, 173, 187, 203
Blogger, 128, 132, 173
Blogs, 35, 61, 67, 127–132, 202
Brand FANS, 46–48, 115
Branson, Richard, 140
Brett, Brian, 34
Brooks Brothers, 60, 61, 213
Brown, Antonio, 54
Brown, Bobby, 147
BROWSERS, 11, 27, 186
Burcher, Nick, 66
Business energy creation, 15, 17–25

Call to action (CTA), 59–61, 105, 146, 165, 185, 213, 216, 224
Campaign Conversion Value (CCV), 82, 86, 87
Carloss, Alex, 146
Catalogs, 61, 62
Cedar Point, 204, 234
Cert, Vint, 111
Change, 93, 94
Chapman, C. C., 203
Chopinot, Régine, 17
Circulars, 219, 220
Clark, Tony, 204
Coca-Cola (Coke), 72, 247
Co-Marketing, 221
COMMENTERS, 11, 31, 67, 186
Comparative Incentive Value (CIV), 83, 88–90
Compendium, 132
Connect: The Professional Women's Network, 141
Consumer-controlled social channels, 40
Contagious: Why Things Catch On (Berger), 204

Content development, 93
Content Marketing, 11, 28, 61–63, 104, 202, 203
Content Marketing Institute, 63, 203
Content Rules (Handley and Chapman), 203
Contests and giveaways, 165, 207, 222
Converged Media, 68, 69, 93, 95, 125, 141
The Converged Media Imperative (Altimeter Group), 68, 69
Conversion, 30, 60, 82, 86, 87, 104, 105, 125, 209, 239
Conversion Voodoo, 209
Convince & Convert, 208
Cost per acquisition (CPA), 87
Cost per click (CPC), 21, 87
Cost per thousand (CPM), 21, 87
Costolo, Dick, 121
Coulton, Jonathan, 36
Coupon codes, 217
Creativity, 9, 95, 128
CREATORS, 11, 31, 32, 67, 186
Crisis management, 37, 50, 51
Cross-channel promotions, 210, 211
Customer Relationship Management (CRM), 40, 74, 94, 95
Customer service, 78, 118, 123, 124, 228, 229. *See also* Red Velvet Touch
CUSTOMERS, 1, 10, 11, 15, 16, 29, 30, 32, 38, 39, 48, 51, 59, 69, 71, 83–86, 186, 193, 195

Database size, 71, 74, 75
DeVirgilio, Dawn, 156
Dichter, Ernest, 34, 35
Digital Outsider, 210
DINERS, 11, 38, 186, 201
Direct Comparative Value (DCV), 83, 88
Direct mail, 62, 219, 220
Dislikes, 11, 22, 78, 175, 210
DONORS, 11, 38, 159, 186, 216, 220

DOOH (Digital Out of Home), 57, 210
Dorsey, Jack, 126
Draper, Don, 56–57, 93–95, 99, 248

E-commerce checkout, 211
Earned Media, 24, 55, 58, 64–70, 124, 125, 135, 141, 164, 221, 236, 247
Eliason, Frank, 201
Email, 35, 36, 44, 45, 55, 61, 63, 69, 72–77, 79–80, 109–113, 136, 206, 218. *See also* SUBSCRIBERS
Email Swipe File, 156
Eminem, 225
EMPLOYEES, 11, 32, 38, 39, 140, 142, 165, 169, 186, 191–193, 196, 229
Engagement, 70, 77–82, 109
Entrepreneur Magazine, 221
Erving, Julius (Dr. J), 26
Events, 224, 225
Everlapse, 137
ExactTarget, 43, 131, 156, 228, 229

Facebook, 13, 29, 33, 35, 47–49, 51, 52, 55, 59–61, 62, 65, 69, 71, 72, 74, 75, 77–79, 85, 93, 112, 114–120, 122, 124, 135, 136, 207, 213–215, 223, 225. *See also* Instagram
FAN-to-FAN Customer Service, 118
FANS, 1, 2, 7, 8, 10–12, 14, 15, 22, 24, 30, 38–43, 45–51, 55, 59, 60, 62, 64, 67–69, 71, 72, 74–76, 78, 79, 81, 85–88, 186, 190–191
Fascinate: Your 7 Triggers to Persuasion and Captivation (Hogshead), 204
Fish, Matt, 48
Fisher, Roger, 221
Fishkin, Rand, 151
Flickr, 29, 164
Flip the Funnel (Jaffe), 16
FOLLOWERS, 1, 2, 11, 12, 14, 15, 24, 25, 38, 39, 41, 42, 51–55, 59, 60, 62, 64, 67–69, 71, 72, 74–76, 81, 186, 190–191
The Four Rights (right message, to right person, at right time, through right channel), 40
Foursquare, 29, 35, 173

Gates, Bill, 140
Geofencing, 218, 219
Getting to Yes (Fisher and Ury), 221

Gmail, 76, 79
Godin, Seth, 16, 39
Goldsworthy, Andy, 17
Google, 29, 132, 144, 147, 207, 212, 213
Google+, 1, 52, 65, 74, 75, 149–152
Google Ad Extensions, 213
Google AdWords, 60, 212, 215
Google Alerts, 192
Google China, 172
Google+ Hangouts, 149, 150
Google Images, 29
Google Maps, 29
Google Mobile Maps, 215
Google Official Blog, 131
Gundotra, Vic, 150
Gunther, Rob, 236

Hall, Justin, 132
Halpern, Derek, 45
Handley, Ann, 203
Hansen, Beck, 235
Harmon, Jeffrey, 145
Hashtags, 223
Home field advantage, 64
House, Chip, 228
"How Word-of-Mouth Marketing Works," 34
Huffman, Kristina, 156
The Human Face of Big Data (Smolan), 74
Hybrid Marketing Era, 23, 24, 58, 66, 99, 180, 201, 215, 247

Improvisation for the Theater (Spolin), 91
In-app mobile advertising, 214, 215
Inbox Insight, 73
Inbox Tabs, 76
INFLUENCERS, 11, 31, 67, 126, 140, 142, 151, 169, 170, 186, 189, 190
Instagram, 29, 30, 35, 52, 53, 60, 61, 65, 75, 78, 119, 134, 137, 163–167, 223, 225
Instant messaging, 35. *See also* SMS (Short Messaging Service)
Interactive Advertising Association, 215
Internet, 9, 22, 96
Internet Retailer, 212
Interruption marketing, 39

Jaffe, Joseph, 16
Jenkins, Simms, 206
JOINERS. *See also* specific audience channels
about, 11, 26, 29–30, 36–40, 42, 55, 62, 63, 74, 245, 247

and Red Velvet Touch, 231
and strategy, 184, 186–190
and tactics for building and engaging proprietary audiences, 201, 202, 210–217, 220, 222, 223, 225
types of, 11, 186. *See also* specific subgroups
Jones, Kristopher, 203

Kakao Talk, 173
Kickstarter, 41, 42
Kopp, Tim, 228

Lady Gaga, 174, 225
Laipply, Judson, 147
Landing page, 28, 57, 107–108, 125, 185, 188, 191, 215, 220, 222
Lee, Stan, 36
Lieb, Rebecca, 68
Lifelong learning, importance of, 99
Lifetime CUSTOMER Value (LCV), 82–85, 183, 188, 191, 222
Lifetime Incremental Value (LIV), 82, 84, 85
Like button on Facebook, 49, 69, 78
Line, 173
Link-baiting, 97
Linked content, 218
LinkedIn, 1, 52, 53, 61, 65, 74, 75, 139–143, 234
LinkedIn Groups, 141
LinkedIn Influencers, 140
LinkedIn Today, 140
LISTENERS, 7, 11, 27, 168–171, 175, 186–188, 218
Locklear, Heather, 33

Mackay, Charles, 46
Macromedia, 129
Magazines, 174
Marketer-controlled social channels, 40
Marketing as a service, 230
Marketing automation, 213
Marketing Experiments, 212
Marketing Sherpa, 112, 206, 209
Marketing tactics, 57, 58, 62, 200–227
MarketingProfs, 202
Maron, Marc, 168, 169
Martin, George R. R., 36
Mass Relevance, 225
McCullough, Nick, 154–156
McHale, Joel, 14, 15
Medium.com, 173
Melt Bar & Grilled, 48, 235

Messina, Chris, 223
Metrics, 98, 239, 240
Midsummer Snowballs
  (Goldsworthy), 17
Misinformation, 96–98
Mobile Ads for Apps, 214, 215
Mobile apps, 35, 44, 61, 62, 75, 77,
  81–82, 117, 119, 120, 130,
  133–138, 154, 161, 163, 164,
  202, 210, 214, 215, 217–219,
  225, 232, 235, 236
Mobile devices, 93, 104, 112, 137,
  150. *See also* Smartphones
Mobile First, 137
Mobile Marketer, 218
Mobile Marketing Association, 215
Mobile Marketing Magazine, 218
Modified Shannon-Weaver model,
  66, 67
Mosaics, 225, 226
Musk, Elon, 24, 25
Myspace, 47, 49, 173

Narcissistic brands, 79
Negative reviews and comments, 37,
  50, 51, 117, 118, 126
Net Equivalent Value (NEV), 83, 87
The New Inbox (Jenkins), 206
The New York Times, 34, 35
News Feeds, 77, 78, 115, 116
"Next big thing," 96–98
Nielsen, Jakob, 103
Nike, 133, 144, 164, 165
"Not my job" attitude, 94, 95

The One-to-One Future (Peppers and
  Rogers), 16, 233
Online communities, 28, 44, 174
OOH (Out-of-Home), 57, 160, 185
Opt-in, 12, 61, 62, 89, 104, 105,
  108, 132, 159, 160, 162, 185,
  186, 190, 197, 205–207,
  209–213, 215, 218, 222, 224
Opt-out, 12, 22, 45
Orabrush, 145, 146
Oreo, 117, 165
Organic growth, 204
Organizational value, 90
OTT (Over the Top), 57, 160,
  161, 173
Overlays and pop-ups, 209
Owned Media, 24, 55, 58, 61–64,
  68–70, 103, 125, 135, 141,
  146, 159, 210, 211, 221, 224,
  225, 232, 247
Owyang, Jeremiah, 68

Paid Media, 2, 21, 23–25, 55,
  58–61, 64, 68–70, 87, 94–96,

107, 110, 120, 125, 135, 141,
  159–160, 184, 185, 193, 194,
  197, 210, 214–215, 224, 247
*Paid Owned Earned: Maximizing
  Marketing Returns in a Socially
  Connected World* (Burcher), 66
Paladin, Seth, 54
Palmer, Amanda, 41, 42
Papa John's, 59, 194
PARTNERS, 11, 32, 38, 39, 124,
  140, 142, 186, 191–193, 196
Path, 173
Pay per click (PPC) advertising,
  212, 213
Peer-to-peer messaging, 58, 160,
  161, 173
Peppers, Don, 16, 232, 236
Peralta, Len, 36
Permission marketing, 37, 39, 40,
  80, 226, 228, 229. *See also*
  JOINERS
Permission Marketing (Godin),
  16, 39
Personalization, 232
Pinterest, 29, 35, 52, 53, 60, 61, 65,
  74, 75, 153–157
Podcasts, 44, 61, 67, 168–171
Pop-ups, 209
Post-purchase confirmation and
  communications, 211, 212
Presley, Elvis, 247
Print advertising, 219, 220
Priority Inbox, 76
Privacy issues, 120, 226, 242
Product packaging, 204, 205
Proprietary Audience Development
  (PAD)
  audience and customer
    relationship, 16
  Audience Imperative, 10, 70, 247
  audit of existing efforts, 184–193
  and business energy, 15, 17–25
  and complexity of marketing,
    238, 239, 244
  and Content Marketing, 63
  defined, 10
  goal setting, 194–196
  hybrid marketing approach,
    22–25
  importance of, 8–11
  and Paid Media, 59. *See also* Paid
    Media
  perspective on, 244, 245
  potential audiences, 11
  soccer, lessons learned from his-
    tory of, 240–244
  strategy, 196–199
  tactics for, 200–227
  team, 179–184

testing, measuring, and assessing,
    238–240
Proprietary audiences. *See also*
    specific audiences
  about, 1–3
  benefits of, 10
  development. *See* Proprietary
    Audience Development
  owned audiences compared,
    14, 15
  types of, 11, 186
  value of, 12, 13
PROSPECTS, 10, 11, 16, 27, 71,
  135, 142, 169, 186, 201, 213,
  218, 226, 231
Pulizzi, Joe, 63
Push messaging, 136, 218, 219
Push notifications, 82

Qihoo.com, 172
QR codes, 220
Quora, 28, 35
Qzone, 174

Radian6, 192
Radio advertising, 216, 217
READERS, 1, 7, 11, 27, 108, 186,
  205, 218, 220, 231
Red Bull, 145, 146, 174
Red Velvet Touch, 229–237
Reddit, 174, 236
Relevance, 40
Renren, 174
REPORTERS, 11, 31, 67, 186
Responsive Design, 137
Return on investment (ROI), 82,
  104, 112
Return Path, 73
Retweets, 35, 121, 124, 125
REVIEWERS, 11, 31, 67, 186
Richman, Adam, 235
Rogers, Martha, 16, 226, 232
Rosen, Jay, 32
Rossio, Evan, 115, 116
RSS (Really Simple Syndication),
  44, 129, 132

Salesforce.com, 228, 229
Santana, Ever, 158
Sasso, Will, 166
Schultz, Howard, 133
Search advertising, 212, 213
Search Engine Land, 204
Search Engine Optimization
  (Jones), 203
Search engine optimization (SEO), 22,
  28, 29, 62, 104, 108, 132, 151,
  186–188, 197, 203–204, 213
Search Engine Watch, 204

SEARCHERS, 11, 27, 108, 186–189
Security issues, 12, 226
SEEKERS. *See also* specific audience channels
about, 11, 26–30, 36, 40, 61–62, 186, 187, 189, 245
and Red Velvet Touch, 231
and strategy, 184, 186–189
and tactics for building and engaging proprietary audiences, 201, 203–206, 208–210, 212–217, 220, 223, 225
types of, 11, 186. *See also* specific subgroups
SEO Book, 213
Seper, Chris, 140
Sernovitz, Andy, 37, 201, 211
Shannon-Weaver Model of Communications, 64, 65, 66
SHARERS, 11, 31, 67, 186, 189, 190
Shiny object syndrome, 97
SHOPPERS, 11, 27, 30, 62, 159, 160, 186–188, 205, 218, 232
Signage, 61, 62, 64, 210, 225
Silbermann, Ben, 153
Sina Weibo, 174, 175
Skype, 160, 161
SlideShare, 52, 53, 142
Smartphones, 30, 81, 133, 135, 158, 217, 218. *See also* Mobile apps
Smith, Kevin, 36
Smolan, Rick, 74
SMS (Short Messaging Service), 35, 44, 45, 61, 63, 75, 76, 158–162, 217, 218, 224
Snapchat, 35, 161
Soccer, lessons learned from, 240–244
Social Fresh, 223
Social icons, 208, 209
Social login, 207, 208
Social media, 9, 32, 64, 65, 66, 77–79. *See also* specific types
Social Media Examiner, 208
Social Media Explorer, 209
Social Pros Podcast, 169
Social Triggers, 45
Social widgets and mosaics, 225, 226
SocialMedia.org, 225
Sogou.com, 172

Soso.com, 172
Spam, 76, 80, 111, 113, 162
Spolin, Viola, 91
Sponsored Communities, 141
Spotify, 175
Springsteen, Bruce, 7–10, 14
Starbucks, 133, 134, 174
Stewart, Morgan, 43, 228
Streaming content, 75
StumbleUpon, 35, 175
SUBSCRIBERS, 1, 11, 12, 38, 39, 41–45, 55, 59, 61, 62, 64, 67–69, 71–76, 80–82, 185, 186, 190, 191, 194, 197, 198, 202, 203, 205–207, 209–220, 222, 224–226, 228–237, 244
SUBSCRIBERS RULE!, 228, 229
Sullivan, Andrew, 128, 129
Sullivan, Danny, 150
Systrom, Kevin, 163

2013 Quarterly Digital Intelligence Briefing (Econsultancy and Adobe), 91
Taco Bell, 165, 221
Tactics for Proprietary Audience Development, 200–227
Television, 58, 59, 216, 217
Tesla, 23–25, 130
Text messaging. See SMS (Short Messaging Service)
Theatre Is Evil, 41, 42
Thurek, Gary, 111
Timberlake, Justin, 173
Tomlinson, Ray, 110
Tumblr, 35, 129, 130, 132
Turntable.fm, 175
Twitter, 1, 35, 52–53, 55, 59–62, 65, 69, 71, 74, 75, 121–126, 130, 213, 214, 223, 225. See also FOLLOWERS; Vine
Twitter Cards, 122, 125, 126, 206, 215

Unfollows, 11, 40, 210
Unsubscribes, 11, 12, 14, 40, 44, 45, 210
Urban Airship, 219
Urturn, 137
Ury, William L., 221

Video advertising, 216, 217
VIEWERS, 7, 11, 27, 59, 60, 108, 145, 146, 148, 186, 215–218

Vimeo, 175
Vine, 29, 35, 53, 58, 97, 137, 163, 164, 166, 175
VISITORS, 1, 11, 27, 62, 108, 142, 159, 160, 186, 204, 206, 207, 209, 217, 224, 225, 234
VKontakte, 175
Vogel, Robert, 64

Wagstaff, Bob, 145
Waits, Tom, 149
Walgreens, 30, 134
The Walking Dead, 134
We Are Social, 214
Weather Channel, 219, 232
The Web Outside, 210
Website Magazine, 202
Websites, 1, 8, 11, 22, 28, 35, 36, 45, 60–64, 75, 103–108, 137, 202, 203, 205–209, 216, 217, 220, 225
Weiner, Jeff, 139
Welch, Jack, 140
Wendy's, 105, 106, 207
WhatsApp, 161, 173
Which Test Won, 209
White, Chad, 156
White Castle, 236, 237
White papers, 33, 61, 63, 203, 213
Widgets, 62, 225, 226
Williams, Ev, 173
Wilson, Fred, 109
Word-of-mouth marketing, 34, 65, 201, 232
Word of Mouth Marketing (Sernovitz), 37, 201, 211
WordPress, 128, 132
WordTracker, 213
Wounded Warrior Project, 160, 220
Wroblewski, Luke, 137
WTF podcast, 168, 169

Yahoo!, 129, 130, 132, 137
Yahoo! Mail, 79
Yelp, 29, 35, 37, 175, 176
Youtility: Why Smart Marketing Is About Help Not Hype (Baer), 219, 231
YouTube, 44, 61, 144–148, 150
YouTube True View ads, 215

Zuckerberg, Mark, 114, 118, 119, 163
Zuckerberg's Law, 118, 119